WARNING!

THIS BOOK CONTAINS GRAPHIC SCENES
OF REVOLUTIONARY VIOLENCE.
DO NOT CARRY ONBOARD U.S. DOMESTIC
OR INTERNATIONAL FLIGHTS!

Praise for Murdered by Capitalism:

"It is a ripsnorting and honorable account of an outlaw tradition in American politics which too seldom gets past the bouncers at the gateways of our national narrative."

—Thomas Pynchon

"Ross is bold enough to point out what most writers choose to ignore, for fear of upsetting those who proclaim the Great Virgin's Eternal Innocence . . . his description of the bus trip to Baghdad is priceless."

—Alex Cox, director of *Repo Man* and *Sid and Nancy*

George
E. B. SCHNAUBELT
BORN
APR. 5. 1855
DIED
MAY. 22. 1913
MURDERED
BY CAPITALISM

Also by John Ross

Rebellion from the Roots—Indian Uprising in Chiapas (1995)
In Focus Mexico—A Political Guide (1996)
We Came to Play, an Anthology of Writings on Basketball (with Q. R. Hand) (1996)
The Annexation of Mexico—From the Aztecs to the IMF (1998)
Tonatiuh's People, A Novel of the Mexican Cataclysm (1999)
The War Against Oblivion—Zapatista Chronicles (2002)

ANTHOLOGIZED IN:

Nuclear California (1984)
Third World Ha Ha Ha (1995)
The Zapatista Reader (2002)
Puro Border (2003)
Shock and Awe (2003)

POETRY CHAPBOOKS:

Jam (1974)
12 Songs of Love and Ecocide (1977)
The Psoriacis of Heartbreak (1979)
The Daily Planet (1981)
Running Out of Coastlines (1983)
Heading South (1986)
Whose Bones (1990)
Jazzmexico (1996)
Against Amnesia (2002)

Murdered by Capitalism

A Memoir of 150 Years of Life and Death on the American Left

John Ross

Nation Books
New York

MURDERED BY CAPITALISM:
A Memoir of 150 Years of Life and Death on the American Left

Published by
Nation Books
An Imprint of Avalon Publishing Group
245 West 17th Street, 11th Floor
New York, NY 10011

Nation Books is a co-publishing venture of the Nation Institute
and Avalon Publishing Group Incorporated.

Library of Congress Cataloging-in-Publication Data is available.

ISBN 1-56025-578-1

9 8 7 6 5 4 3 2 1

Book design by Kathleen Lake, Neuwirth and Associates
Printed in the United States of America
Distributed by Publishers Group West

FOR THE OLD BONES (PARTICULARLY THOSE OF Q. R. HAND WHO SHARES MANY OF THESE MEMORIES) AND THE NEW BLOOD (MY KIDS CARLA AND DANTE AMONG THEM) WHO ARE DOOMED TO PERUSE THEM

• • •

"Where will we go after the last border? where will birds fly after the last sky" —Mahmoud Darwish from *Earth Presses Against Us*

• • •

"And its back to back
and belly to belly,
I don't give a damn
'cause I'm done dead already"

—*from "The Zombie Jamboree" introduced by Lord Intruder at Trinidad carnival 1953 and popularized by "The Charmer" (AKA Louis Farrakhan) on the jukebox at Johnny Romero's, Minetta Lane, Greenwich Village, circa 1956*

• • •

with gratitude to my editor Carl Bromley who believed in this crazed project from the get-go, Elizabeth Bell for the usual reasons, Elaine Katzenberger who finally gets to read this book, Carolyn Aspaugh for her wonderful biography of Lucy Parsons and Franklin Rosemont for his invaluable anarchist archives, Bolerium Books who supplied prime material as did Edie Butler who directs the Humboldt Room at Humboldt State University, Ned Simmons and Mark Rogovin who showed me the cemeteries and Sid Dominitz and Carol Mone who did leg work, Irma Nelly Guadarrama for the frontispiece photo, as well as my colleagues at the Hotel Isabel, the Cafe La Blanca, and X Copias here in the Centro Historico of Mexico City

—JOHN ROSS, TENOCHTITLAN, DECEMBER 2003

Contents

A Brief Introduction to E. B. Schnaubelt

Up against the splintery redwood fence at the top of the blazing green jewel box of a cemetery in the tiny fishing port of Trinidad, California, a few dozen miles short of the Oregon line, amid daffodils and daisies and the family plots of dead burghers and loggers, drowned fishermen and Christianized Indians, a solitary cenotaph wobbles in the Pacific wind like a peg-legged sailor:

"E. B. Schnaubelt
Born April 5th 1855
Died May 22nd 1913
MURDERED BY CAPITALISM"

the simple furious epitaph shouts. Along the beveled edges of the column, an anchor has been molded to the stone, implying that E. B. endured a watery death. Nothing could be farther from the truth. Edward Bernhardt Schnaubelt died from a projectile maliciously fired upon his person by the minions of his class enemy. But in Trinidad, where nibbled cadavers wash up from the sea in the stormier seasons and others are swallowed whole by the deep and never heard from again, the tombstones come prefabricated with maritime emblems. Eddie Schnaubelt was no fisherman—in fact he hated fish.

He told me so himself.

Like other outlaws, scoundrels, and low-life villains who have landed on this lonely shore, E. B. Schnaubelt migrated to this damp neck of the near north woods on the run from the big city police. In Chicago there had been labor troubles, the terrible McCormick strike, the agitation for the eight-hour day, anarchists with black bombs. His brother Rudolph had been accused of tossing the bomb that blew up a cop at the Haymarket Square police riot of May 4th, 1886. After that, the three Schnaubelt boys hit the road in a big hurry—Rudolph to the pampas of the Argentine, Eddie and young Henry to the Barbary Coast of San Francisco.

Before long, Ed and young Henry caught on in a lumber camp up by Santa Rosa but the younger man didn't take to it at all and returned to San Francisco where he became a cop and later changed his name to "Snowball."

"After he was growed and on his own, I never had much use for him," Ed Schnaubelt confesses.

By the mid 1890s, now a family man but still with a stubborn anarchist streak in him, E. B. went gold-mining up on the Trinity River and when that didn't pan out, he showed up in this fog-bound harbor, put down his hard-earned money on a few acres Old Man Brizzard, the local land baron, was temporarily willing to part with, and built himself a shingle mill from scratch. A talented machinist and carpenter who had learned his trade in the maw of industrial Chicago, he hand-tooled his own saws, his bands and his belts, organized his logger neighbors into a co-op, and went to work.

The mill earned the men and their families a slender living but timber prices collapsed in the depression of 1908 and the business went belly-up. For a few years, his neighbors scattered to find work in other clearings in the great forest.

Now Brizzard and his henchmen in the Big Lagoon Timber Company wanted the land back to connect-up their properties. The old bastard went to court down in Arcata, got a court order, foreclosed on the mill. Said it was his in lieu of monies owed and posted a guard who was ordered to dismantle E. B.'s cherished shingle mill.

But Eddie Schnaubelt was not going to be a pawn in the class war. One night, he packed up his tools and stomped out to the mill site to retrieve his machines. That's when Brizzard's gunsill, Kelly, plugged him.

The Schnaubelt family was schooled in the hardness of a world where the struggle between the classes never, ever abated, even here in this leafy paradise. Every evening after dinner, what little there was, Edward Bernhardt Schnaubelt had dug out his mildewed copy of *Das Kapital* and read to them in his native German how the working class had nothing to lose but its chains. The revolution was coming as sure as was the dawn. They would all live to see it. He spat into the wood stove and his spittle sizzled on the fiery logs.

So when his wife Tina and the five kids had collected the old radical's corpse and sent to frame a coffin and carve a tombstone, the epithet they chose came naturally.

For much of the 20th century, the tomb was a local oddity among the Okies and Arkies who settled in with the Christian Indians and cut down the rest of the trees and fished the sea clean of salmon. Every few years around the date in May Eddie had been cut down, a reporter would pull out the file and write a half-baked story about the origin of the tombstone, but for the most part Schnaubelt lay up there alone and ignored.

Then in the 1960s and '70s, the North Coast of California was resettled by budding Wavy Gravys and Thomas Pynchons (Pynchon himself lived down the road from Schnaubelt for a few years while polishing up *Gravity's Rainbow*), burn-outs from the big-city political wars, and tribes of New Age acolytes who seemed to have run out of gas between Grateful Dead concerts on this stretch of coastline. "Murdered by Capitalism" became a kind of perverse tourist attraction. Wine bottles and the stubs of marijuana cigarettes were often to be found at the foot of the tomb. Each year on May 1st, the month of E. B.'s martyrdom, and the day when International Working Men and Women honor the industrial proletariat everywhere in the world except in the land where this celebration had its roots, red roses would appear on Schnaubelt's gravesite, as if he was some sort of West Coast Edgar Allen Poe. A doctor named Eugene Debs Robbins is thought to be responsible.

Whenever I have occasion to pass through what's left of the northern woods, I have visited with E. B. to tell him of my travels and my troubles, leave him with my new book, wedge a revolutionary poem under his anchor, kick back a jigger or two of Dago red, and give his old wobbly cenotaph a pat on the back. A few years ago, I dropped by to tell Schnaubelt all about the Battle of Seattle, demon globalization, the evil World Trade Organization, the heroic continuity of resistance. The revolution was really coming this time, I assured him.

"Where have I heard that one before?" a voice the color of moss rumbled back from inside the stone, "anyway, I was in Seattle, too—or at least my spirit was. I didn't see *you* there. . . ."

Book One

Haymarket

Preamble to the Death of Schnaubelt

Trinidad, California boasts that it is the smallest incorporated city in the Golden State—400 souls marinade here suspended in a fog-bound aspic where seasons are governed by salmon and crabs, Winnebagos, and well-heeled tourists. Spacious seaside homes overlooking the emerald bay and deep blue ocean house real-estate moguls, prosperous merchants, retired law enforcement officials, and tenured professors from the nearby state university. The fishermen themselves tend to live on their boats or down the highway in McKinleyille, a one-time shantytown often dubbed "Oklahoma By the Sea," and named for a former U.S. president, the father of Yanqui Imperialism in fact.

Trinidad is a watchful community. The transient population out in the surrounding unincorporated woods comprises vagabonds and tweakers, trailer trash, traveling freaks, and an occasional homicidal hitchhiker dropped off on the U.S. 101 exit ramp with a hankering to throttle and dismember female joggers. Robert Durst, the alleged Butcher of Galveston, was in residence for a stretch. The Pelican Bay Maximum Security Prison, where angry men of color are in cages 24 hours a day, is just an hour's drive north, and Trinidad's large, shiny COP WATCH sign offers numbers to call in case suspect strangers are spotted inside the city limits—the icon for such suspects has shaded features and a dark complexion, suggesting African or Latino or Indian heritage.

Indians are the usual suspects around Trinidad Bay and have often been the victims of massacre and malice—such as the prototypical killings of hundreds of Wiyots out on Indian Island back in the 1860s. But now the thirty surviving members of Trinidad's Tsurai band have taken their revenge on the white settlers who rubbished their culture, in the form of a glitzy casino just south of town that has made them the kingpins of this tidy port. The casino's Firewater Lounge is a popular watering hole for Trinidadians of all ethnic persuasions.

Alcohol is an ice-breaker in this small-minded way-station, and like many a denizen I used to toss back my quota in the local gin mills. An early morning drunk, I would be scouting a spot to nap by noon and the Trinidad town cemetery, with its cathedral Redwoods, gently sloping knoll and quiet company was always an inviting flop. Schnaubelt's tomb up on the crown of the sun-splashed hill was a prime location.

Back in the 1970s my drug of choice was a chemical slop assembled by Ernesto and Julio Gallo and marketed by the gallon under the "Red Mountain" label. When combined with such proscribed substances as PCP and Seconal, it was sort of the crack of its time.

So I would haul my jug up there to hang out with old "Murdered by Capitalism" who provided a politically correct head-rest against which to doze or read or scribble screeds, weave joints, and tipple the house red. Schnaubelt was the perfect host, guarded and dignified. I would sometimes quiz him about his life as an anarchist—I myself was a recently lapsed Maoist—but never really anticipated a response. He was dead, after all, had been so since May 22nd, 1913. "Na na," I would mock his reticence, quoting from August Spies on the gallows for the Haymarket affair back in 1886: "The day will come when our silence will be more powerful than the words you throttle today."

Then, one spring morning (it must have been soon after Decoration Day because the gravesites of the veterans of foreign wars were adorned with small American flags and their plastic flowers had been recently freshened) I lied down amid dandelions and buttercups to savor the soothing thud of the surf against the shoreline, and, in a paroxysm of seasonal ecstasy, kicked over my gallon jug of Red Mountain.

"Umm good! More!" rumbled a moss-green voice from inside Schnaubelt's tomb. "Good! More!" it kept rumbling. "Skol! L'chaim! Salud!" Now the cenotaph was trembling like it had the DTs. "Coming right up, Brother Schnaubelt," I assured the dead man, "but could you please tell me exactly where your mouth is at?"

"Just pour it out on the ground and it will soak in," he instructed. I tipped the jug over and watched the wine run through the grass, saving myself only a small swallow for the tete-a-tete I felt sure the elixir would finally stimulate.

But to my chagrin, the conversation died right there. I put my ear to the ground and thought I heard a sort of burp from the earth, a distant subterranean snoring, the purring of the contented dead. . . .

When I awoke, the starry sky was wheeling overhead like a Van Gogh canvas and Schnaubelt was still encased in the sleep of the deceased.

I came back many times after that and kicked over many wine bottles. Sometimes it jolted him awake and sometimes it didn't.

Meanwhile, just on the other side of the redwood fence, Glen Saunders (not his real name), a local supermarket tycoon and 21-gun-salute patriot who flew the Stars and Stripes from his hilltop home long before 9/11 was even a gleam in bin Laden's rheumy eye, filmed and took extensive notes of all subversive activities that took place in the Trinidad graveyard.

"Glen Saunders" knew all the dirt on Schnaubelt, the bomb throwing stuff in Chicago, the murdered cop, the fling with that black girl, and he kept files on everyone who visited the tomb, perhaps hoping to nail the long-lost Rudolph for whose arrest there had once been a sizable reward. Every Friday, "Glen" would drive 20 miles south to the city of Eureka and turn his notes over to the FBI agents in brown wing-tip shoes up in their stuffy little office at the top of the old brick courthouse.

Death of Schnaubelt

So we would sit up there in the warm sun with "Glen Saunders" eavesdropping on the other side of the fence, and snooze and schmooze, two old men, one long dead, the other not quite, carousing the afternoons away.

"What's it like being laid out in a place like this?" I questioned a momentarily garrulous Schnaubelt one balmy Saturday afternoon—he had already sucked up half a gallon of groove juice and was now demanding that I smoke joints and blow the smoke on his column.

"Oh, it's restful all right. I have lots of time to plot. But it's too dark to read and the damp is driving me batty. Mostly, it depends upon where you're fixed. My neighbors over there, the Nortons (William 1902–1931), Beulah Ann (1908–1977), Clara (1888–1958), and Lewis Caldwell (1948–1995) are all right. They're Indians. They keep to themselves. But I don't care much for the Harringtons—Clinton (1888–1914) and Maude (1880–1930)—they've always been right-wing assholes and snitches for "Glen Saunders" . . .

"What's really great here are the kids. Stella Rae Johnson (1900–1902) down there is really adorable and Caspar (son of Marvin Simmons, 1913–1919) is like my own dear boys. I love to be around dead children. It keeps me young!"

Eddie Schnaubelt called enthusiastically for another flagon. He wanted to toast the dearly departed. It was broad daylight and he was dead drunk. "Shaddup" his neighbors shushed in unison, "or it's just not going to be Capitalism that killed you. . . ."

"It was Capitalism with a capital K that killed me, all right. Stinking Kapitalism—you could smell it everywhere, it was up your nose and the taste was on your tongue. It was the stink of sweat and wage slavery and excrement and rotting meat, the stench of slavery. The Chicago River stink, fetid wastes of industry and desperate humanity curdling on its foul bottom.

"You lived with that stink everywhere, in the streets and tenement buildings lining the river. You couldn't breath inside those rooms so filled with pale children coughing up their little lives, three and four families so crammed into a crawl space the men had to sleep in shifts.

"And the stink came at you from the stockyards, wallowing up to your waist in hog shit and blood on the killing floor. And the stink came at you from your own heart. And the stink never ended until you were dead too. You couldn't breath for it. It was the stink that finally got Rudolph and the rest to think about killing, rather than being killed, by Capitalism. . . .

"Out here in California at least there was some air. When you sucked it in, it tasted green. It was the breath of the trees. The trees exhaled and gave me my breath back. It wasn't like Chicago.

"I knew me and the trees had to get along but my job was to cut them down, kill them, mill them with my own hands. We only took the tallest trees, the first ones, sending them crashing to the earth with a thunderous *woosh*—50 loggers could jig on its stump when they were done. Like they were dancing on the back of a dead whale. . . .

"It smelled better out here in California but there was still plenty of killing to be done. Ya, the throats of many capitalists still to be slit. Old man Brizzard for one. The Capitalist son-of-a-bitch had sold me this land and now he wanted to take it back. By then all my neighbors had deserted me, my own comrades! You're standing in the way of progress and you are going to be removed," the Big Lagoon Timber goons had threatened. They coveted the parcel because it stood between their holdings."

Now Brizzard was coming to him in his dreams. The old man didn't say much, just stood there by the side of his cot laughing and dangling the $1000 bill he had offered for clear title. Schnaubelt had spit at him and in the dream, his spittle sizzled. . . .

He often thought how he would kill Brizzard. How he would go to San Francisco on the packet boat and walk into his office and stuff a bomb in the old man's mouth like Lingg had done, like Berkman when he shot that prick Frick!

"I knew I was as good an anarchist as them—no matter what Tina said about it. . . ."

The boys led the way through the logged-out copse, disappearing in and out of the low-hanging night fog like little Casper the Friendly Ghosts. He knew this stretch of the woods, every stump and root—he had cut down a lot of these trees. He understood the nuance of each shadow, the Braille of the ground, the brush and scrape of each branch.

"That night for once I wasn't thinking to murder Brizzard, not just yet anyway. I only went out there to get my stuff back, my saws and my bands and the rest of the tools. The watchman Kelly was already taking the mill down and they said in town that Brizzard had sold it to Phineas Bell down there in Freshwater.

"Over my goddamn dead body he would," E. B. Schnaubelt spat hotly.

"Tina had been all over me about the kids again: Why was I taking the boys along on this foolishness. If I wanted to get shot over a bunch of metal scraps, that was my business. Just leave our children out of it!

"She had stayed with Adolph the arm baby and the girls and you know what, I didn't miss her one bit. She called herself a socialist but she was turning into a damn fishwife." He needed a real revolutionary woman for this work, a Lucy Parsons, the Black Angel, or Red Emma in her sensational red bloomers. . . .

"Papa! Papa!" Henry came running up to him, "Eddie's got scared and run home to Mama." Shit, even his own kids were deserting him now. "Listen, you wait here," he said to the boy, "if you hear anyone coming or see a light, whistle. You be the lookout guy." He patted his son on the back of his scrawny neck. "You'll do fine."

The shingle mill was framed before him in the moonless night, a black hump illuminated only by dim starshine. He dropped his bag of wrenches on the damp ground and they clanked. He ran his fingers along the sharp teeth of the saw blade. A dog barked lazily down the property. An owl hooted in the crotch of the dark branches above him. "Stop!" he heard someone shout. "Stop or I'll shoot." Stop what? he thought. This is my place. These are my saws.

The bullet slammed into his chest and he remembered what it was he had forgotten all these years and then he forgot it all over again, this time forever. Suddenly, he was dead like all the others, like Spies and Parsons and poor Lingg, Fischer and Engels, at last he was perfectly dead. . . .

"You killed me, Kelly," he was supposed to have gasped at the watchman but it could have been anything, Capitalism or Brizzard or Cyrus McCormick. The newspapers don't tell the truth. "The tragedy ended years of turmoil and litigation" reported the *Arcata Union*. "A crushed artery." "The death of Schnaubelt was instantaneous." "The victim left a destitute wife and many small children."

"They said he was an anarchist. I had to get him before he got me" sobbed Kelly the watchman at the inquest.

"It got weird after I was dead. My soul flew up to the top of a burnt snag and I watched over my body until it was taken away for the inquest. After that, I was alone up there. I felt lost. I didn't know where I had gone to. Then finally Tina put up this marker and I found myself again . . .

"She sure took her sweet time about it. Oh, I know she hit a rough patch in there. One lawyer was mysteriously poisoned. Another sold out to Brizzard. Then the mill burned down under 'unexplained circumstances,' though I favor the boys did that.

"All I know is that she would come up here to the graveyard and mope and moan all day long. C'mon girl, I'd tell her, don't mourn!

Organize! This was something I picked up from Joe Hill down here after the copper bosses had him put up against the wall to be gunned down by the firing squad.

"Y'know, the truth be told, I was glad when Tina finally moved away and was gone. After that, I could get some rest. Like the sign says up here, RIP, Rest In Peace. It's supposed to be zoned for that."

Death on the American Left

American martyrdom came with the territory and those who fought back were welcomed with genocide. From the Abenaki Indians proffered blankets saturated with plague by Lord Jeffrey Amherst, to Cochise and Chief Seattle and Ishi and Leonard Peltier, with stops along the way at Sand Creek and Wounded Knee and the Trail of Tears, the blood of the first martyrs soaked the American earth and never dried clean. This land is My Land, not your land. Anymore.

Cinque was crucified upon the main mast in the Middle Passage even before the slave ships put into port. Nat Turner and Denmark Vesey rose like the cotton and were chopped down with it. John Brown took up the gun and became a golden trumpet.

The working class suffered grievously. The strikers murdered at Homestead and Republic Steel were no less martyrs than the men hung for Haymarket. Nor were Joe Hill or Frank Little or Wesley Everett, Wobbly brothers lynched by the bosses.

Sacco and Vanzetti, Julius and Ethel, Malcolm and Martin and Medger Evers. Those who walked through Alabama and Mississippi with blindfolds on their eyes—William Moore, the dead postman, Viola Liuso, Schwerner, Cheney, and Goodman. Fred Hampton dead in his bed in Chicago with 40 slugs in his head. The Baby Panther, Little Bobby Hutton, spread-eagle naked in an Oakland gutter. Four little girls blown up in a Birmingham church, the Weather dead torn apart in the Townhouse. Sam Melville and two score more martyrs at Attica. The students gunned down at Jackson State. Four Dead in Ohio. James Rector taken at Peoples' Park. Comandante George Jackson, the man-child Jonathan—the suffering runs through us like a big bloody river.

Judi Bari and Gypsy Chain—murdered by Big Timber. Brian Willson's legs, the bones of nuns in Salvador. Wilhelm Reich buried alive in his orgone box. The Mexican anarchist Ricardo Flores Magon strangled in Leavenworth. Norman Morrison exploding into flames on the steps of the Pentagon. Rachel Corrie buried alive under the bulldozers in Gaza . . .

Martyrdom is as American as apple pie, peanut butter, baseball, Jeffrey Dahmer, and John Ashcroft. On the top rung of this stained, sainted altar are those hung for Haymarket—August Spies, Albert Parsons, Adolph Fischer, George Engels. Louis Lingg was blown up in his death row cell. E. B. Schnaubelt's murder is only an interesting footnote to those heroic deaths. And his brother Rudolph has been erased from the history books entirely.

Life of Ross

I have worked for many years as a freelance foreign correspondent, a job description that dignifies the trivia of political exile. Social strife in the Third World is a particular attraction. Which is to say, for a long time now I've been moving around Latin America looking for trouble.

In the spring of 1986, I touched down in Santiago, Chile, eager to celebrate the 100th anniversary of International Working Men and Women's Day tentatively set for that southern-cone city's Alameda Boulevard on the morning of May 1st. But Chile was then in its 13th year of the Pinochet dictatorship and the marches of workers were seriously discouraged.

Defiantly, the workers vowed to march.

We gathered in the dawn at the dimly lit offices of the United Workers Central, our red kerchiefs soaked in freshly squeezed lemon juice to ward off the effects of the tear gas. The first contingent retreated from the Alameda bleeding, some with buckshot in their behinds—the pinche "Pacos" had opened fire with shotguns. But a second and third wave of workers took to Alameda and began marching north. The tear gas was pungent and the lemon juice didn't much cut it. I was wearing a T-shirt that had been popular in El Salvador that year: "Periodista! (Journalist!)" it advised, "Don't Shoot!" "Take that off before you get us all killed," a colleague warned.

Our destination was the Leatherworkers Union Hall, where two desperate workers had hung themselves with their shoelaces the week before. Rudolfo Siguel, then the leader of the nation's copper miners, was struck by the symmetry of death and was determined to read the words of the "Martyrs of Chicago" to honor all of those dangled by Capitalism.

The melee outside the union hall was a wonder to behold. The hall was ringed by armored vehicles, tanks, and those peculiar living water cannons called *guanacos* that spit out filthy water to quell civil disturbance—Chileans are well-dressed people and the threat of being splattered by the *guanacos* (actually a species of llama) may well have been Pinochet's ultimate weapon.

Heavily armed police and army troops milled in front of the gated entrance but the workers were at such close quarters that the usual tear-gas grenades were of little use. Suddenly, Siguel's people put all their shoulders together in one stupendous push and we broke through the cordon of security agents. Once inside the hall, Rudolfo leapt up on a chair and began to recite the famous litany of August Spies: "The day will come when our silence will speak louder than the voices you throttle today. . . ."

Here, at the other end of the Americas, almost to the South Pole for chrissakes, workers took turns reading the gallows speeches of the Haymarket martyrs and their words never rang more true.

Meanwhile, up in El Norte, my own country where these men were once hung by the neck until dead for the crime of seeking justice for working women and men, the agonies of *Los Martires de Chicago* have been erased from collective memory. May 1st, which everywhere in the world save the country of its origin honors the battle for the eight-hour day and the industrial proletariat that won it from the Capitalist class with its breath and its blood, was converted by Richard Nixon, a pathological lawbreaker, into "Law Day," a date devoted to the memory of law enforcement officers slain while carrying out their duties. That is to say, in the United States of North America, the day that once honored those hung at Haymarket now honors those who framed them.

• • •

I was introduced to the Haymarket martyrs at an early age by Howard Fast, a commie author—the book was *The Americans,* really the story of Governor John Peter Altgeld, who destroyed a promising political career by pardoning the three surviving Haymarket defendants, Samuel Fielden, Oscar Neebe, and Michael Schwab, who was married to Maria Schnaubelt, the younger sister of Rudolph and E. B.

Howard Fast and my mother were comrades. They had worked together on the Joint Anti-Fascist War Relief Committee raising funds for anti-Franco fighters in Spain and France and when they refused to name names before some two-bit congressional committee, Howard Fast was railroaded to jail for contempt. We visited him in a Danbury, Connecticut federal penitentiary, my debut performance in an American prison. Soon enough, there would be many more opportunities to review American justice from the inside out.

Howard Fast wrote a number of books about American history—*The Unvanquished, The Last Frontier,* and *Citizen Tom Paine,* among them. My all-time favorite was *Freedom Road,* which, like many of Fast's better titles once he emerged from the blacklist, was made into a major Hollywood extravaganza starring yet another American martyr, Muhammad Ali.

I found Fast's books in the library of Elizabeth Irwin Junior High School on Charlton Street in the Greenwich Village neighborhood where I grew into adolescence, the upper-grade extension of the infamous Little Red Schoolhouse (whose facade was painted the color of its politics). I realize now as I rethink Haymarket and try to fit Schnaubelt's revelations in place, that Howard Fast forcefully colored my skew on American history, twisted and perverted my mind and my heart, and made me want to overthrow the U.S. government from a very early age. I thank him for it now.

My formative years lurched by in a thoroughly dysfunctional household fronted by New York showbusiness Jews who had joined the

Communist Party U.S.A. in the mid-1930s when it was both a fashionable and, in some circles, a career-boosting, move to sign up. My father, an entertainment columnist ("So This Is Broadway") at the *World Telegram* came to the CP-USA through the Newspaper Guild, founded by his colleague Hayward Bruin. My mom, a pushy Jewish-American Princess and Marjorie Morningstar look a like, who claims to have been a suffragette at age ten, barged into the party and organized a theatrical publicists union—in addition to taking many fascinating lovers, whose sexual skills (or lack of same) she never tired of touting. Dorothy Ross was the first certified woman press agent on Broadway and I was born in Walter Winchell's column: "It's a boybee for the George Rosses."

Working under V. J. Jerome in the cultural section of the party, Mom flacked for the Hollywood Ten, Paul Robeson's disastrous 1948 Peekskill concert, and the Herbert Biberman labor classic *Salt of the Earth* when that blacklisted film opened at a seedy Manhattan location. She hyped Henry Wallace in his 1948 Progressive Party campaign for president, and ballyhooed the candidacy of crusading San Francisco attorney Vince Hallinan when he ran on the American Labor Party ticket in 1952. I was gaga for Adlai Stevenson that year. "You were ashamed of your mommy the commie," Dorothy loved to taunt me in later life.

And she marched with the cast of "The Cradle Will Rock" in 1938 after the House un-American Activities Committee had shuttered the Federal Theater because of Marc Blitzstein's left-wing libretto. One of my final and fondest memories of my Mommy the Commie was huddling before a VCR on the southern coast of Spain watching Tim Robbins' film of the staging of that play. Although she could barely remember anything anymore, least of all where the bathroom was located, she explained to me and my sister in careful detail why the cast had performed from the audience in the theater that was rented after HUAC shut down the Federal: "It was a lousy scab house and no one would be caught dead performing on that stage. . . ."

HUAC was a terrifying presence in my parents' lives. Every time the committee would visit New York to investigate Red infiltration of the Great White Way, Dorothy and George would head for the closet with a bottle of Scotch. While Pete Seeger and Jay ("Brother, Can You Spare A Dime?") Gorney sang mordant ditties for the red hunters, mom and dad grew progressively closeted.

The persecution and execution of the Rosenbergs, commie Jews like themselves, drove them to excesses. Some will say that George Ross named names, but Mom was a stand-up guy. She eventually left the CP in 1956, after Hungary, with the John Gates faction. Our free subscription to *The Daily Worker* was canceled.

Mom had a life-long tryst with Spain. She kept it a secret, fleeing there only when she needed a substitute lover. After the Spanish Civil War, the veterans of the Abraham Lincoln Brigade would sometimes gather in our living room and Mom always boasted of smuggling thousands of Yanqui dollars to the loyalists in Barcelona in her underwear, the summer of '37, "the year before you were born Johnny."

In the mid-1970s, Mom moved to Fuengirola on the Costa del Sol of Andalucia permanently. Although she had sworn never to set foot on Spanish soil until Franco was six feet under it, she couldn't wait, and spent the last decades of her life drinking herself into oblivion in a garishly messy condominium that had once gazed out on the Mediterranian before the Costa Building Boom took off. She still loved to tell the old stories but every once in a while, her memory collided with the truth. One evening, close to the bottom of the Soberano brandy bottle and before her head hit the table, she confessed her sins. "You know what, Johnny?" she slobbered through rubbery lips.

What, Mom?

"You know what?"

You said that, Mom . . .

"You know none of it was true. There was no Barcelona. There was no money. There was no underwear."

Goodnight Mom.

• • •

The crowd had a profoundly human scent—sour and bitter and cloyingly sweet, part perspiration and urine and feral fear, the flavor of rats crowded together on a sinking ship. It clung like damp nicotine-stained gauze to Union Square that airless June dusk, as if the oppressive Manhattan evening was not enough to smother us.

Those who had chosen to come to the death watch could not get away from the smell. They paced and spat, smoked, and did not pay much attention to the orators. "Free Ethel and Julius!" It almost sounded silly now.

The hands of the big illuminated clock atop S. Klein's drew closer, like pincers. There was no avenue of escape left to bust them out of Death Row. That morning, the Supreme Court had refused to hear their final appeal. Now the Constitution offered only last rites. Up at Sing Sing, ol' Sparky was being greased up for the kill. The Jew commie bastards would at last burn for their sins against America.

I was 15 and wondering whether they had shaved Ethel's head yet. How would my mom look if she was bald? The government said the Rosenbergs had stolen The Secrets of The Bomb but there were no secrets. Physical force is in the public domain. Ethel and Julius were traitors and spies J. Edgar Hoover yapped, they would get what they deserved. "It's all an anti-Semitic plot," my mother swore.

I had been reading Howard Fast about other spies, about August Spies, the rest of the men hung for Haymarket. The two sets of executions seemed to be taking place on the same page.

Before sundown, because it was the Sabbath, the warden had come to their cells with rabbis but they sent the rabbis away. They would fry together for socialism—Glorious Socialism! Paradise was just through the door at the end of the Last Mile.

People drifted off into the stinking twilight, impatient with waiting for the inevitable. Those who had stayed just sat down in the street now, slumped over, their heads between their knees. The clock atop S. Klein's closed to a deadly kiss. Julius and Ethel could not tear their lips away as the electricity coursed through their writhing bodies like it was a vengeful god, charring their internal organs and stopping their hearts until they were free at last. Free at last. Little puffs of smoke rose from their scalps. The crowd inhaled and uttered an audible sob.

"They're dead. It's all over" someone said. "Let's go. There's nothing we can do here." I stumbled to my legs. In the back of the street, a cracked voice began to sing: "Arise Ye Prisoners of Starvation! Arise Ye Wretched of The Earth!"

Goodnight Mom.

Life of Schnaubelt

"Our mothers held similar convictions. The flame of the Communes of 1848 raged across Europe from Paris to Frankfurt and Dresden like the red plague. My mama Rebeka never forgot it. Her own dear brother, the first Rudolph, had been killed on the barricades but his hot blood spurted through her veins and she marched for the emancipation of the downtrodden all her days.

"At mid-century, when she was 22, Rebeka married our father, a guildsman, and moved to Vienna where she delivered him five surviving mouths to feed and then watched Heinrich Schnaubelt, the first Henry, plunge into numbing despair as his business collapsed under the weight of British imports of cheap cutlery. Heinrich died apparently by his own hand. Having stabbed himself in the eye with a badly made English steak knife in a fit of despondency, the old man succumbed to gangrene after many days of agony, leaving Rebeka a widow with five squalling orphans while still in her early thirties.

"The second commune rose and was crushed in 1872 and the phantoms of 10,000 slaughtered workers haunted Europe. The children began to run off to America one by one. They imagined freedom from the old walled-up ways of Austria and Germany, a dream they quickly learned was a lie. By the mid-1870s, Rebecca and my older sister Ida had come over and the Schnaubelt family reassembled itself in the German slums of north Chicago.

• • •

"I was terrified by the fires. The houses were all made of wood and whole blocks would go up in flames if someone so much as accidentally knocked over a candle. I never slept from the time I came to America when I was 16. I would lie there on my pallet and listen for the crackle of the fire in the walls. I could feel the heat licking my face. A house across the street had burned up and when the fire wagons came and took the babies out I saw that they had been burnt black, as if they were black babies.

"Those were terrible times to be coming to Chicago. The depression came down like a guillotine in '74 and not even the native born could get any work. When you could find it, the men were paid two dollars a day and the women if they were lucky, $1.40—kids like me might bring home 70 cents. But there wasn't any work. Every morning, you could see them crowding up around the gate in the packing-house district down by the river, scrapping with each other to work for a few pennies an hour. It made you sick to see it.

"And don't think there was any relief from the government. For the Capitalists this was the Gilded Age of America. Ya, sure, maybe for them. They kept us in their cage and we couldn't bust out.

"The Civil War veterans marched for a crust of bread and work. Then the women marched—my sisters, Ida and Maria and my mother Rebeka who never forgot. Rudolph and I and little Henry went to see what it was like and we liked what we saw. There was a great hullabaloo at the Relief Board and it was there for the first time that I laid eyes on Lucy Parsons, a black woman as tall and as straight up as a tree trunk with a voice like dark honey and a tongue of fire. She was going to take all the women inside but they barred her way and she shouted up at them 'I was a slave and now I'm still a slave to the Capitalist class.' Rudolph and I went over to her and said we wanted to sign up. We didn't know what we was getting into yet. . . .

"I took my baptism in the class war in the general strike of 1877. It was only six years after the second commune had fallen and there were plenty in Chicago then who wanted revenge for that bloodletting. The strike was more violent than any the older men had ever seen. Both sides were armed: the cops and the militias, and the workers too. The German workers had stockpiled rifles in the Turner Halls, which were sort of gymnasiums where socialism and anarchism were preached.

"The strike had started on Jay Gould's railroad in West Virginia. The engineers just unhooked the locomotives and took them back to the roundhouse. By the time the strike rolled into Pittsburgh, Gould and Frick and Carnegie and Mellon, Pullman, the rest, called out the militia but the militiamen saw that the strikers were white working men like themselves and they stacked up their guns and turned them over to the brothers on the railroad. . . .

"So the strike came into Chicago with a full head of steam. In July, I saw 40,000 strong march up Milwaukee Avenue singing 'Les Marseilles.' My poor old mother and my two sisters went with the women to Halsted and tore down the trolley and the telegraph lines and the cops didn't dare come into the neighborhood because the sisters were throwing garbage and bricks down on them from the roofs. . . ."

"But the cops were no creampuffs, either. Most were rogue Irishers. The Irish spoke a sort of English. They could understand what the bosses told them and were willing to take their orders, so they became the cops. There was a lot of money to be made if you were a cop back then in Chicago."

The police worshiped the slave-masters of Capitalism—Swift and Armour, Marshal Fields, McCormick, the big bankers who ran the city. They would do anything for them. They beat and jailed the strikers by the thousands. It wasn't all that different than the time of Boss Daley and the Democratic Convention of '68. 1968 that is. . . ."

Wait, Comrade Schnaubelt. The Democratic Convention was almost 100 years after all this happened. You were already mouldering away up here for a good 55 years. How do you know what happened in Chicago in 1968?

"The dead keep their ear to the ground, boy. Now where was I?

"Oh, yeah—So Rudolph and I began to go to their meetings and smoke their cigars. We began to see August Spies and Albert Parsons, and that black firebrand Lucy. The Parsons had been arrested for inciting to riot during the 1877 strike and every one knew their name now. . . .

"They had met in Waco, Texas, after the Civil War. I think Parsons fought with the Rebs but got a bad conscience from it. She was an ex-slave and already the woman of another ex-slave, Oliver Gathings, but Parsons took her away. Then they both were run out of Texas for miscegenating the Caucasian race and came to Chicago to make trouble.

"Parsons was a short guy with sandy hair and a turkey neck. But he had the gift of gab all right, although his palaver was social democratic, all horse dung and snake oil. Lucy was the more radical of the two. She was an anarchist and she believed in dynamite. She called it 'the great equalizer.'

"The Germans came to Chicago from all over the old country and there were more of us in that city than the native born, about a third of all the workers there at the time. But we had no kind of political power. Even the Irish had more juice than we did and with their boodling and their bribing, they manipulated City Hall against us. They stole the elections even in the German wards. Sent in their goons and stole the ballot boxes. We could never win.

"The German people for the most part were cultured. We had an education and a trade. We worked indoors. The Irish were lumpen. They came over here because their potatoes went bad. They worked outside. They'd go from factory to factory with their roving strikes and call the workers out.

"The bosses put the working class at each other's throats all the time. That's the way it was in that hellish melting pot. Who could you trust? The Harps? The Bohunks? The Sqareheads? The Jews? Parsons and his Lucy were native born and they were above us even if she was a colored lady.

"But although we hated each other and the only other bond between us probably was swilling beer, we were all stuck in the working class and we had to hang together to get the bosses off our backs. There was bad blood, ya, but we tried not to take the bosses bait.

"I worked at a lot of different jobs and I saw bad things every day. I was a knifeman in the slaughterhouse swimming in the blood of hogs. I worked in the lumberyards and in the iron mills and one summer on the railroad, building it west to Nebraska. I was a carpenter, throwing up cottages on the north side for those families just coming out of poverty. With all the fires in Chicago, carpentry earned you a steady living. I apprenticed as a machinist and went to work for Cyrus McCormick.

"Everywhere I worked under a yellow dog contract that said we couldn't have a union, that we had to work for as little as they paid us for as long as they told us to work. So we began the battle for the eight-hour day.

"Ten hours pay for eight hours work! Eight hours for the boss, eight hours for yourself and eight hours to sleep with your woman or your wife! The anarchists argued that it was just a handout. Asking for the eight-hour day admitted that the boss owned your time. But Rudolph and I got right in the thick of it.

"The agitation ran high in 1885. People were striking everywhere and the ruling class wanted us dead. Give 'em the rifle treatment, laughed Pennsylvania governor Tom Scott. The *Chicago Tribune* advocated using hand grenades against sailors that were just getting unionized on the Great Lakes. 'The best meal for a ragged tramp is lead,' the *Tribune* advised. The *Times* prescribed strychnine. So you can see what we was up against.

"The Citizens' League, which was just Swift and Pullman and the rest of those skunks, put the police on us and they would break up all the street meetings and there was no such thing as free speech. The worst of the lot were Black Jack Bonfield and the German turncoats Schleuter and Schatz—they were all thrown off the force later on for stealing from prostitutes. They would come into the meetings with their clubs swinging, take away the speakers, and charge them with disturbing the peace. We saw it happen many times. Rudolph and I got into a lot of scrapes ourselves but we're big men and we could dish it out.

"By then we had soured on the electoral system. The Socialistic Labor Party gave you a lot of blah blah blah but once they got themselves elected, they forgot the workers even existed. We were more interested in action, direct action. What the anarchist orator Johan Most called 'the propaganda of the deed.' It was what Lucy preached too.

"Rudolph had gotten thick as thieves with young Louis Lingg. They had both joined the German Socialist militia, the Lehr and Wehr Division. They trained with guns like the Black Panthers. They were streetfighters long before the Days of Rage.

"Lingg drank a great deal. Beer and dynamite. He was a powder keg—you could see it in his eyes. Lingg built bombs. Big black ones like you saw in the funny books. But he was serious about them. He preached the bombs. He said we couldn't win anything worth winning without using force.

"In February 1886, the workers at McCormick Harvester got organized and demanded the eight-hour day and guess what? Cyrus McCormick gave us the finger and fired us all. He brought in the Pinkertons to force us out and the scabs came in to take our place—some of them were black men. We went and fought with them every day when the shift changed. I had been a knifeman and those scabs knew I could use my pig sticker pretty good. Every day that spring, the cops would come and I got to know Bonfield pretty good.

"By 1886, the eight-hour day movement had grown so big they couldn't hold it back anymore. The Knights of Labor under Terrance Powderly were mostly Harps. They had a lot of secret handshakes. But that winter and spring, everyone was signing up, even the Germans. The Knights grew from 70,000 to 700,000 members in just a few weeks.

"Powderly and his boys called for a general strike to begin May 1st and last until we had won the eight-hour day. That Saturday afternoon, 80,000 workers marched up Michigan Avenue to the lake and it was like a big birthday party to see all those people there, a sea of working stiffs and their families in their Sunday best. My whole family came out—Mother Rebeka and my sisters Ida and Maria with her husband Herr Professor Schwab and, of course, Rudolph and me and my little brother Henry. We all were there and each of us felt like we owned a little piece of history to have marched in the first May Day. Even six feet under down here, I still feel it in my old bones.

"Spies was there with his whole family, too—his mom and his sister Gretchen and the glamorous Nina Van Zant, who became his wife on death row. And the Parsons with their two little kids, Junior and Lula, skipping ahead. I saw Lucy talking with Johan Most and rumor had it that both Mother Jones and Mother Bloor marched that day. A young railroad worker named Eugene Debs. And Grand Master Workman Powderly who, like all piecards in history, was already planning to sell us down the river.

"The only comrade I didn't see that day was Louis Lingg. The eight hour a dayers were leading the sheep to slaughter, he argued. When it was all done, we'd still be slaves.

"That Monday we went back out to McCormick's to try and shut the place down. In the next field, there was a big meeting of Bohunk lumbershovers—maybe 6,000 of them there. Spies was spieling at them. He could sure rattle your timbers. Then we saw the scabs coming and rushed back to the McCormick fence. But this time it was a trick.

"Just then, that brute Bonfield and his men swung around a corner with their revolvers blazing and began shooting into the throng of strikers. Six were gunned down that bloody afternoon although the papers claimed it was only one. Rudolph and I picked up one poor girl—she couldn't have been more than 15 and they had put a bullet in her belly. She was talking in German, crying out for her mama, but she died before we could get her to the hospital.

"Spies, who had witnessed the attack from the speaker's wagon was so upset he went mute. Then he retreated to the office of his newspaper, the *Arbeiter-Zeitung,* and drew up a circular calling for a protest meeting the next evening in the Haymarket. This wasn't going to be just any meeting either. "Destroy the Hideous Monster Before It

Destroys You!" Spies scrawled, "Working Men Arm Yourself And Appear In Full Force!"

"Although only a few of the circulars got distributed before Spies decided to tone down the call for revenge, Louis Lingg was glad to receive one. In his workshed down by the river, he pulled out his trunk and carefully removed the bombs. Big bombs, little bombs, fuse bombs, concussion bombs, compression bombs, pipe bombs, spools of wire and the blasting caps. He set them out on the workbench before him and studied the bombs and considered their uses. Now there was no turning back. Soon the comrades would knock on the cabin door and it would be time for action. For the propaganda of the deed to begin. . . ."

He stared at his pocketwatch and shook it rudely to make sure it was still ticking. He couldn't understand it. Where were all the people? Was not this the night the proletariat would rise and smite the butchers of their brothers and sisters? Was not this the hour the slaves would take their vengeance against their masters? He could already savor the warm blood against the back of his palate. It tasted rich and comfortable, like expensive wine, and he smacked his lips for more.

He was sweating like a pig under his heavy overcoat. He felt like he was on fire.

The meeting was set for 6 p.m. on Desplaines Street, between Lake and Randolph, a few blocks off the wretched Chicago River. There were hardly any workers at all, maybe a thousand if you gathered them all together in the middle of the long, narrow street where the speaker's wagon had been parked, at the corner of Crane's Alley. After all that had happened he could not get it into his head why there were so few of the comrades here.

He checked the leaflet to make sure of the time and if he was in the right place and then jammed it into his overcoat pocket again. He could feel *It* there, cool and impervious to the touch.

By now, Spies was speaking about what he had seen the day before at McCormick's. He always stayed so clean in his collars and arm garters, never got his fingers dirty or his palms smeared with the blood of the workers he was always preaching to. Later Parsons would mount the speaker's wagon and spout his Social Democratic hogwash. Talk! Talk! Well, after yesterday, the time for talk was dead and buried. Now our word would be delivered in a new format: The propaganda of the deed!

When, at dusk, the sky darkened and rain began to fall in cold drops, most of the crowd showed its true colors and went scurrying home. The mayor, Carter Richardson, a fat hog of a politician with many stomachs and chins, had been there to see if the rally constituted an illegal assembly and when he waddled off with the others, that was the signal.

There were maybe only 200 left on Desplaines when Bonfield and his hitters surged out of the stationhouse up the street and began clubbing the citizens that lingered there into the sidewalk. Samuel Fielden, the large Englishman who had once been a Parson was on the wagon sermonizing away and was so hypnotized by the sound of his own voice that the beating of the people did not disrupt his speech.

Someone had to stop them.

The wooden match flared and kissed the fuse. One revolution Two revolution Three revolution Four revolution. . . .

The bomb sailed out of the mouth of the alley like it had been spit straight up from the pit of the night, a sleek black comet, its rouged tail glowing in the slowly shattering darkness.

The Great Equalizer smashed against the paving stones and its voice spoke loud as Jehovah proclaiming justice and eternal damnation upon the evil Capitalists who devoured the earth.

Then there was light.

Then there was nothing.

Then there were groans and sobs, smoke, glass, twisted metal, bloody stumps of meat, a crater gouged in the street.

What remained of Bonfield's police opened fire for fifteen straight minutes. Many workers were murdered in the fusillade. Seven of them and seven cops, all but one, Matt Degnan, gunned down by the officers' own crossfire. The battle of the Haymarket was a kind of draw.

• • •

"I was not there, exactly. Like the others, I left when it began to rain and took refuge in Zyff's saloon at the north end of the street where I could still keep an eye on the action. There were always meetings of the Socialistic Labor Party at Zyff's and I suppose he was friendly to the revolution.

"I ordered a beer and waited for my brother. Parsons was there with Lucy and the children and her friend, Lizzie Holmes. Adolph Fischer came over with his beer and I sat with them too although they knew I was not on their side. Parsons explained that he had just gotten in from Cincinnati where he'd gone to talk to the dockworkers on the Ohio River and the moment he'd come home, Lucy and Lizzie had whisked him off to a sewing women's meeting at his offices in the *Alarm* newspaper. He hadn't even known about the Haymarket meeting until Fischer had come and asked him to speak.

"I couldn't take my eyes off Lucy. Her cheekbones gleamed like the blades of a straight razor and her black skin radiated daggers. It felt like something very dangerous was about to happen.

"'There are too many meetings,'" I complained to Fischer and Parsons. 'Regular meetings, special meetings, mass meetings, secret meetings. I'm sick of meetings. We need fewer meetings and more direct action.' Lucy just looked at me like I was a crazy man.

"Lucy and Parsons and their party definitely went home before the bomb went off. I watched them leave and ordered another beer and then the window fell in and glass was flying everywhere and the building kind of settled back on its haunches. When I finally came out from under the table and ran to where the window had been, the police had opened up. Bodies were falling everywhere. Women crumpled to the stones like rag dolls, the children crushed upon the breasts of their dead mothers. A typical American massacre.

"I waited there at Zyffs for my brother but he never came. I was convinced that he had been murdered in the police fusillade and all I could think of was to get back to the room we had rented off

Halsted—we had moved from Mama Rebeka's so that our work would not draw any heat to her home.

"At last, the police reholstered their revolvers and now there were sirens and the ambulances and fire wagons galloping to the scene. No one noticed when I slipped off into the night.

"When my brother didn't come home, I was sure that he was dead and began rehearsing to tell our mother what had happened. Then I heard a crack on the stairs and there he was, more dead than alive, both his eyes blacked and an ugly red gash running across his scalp. He had been grabbed in the Haymarket and taken to the Desplaines station where Bonfield had personally brutalized him with his blackjack and then had him thrown in the crowded tank cell with the other comrades.

"Around three in the morning, a man in a suit, whom my brother did not know, came to the bars. 'Psst,' he signaled, 'we're going to let you go.' Lack of evidence. The screws took him out of the cell. My brother didn't understand it and it spooked him—it was like they were trying to set him up. By then, everyone but Lingg and Parsons had been pinched. Spies and Engels and Fischer and Fielden had been picked up at the *Arbeiter-Zeitung* offices. Schwab and our dear sister Maria too. 'Get out of here,' the cops ordered my brother. By now, Rudolph smelled a rat.

"I dressed my brother's wound and put a hat on his head to keep it clean. He had his bag all packed for just such an emergency exit. I walked him to the depot but when we saw the plainclothes cops at the train gate, we hesitated and exchanged identification papers. My brother had his collar pulled up and his hat slouched down over his eyes and that way the inspectors allowed 'Edward Bernhardt Schnaubelt' to board the train that day.

"My brother holed up at George Meng's farm on the Illinois–Wisconsin line until it was safe to move on. Meng was a member of the same circle as Lingg—some historians even say that Meng was the real bombthrower. George Meng was fearless and probably crazy. He drank like the devil and cursed God and would tear open his shirt and dare the Lord to strike him dead. He perished in a saloon fire years later brooding over a beer and the secret of the Haymarket. But George Meng did not throw the bomb.

"I never saw my brother again. Legend has it that he first went to Canada and then England. He wound up in Argentina. Some say that he became a cattle rancher, a gaucho on the Pampas, and others that he kept a metal shop in the port of Buenos Aires. I don't know if he ever learned to dance the Tango. He never wrote.

"Years later, maybe 20, Frank Harris, a bald-faced liar, thief, and yellow journalist, wrote a book blaming Rudolph Schnaubelt, "the man who disappeared," for throwing the bomb at the Haymarket. The name of the book is *The Bomb* and it is probably *as* dangerous to carry it in your hand luggage onboard domestic and international flights (as it is to carry this one aboard). *The Bomb* is a calumny and a fabrication from page one to the back cover and Harris ought to fry in boiling fish oil for an eternity for having written it. He has branded my brother as the Haymarket bomber for all of history. Let's get this straight now: My brother did not toss that bomb."

Life of Ross

My mom thought she was the Union Maid. Sufficiently lubricated by poisons of her own choosing, she would yawp at me in her grotesquely off-key voice, of "goons and ginks and company finks and of the sheriffs who made the raids." She had once helped the CIO organize a union of theatrical managers and press agents, not exactly an industrial powerhouse that would bring the Capitalist economy to its knees.

Unlike you, Eddie Schnaubelt, my roots were not in the industrial proletariat. I was not whelped down in the stinking miasmas of the Chicago River wards amid roughneck wage slaves, but rather at perfumed addresses on Central Park West and the grittier but no less blessed West Village.

Maybe Mom wasn't a steelworker or a lumberjack but she knew "Solidarity Forever" by heart and she militantly tramped the snow drifts (or took cabs) when Mike Quill called out the transit workers at midnight on January 1st, 1952.

She fought Taft-Hartley and chastised friends who crossed the picket lines of striking bank workers and department-store employees. Once, when my preteen sister Susan arrived home with a Macy's shopping bag on her arm during a particularly vicious strike at that Herald Square emporium, my mom chased her all around the loft with a mop. Years later, guilt-ridden because I had inadvertently crossed a city workers' picket line to attend a San Francisco Giants home opener, I recalled Mom and her mop on the pages of "California Living," the Sunday magazine of the *San Francisco Examiner*.

"What's a mop?" Mom puzzled when she read the clip.

My own personal chapter of *Labor's Untold Story* is a checkered tale. When I was 12, I organized a union of wagon boys out on Fire Island, a favored getaway for hassled Manhattanites—during the summer-vacation months, we would meet the ferries and haul visitors' suitcases and groceries to the bungalows in our little red wagons. But some of the brothers (there were no sisters) had taken to undercutting the base 75-cents-a-run rate and it hurt business. Then Chris Stone broke away and organized a scab union and I had to send the education committee to teach him a lesson—we dumped Chris, the son of I.F. Stone, the first radical journalist I ever met in the flesh, in a downtown Ocean Beach garbage can to show him some labor etiquette. When Izzy, serenely deaf on the sun porch, got word of the wagon boys' revolt, I like to think he took Chris aside and lectured him on labor solidarity.

My baptism of fire in the class war, like yours, E. B., came during a desperate strike. In 1960, in between Mexico sojourns, I went to work on the barges in New York Harbor. It was a time-honored Greenwich Village job and the slots were passed around between boozed-up seamen and Beat writers in dingy saloons like the Kettle of Fish and the Riv. During the spring and summer months, we ran the Hudson River from Albany to the Long Island Sound and out to Port Jefferson, Long Island, a slow crawl, hauling sand and gravel for the construction trade. We were all captains only because we were the sole crew aboard these ancient leakers, which were not barges at all, but rather scows with the load up on the deck.

We lived in ragged wooden shacks in back of the load and our job was to keep leaky old eelpots afloat so the insurance costs wouldn't go up for the sand-and-gravel companies. Too often, we had to crank the bilge hand pump all day and all night and never made a dent in the level of water that gushed through the bilge walls. In classic maritime tradition, many a hapless captain went down with his scow.

When orders were slow, your scow would get tied up on a barge anchored in the middle of the Hudson River and you could not get to the store for a week. I have survived on canapés of dog food under such degrading circumstances. But most of the time, we couldn't eat for the stench anyway, as the tugs hauled us through the putrid industrial scum of the Newark River or the Gowanus Canal, and if we were fortunate enough to tie up on terra firma, it was on creaky piers at the stinky feet of the city. We were like wharf rats and we smelled too bad to go home.

For being allowed to experience this colorful lifestyle, the members of Deck Scow Captains Local 410 were paid by the barge companies $1.25 the hour, then the minimum wage—half that for mandatory overtime when you were staked out 90 feet off the East River Drive and couldn't get off the boat to scavenge for food.

Local 410 was a wholly-owned subsidiary of Boss Joe Curren's National Maritime Union (NMU)—Curren had red-baited every progressive seaman off the ships long before Joe McCarthy was scouring the Army for purported commies.

For all of those reasons and more, one hot July day in 1960, 300 ersatz captains walked or swam off their scows and declared themselves on strike for a new contract. It wasn't exactly a spontaneous wild-cat strike though—our dues were being wooed by Curren's rival, the Seafarers' International (SIU), an even more rabidly anti-red bunch that had hoodwinked us into signing pledge cards.

Because the scows carried the bulk of materials used to mix concrete for the short New York construction season, we had a lot more clout than our dismal status as bedraggled wharf rats belied. I ran with Tommy Crowley and Big Bill from Barra de Navidad, sailors with a thirst for action, and they showed me the ropes. Down on the 40th Street Pier, we clamored down into the bilges of one New York Traprock leaker and chopped a big hole in a side wall with our axes. Then we scampered up top and cut the hawsers free and sent the old scow wheeling to its watery grave in the middle of the shipping channel. Wowee! Sabotage! What a rush!

Tommy and Big Bill taught me how to sugar the gas tanks of the cement-mixer trucks the bosses had lined up along the waterfront, waiting for the strike to fizzle. We fought mounted police down on South Street dock and ice-picked the tires of New York's Finest patrol cars. Finally, the union bosses figured enough was enough and George Meany himself, the AFL-CIO head goon, summoned us to the SIU hall in Brooklyn and ordered us back to work without a new contract. That November, when the river froze up, all the captains were taken off the scows and no one ever went back to work. I packed up my wife and kids and headed straight back to Mexico.

By the time I got back from south of the border and lit down in San Francisco, it was 1964, the genocide in Vietnam was in LBJ's pipeline, and black people were marching and singing all over America. An old comrade, Barton Stone (no relation to Izzy and Chris), who had just been sprung from the federal poky for sailing into the South Pacific nuclear test zone, signed me up for the Industrial Workers of the World, the One Big Union, and I became a Wobbly with my own little red dues book filled with row after row of neat retro stamps.

By 1964, the IWW was really retro, reduced to organizing workers at a San Francisco Cedar Alley cafe owned by Malvina Reynolds, the "Ticky Tacky Box" lady. I felt like I was part of the end of what had once been something important.

"I know something about the Wobblies, son. The Industrial Workers of the World first saw the light of day where else but in Chicago, the most proletarian city on the U.S. map. The year was nineteen-ought-five and I caught a train clear across country just to be there.

"Big Bill Hayward, the one-eyed miners' leader from Colorado, was elected secretary general at the founding convention—he called it the 'Continental Congress of the Working Class.' Lucy Parsons, Albert's wife, now 52, but still sharp-tongued and on the front lines of labor's eternal struggle, was right there on the stage by his side and it filled me with pride to see her there. Lucy was the second woman to sign up in the IWW—Mother Jones was the first and Emma Goldman and Elizabeth Gurley Flynn, "the Rebel Girl," were third and fourth. Joe Hill was up there too and Gene Debs and, it goes without saying, so were the ghosts of the Haymarket Martyrs.

"And me too—I was there and never will forget it."

Tell me more, Brother Schnaubelt.

"Well, the Wobblies weren't communists and they weren't anarchists. They called their way of thinking 'anarcho-syndicalism.' That meant the factories and the fields were the basic units of organizing how society would be run once the Capitalist class was overthrown. 'An injury to one is an injury to all' was their motto and they stuck to it. The Wobblies mocked the official unions and the political parties. Their tactics and strategies were the Black Cat and the Wooden Shoe, industrial sabotage, the sit-down strike, and monkey-wrenching the Capitalist system. They organized blacks and Mexicans and Italians and American Indians, Hunkies and Polacks and Women and Just Plain Americans. They hated the wage system and they were pledged to bring it down.

"Out here in California, the IWWs were chased up and down the coast for demanding their right to be heard, 'free speech' is what we called it. Us Wobblies would go to a public square or park and sing Joe

Hill songs out loud to agitate the workers and the sheriff would come down and haul us off to the can until the jails were so full they had to let the Wobs loose and we would go on to the next stop and preach free speech all over again.

"The Wobblies were fearless. They rode the boxcars and sang with T-Bone Slim, 'Hallelujah I'm a Bum! (Bum Again!') and 'There is power, there is power in a band of working men/when they stand hand in hand (One Industrial Union Grand!)' They followed the crops, organized whole harvests, and were gone with the dust in the morning. They were bindlestiffs and popular Wobblies, grifters, drifters, pickers, and streetcorner poets. They organized the iron miners up in the Mesabi range of Minnesota, the hard-rock miners in Idaho and Colorado, timber workers in the Great Northwest, the waitresses of Los Angeles. They battled the Colorado militia, the Arizona and the Texas Rangers, the Pinkertons, the scabs, the railroad bulls, and the local flatfoots. That's just how it was."

Thank you, Eddie, for that background report. I'm sure that those who are still with us appreciated hearing your recollections.

Phil Mehlman was a young Wobbly organizer when he got sent up for "criminal syndicalism." For ten years, the State kept him locked up in San Quentin out there on San Francisco Bay. By the time I got to the Bay Area in 1964 on the lam from Michoacan timber wars, Phil, then in his 70's, had been introduced to Sandoz Acid and his Dearborn Street digs in the Mission were always filled with blissed-out young folks who eagerly gobbled up his stories.

Inspired by Phil to reinvent the IWW, we scheduled the first Wobbly street meeting in San Francisco in 30 years. Barton and his pals tuned up their guitars and banjos, promising authentic renditions of "Long-haired Preachers Come Out Every Night" and "Might Is Right" and "We Have Fed You All For A Thousand Years." Back then, we thought we could drive the ruling class mad by singing at them.

As luck would have it, this historic event took place the night after the burgeoning Bay Area civil rights movement had occupied the lobby of the swank Sheraton Palace to protest a dearth of black faces on the hotel's employment roster—700 of us were carried off to jail for blocking the revolving doors over by the perfume counter. I was caterwauling "I Aint A-scared of Your Jails Because I Want My Freedom," locked arm-in-arm with a pair of muscle-bound longshoremen on either side of me and when the cops yanked on my legs to break us apart, my pants flew off and I was tossed bare-assed into a waiting paddy wagon.

After we had sung the jailhouse down and were bailed out the next morning, we headed back to the Palace to do it all over again and as we swept up skid row, where the first Wobbly rally in 30 years would happen that night, I reminded the dazed denizens not to miss it.

The fireworks got under way in a slimy drizzle outside a Chinese grocery store on Third and Howard. There were few witnesses: three winos, the Chinese grocery store owner and his family, and ten squad cars of burly men in blue. "What do we do now," Barton whispered anxiously. I mounted the soapbox, really a milk crate of eclectic origins that the cops eyeballed as possible stolen property, and offered the throng my recitation of the preamble to the IWW Constitution: "The working class and the ruling class have nothing in common. There can be no peace between them as long as hunger and want are to be found among millions and the few have all the good things of life . . ."

"What the fuck did he just say?" I could lip-read the pigs muttering.

"Between the two classes, a struggle must go on until the workers of the world organize as a class, take possession of the means of production, abolish the wage system, and live in harmony with the earth . . ."

"Live in harmony with the earth?" It sounded like commie propaganda to the cops. They stroked their batons like they were masturbating.

Then Barton and Don Auclair pulled out fretted instruments and began to croon "You will live by and by/in that glorious land beyond the sky/work and pray, live on hay/you'll get pie in the sky when you die (that's no lie!") and bam! the guardians of law and order were in our faces. Did we have permits to sing this commie crap in the street? Weren't we the guys that started all that shit at the Palace? We were disturbing the peace and they were seizing our instruments as evidence. Oh-no, not the guitars, the musicians groaned.

We caucused. I asked the comrades what Joe Hill would have done in this situation, or Ralph Chaplin (Chaplin, who wrote many Wobbly anthems became a lunatic anti-Communist in later life). But I was a minority of one. The musicians packed their cases and we slunk home.

Disgusted with this act of surrender, I turned my Wobbly dues book back to Barton, the one with all those pretty stamps. I was looking for the revolution, I told him sadly, not a hootenany.

By 1965, after a few seasons at Terminal Island Federal Penitentiary for flipping off Johnson's brutal war against the Vietnamese people ("Hey Hey LBJ, How Many Kids Did You Kill Today?"), I thought I had finally found that revolution, and attached my anarchist proclivities to a vanguard Marxist-Leninist-Maoist conspiracy to overthrow the pinche U.S. government, the Progressive Labor Party. Although the word "labor" appeared on our mast-head, few of us had actual jobs.

The "Progressive Labor" handle was the brainstorm of a couple of Buffalo, New York steelworkers who had been booted out of the Communist Party USA for espousing the "Albanian Tendency" and, in the process, had embraced not only the glorious thoughts of Enver Hoxna but that of Mao as well. Progressive Labor talked tough, worked arduously at building a base for the coming revolution, and popularized Mao's *Little Red Book* before anyone else saw its commercial possibilities. Indeed, we lived by and for the *Book*. What is to be done? Here, read this. One step forward and two steps back. . . . Or is it two steps forward? I could never get it right.

We studied Hegel and took target practice out at the Coyote Point police range right under the snouts of the pigs and held secret meetings at the International House of Pancakes where we wondered if it was time to go underground yet. Mostly we criticized ourselves and each other for not being revolutionary enough.

Oh sure, we could make a mess for the ruling class, like the time my then-wife dumped hundreds of cockroaches all over the San Francisco

Health Department chambers to protest slumlord deprivations, but you couldn't win the revolution with cockroaches alone. We needed the industrial proletariat for that. Building a community base—I ran a tenants' union out in the Mission—was decreed women's work. The guys had to get jobs.

I went right to the heel of the matter and joined the Teamsters. I worked in warehouse and the Teamos and Harry Bridges' once left-wing International Longshoremen and Warehousemen's Union (ILWU) negotiated a joint Northern California agreement together. We had comrades in both locals and formed a caucus to push our wild-eyed demands and convince the working class to support revolutionary communism.

On the night the Great Northern California Warehouse Strike of 1967 was voted up at a San Francisco Labor Temple conclave, Herb Sivocco, a 300-pound Samoan Teamo goon who was called "The Toe" because he could crack an adversary's femur with one swift kick down below, warned me that I would be riding with him on the "education committee" in the morning. The union bosses had been watching US commies like buzzards and were going to keep us in close confinement during the upcoming strike.

At dawn the next day, I found myself wedged between a pair of corpulent educators in the back seat of a goon mobile trolling the South San Francisco industrial-park district for freelance scabs. The first catch of the day was an older black man in a battered pickup, hauling a rug from a Teamster warehouse. "Get the nigger!" Sivocco rasped at me as the goons nonchalantly stopped traffic on one of the Bay Area's most traveled arteries in the middle of morning rush hour. Thankfully, the driver scrambled off before I was forced to pummel him and then we turned his truck upside down in a muddy ditch. "Good work," Herb the Toe cheerfully gurgled.

For the next two weeks, The Toe and I were a team. Herb clapped me on the back when I threw a handtruck through a dispatcher's booth down on Folsom Street, showering the scabs with glass. I watched in horror as Sivocco booted a non-union worker off a loading dock and then tossed a drum of toxic chemicals on top of him. These were serious felonies.

But despite such acts of criminal bravado, in the end, just as George Meany had sold the scow captains down the river way back when, Harry Bridges himself, once a radical red and now a registered Republican, invited us to the Cow Palace and shouted that we'd won and now go back to work. Our fellow workers, the payments on their pick-ups and their Harleys threatened, meekly voted to do just that.

The revolutionary communists caucused and re-caucused, trying to figure it all out. Where had we gone wrong? Why didn't the wage slaves comprehend that they had nothing in common with the Capitalist class? Criticism and self-criticism marathons were mounted. What is to be done? One step forward and one step . . . oh forget it.

By 1969 with the war grinding relentlessly onward and the American proletariat mesmerized by the illusion of a light at the end of the tunnel, I was many more steps behind the Vanguard Party. The practice of "Democratic centralism" and duplicitous conduct during the San Francisco State student strike had curdled me on the Progressive Laborites—although my former comrades always claim that I was excommunicated because (a) I never learned to drive a vehicle (for bank-robbery getaways, I suppose) and (b) I had been spotted puffing on a joint, a cardinal sin in the PL catechism, up in the Haight-Ashbury where the next revolution was revving its spectral propellers.

Life of Schnaubelt

"'We shouldn't be expecting Rudolph back any time soon.' I had to break the news to Mama Rebeka as best I could. She was ailing and anxious about Maria who was still in jail. 'Don't you go off on me now too, Eddie' she pleaded, so I had to stick around although I had made up my mind to leave Chicago.

"Chicago was no place for a labor radical after the Haymarket. Lucy was picked up three times the day after the bombing but Albert had gotten clean away. I was taken down to the central station house twice myself—both times I used Rudolph's papers (he had mine) and both times the detectives just let me walk away. Like my brother, this made me wonder if letting me run loose like that wasn't just a setup and I decided to ditch my brother's documents. His friend George Meng got me new papers.

"The bombing had given Bonfield a license to break up workers' meetings and the bulls busted our skulls every day with their billy clubs when we tried to stand our ground. Many a militant left his teeth on the sidewalks of Chicago during this terrible time. Thousands were packed off in the paddy wagons and taken down to the pens. I saw that the brothers and sisters were getting tired. There was no question but we needed to reorganize.

"Three-hundred-thousand workers had been on strike for the eight-hour day but after the Haymarket bomb, the strike collapsed and the 'respectable' labor leaders like Powderly and Gompers washed their hands of the anarchists. They said we were 'human monstrosities' and ought to be blotted off the face of the earth. Powderly and the Knights of Labor convicted us even before the courts could.

"It was a lynch mob out there, the damnedest red scare you ever saw in your whole life. The bosses' newspapers howled that we were 'vipers' and 'ungrateful hyenas'—though I never saw a grateful one. 'They sneak through the land like midnight assassins bamboozling ignorant foreigners into throwing dynamite bombs.' That's what *The Chicago Tribune* wrote in an editorial. The Illinois legislature and the federal congress in Washington passed a pile of unconstitutional laws that made Clinton's anti-terror law look like a tax rebate."

Pardon me for interrupting, Eddie, but I've read that on May Day 1886, 70,000 workers in Chicago had won the right to the eight-hour day. By the end of the year, only 10,000 retained that right. Some writers argue that the backlash from the bombing signaled the death of radical labor in North America and the ascendancy of milquetoast reformers like Powderly and Gompers. . . .

"Look friend, is this some kind of interview or press conference? I thought I was narrating the story of my life for a book on spec—about which we need to discuss the financial arrangements before we get on much farther with this project.

"I will state, however, for the record—if you want to get this down—that, no, the bomb at Haymarket did *not* squash radical labor or the battle for the eight-hour day. By 1890, German carpenters—and I was a member of this union, remember?—had won the eight-hour day all over again, and radical labor bounced back bigger and stronger than ever with the Wobblies a decade later.

"I would appreciate it if you would hold your questions until the end of what I am telling you.

"Thirty-one indictments were handed down by the end of May and Rudolph's name was right up there on the list. People on both sides talked a lot of stuff about Rudolph and the bomb. Even my fellow anarchists looked at me funny and argued behind my back that my brother must have been a double agent. 'Hadn't Schnaubelt's bomb destroyed the general strike,' they whispered, and now those that can find work are toiling 10 and 12 hours a day again. The 'proof' of Rudolph's guilt was that the police had picked him up three times and let him escape. I wanted to say that two of those arrests, it was me, but held my tongue—after all, wherever he was, Rudolph was me now, and I was him.

"Personally, I always believed the police threw the bomb on themselves. Rudolph, the man they let disappear, was their backup villain for the Haymarket if they hadn't nabbed Parsons. I have to believe that.

"I don't know why they wanted to put it on my brother so bad. After all, they had a real bomber in jail, Louis Lingg, the only defendant found to be with bombs—he had a trunkful of them when Captain Schatz collared him down in his shack by the river.

"Like I said before, of all the anarchists, the one they most wanted for Haymarket was Parsons. Albert left town in a big hurry, shaved off his mustache, boot-blacked his hair, and headed for Lizzie Holmes' husband's farm out in Geneva, Illinois. He and Lucy kissed hard on the lips, so hard that it drew blood. They looked at each other long in the eye. They thought they would never see each other alive again. Lizzie yelled it was time to go.

"If America had had a Most Wanted back then, Albert Parsons would have been number one on it. He laid low as he could up in John Holmes' barn for a few weeks before traveling on to Wisconsin, painting houses for bread and keep. He had no contact with Lucy and for all he knew she was dead. Then he got hold of the Chicago papers and read in there that Spies and the rest were being taken to trial June 21st. The notion that he abandoned them tortured Parsons' conscience so he came back to Chicago to face the music. Walked right into the court room on the first day of the trial and gave himself up. Maybe Parsons thought giving himself up like that would convince the jury of his innocence. He was dead wrong on that one.

• • •

"The trial lasted all through July and most of August. The courtroom was like an oven and the stink from the river crowded through the open windows and made everyone gag, even Gary the judge and the D.A., Julius Grinnell. It was a stink that made you think about killing the whole lot of them.

"Captain William Black was the lawyer for the eight men brought to trial for the Haymarket bombing. Captain Black was a Civil War hero and much respected in civic circles. Parsons had been a Johnny Reb and then turned on the slavocrats and married a black girl.

"Parsons was also the only native-born of the eight, and only for him and Fielden was English their first language. This was a real issue—some of the men could barely follow the trial. Lingg had only been in America for a little over a year. It was a kind of racism against the foreigners—the Germans were the next niggers. They wanted to deport us like they deport the Mexicans.

"The trial was stacked against the Martyrs from the opening gavel. Every time Captain Black tried to object, Judge Gary threatened him with contempt of court. Grinnell handpicked a hanging jury—one was even the cousin of a cop who had been shot at Haymarket. Captain Black tried to disqualify him for prejudice but Grinnell had a roomful of cop lovers waiting to replace him.

"Of course the State had zero evidence that the men had set the bomb besides a few perjured witnesses. They put a notorious scab, Harry Gilmour, on the stand and he lied out loud that Spies had lit the fuse and my brother Rudolph had thrown the bomb. But Rudolph disappeared. He couldn't be there to defend himself. That was all they had. The lies of a filthy scab.

"So the prosecution decided to put the ideas of the men and their words on trial. The jury was read Parsons' speeches, Spies', what the others had written in the anarchist newspapers, and the State charged they were all guilty of the premeditated murder of the cop Mathias Degman because of what they had once said or written. Although only

Lingg had them, all eight defendants were accused of conspiracy to overthrow the government of the United States with dynamite bombs.

"Even though she was not on trial, the D.A. read from Lucy Parsons' articles in *The Alarm* to prove these things. Back in the winter of '84, times had been especially tough and the weather so fearsome that homeless people were throwing themselves in the Chicago River. Lucy thought that was a great waste. She suggested that if the homeless were so damn bent on self-destruction they should tie on dynamite first and take a rich man down to hell with them. 'Let us kill them without mercy!' she had written in one call to arms for *The Alarm*.

"D.A. Grinnell pounded rhythmically on the jury rail. 'Kill-them-without-mercy! Kill-them-without mercy!' Captain Black kept objecting but the judge had dozed off and paid him no mind.

"Suddenly, Mrs. Lucy Parsons was on her feet, a colossal black woman wailing at the top of her lungs that these were her words being read in the courtroom, not her husband's, and she demanded to be up there on trial with him, by his side, and to be hung for her own words. They would swing together! Judge Gary snapped right up and flailed away with his little wooden hammer and the bailiffs rushed in to restrain the distraught Lucy.

"I saw Lucy Parsons every day of the trial, sometimes in the courtroom and sometimes I would wait outside for her if there wasn't a seat at the trial. She let me walk with her and the children and I felt proud to do it. I carried her books and her pamphlets for her and every day we would discuss what we had seen in the courtroom and what it meant.

"In the evenings that summer, Lucy would often take her stepladder and her books with the writings of Albert Parsons in them and the leaflets demanding his liberation, and go down by the lakefront to agitate the crowds that strolled there trying to find a gasp of fresh air, for the Martyrs' acquittal. The cops would come and try and pull her down but I would step in and I'm a big guy and what with the hot night and the working people who rightly sympathized with her, the bulls usually backed down. Lucy would thank me and take my arm after the meeting was done and we would walk along the lake and talk.

"Or sometimes when she had other comrades to carry her things, I would watch after little Lula and Albert Jr. and tell them stories made up of scraps of all I had seen. Only the workers always won in those stories.

"Lucy and Albert rented two rooms down around Lincoln Park. She worked as a seamstress in the midnight hours at home, sewing her fingers to the bone to keep the kids fed and Albert in clean underwear. I don't think she ever slept.

"One night she took me to her bedside and threw back the bedclothes to show what she kept there. I saw three bombs. She said they were Lingo's. After Albert went to prison, Lucy Parsons slept every night with Louis Lingg's bombs.

"Lucy Parsons was a black woman born into slavery. As a young girl, she had been whipped for the sheer pleasure of it by her white master. She knew what slavery was by the lashes that cut her black skin, the original slavery, chattel slavery, and she was still a slave to the wage system. She felt its teeth on her back as deeply as she had suffered the bullwhip of the overseers. Only dynamite bombs could break those shackles.

"After deliberating just three hours—some said they was playing pinochle in there—the jury came back with the guilty verdict. It was the 20th of August 1886, just three months after the bombing and that dog Gary set sentencing for the next day. My sister Maria got hysterical in the courtroom and started screaming that Professor Schwab was innocent and had not even been at the meeting. But it was all in German and Gary didn't pay it much mind.

"There wasn't a soul in Chicago who couldn't have told you what kind of medicine that judge was going to prescribe to cure the anarchists of their disease. Parsons stood by the open window and made a noose out of the window sash. When Gary asked the defendants if they had anything to say before he handed down the sentence, the men said yes, they had plenty to say. I missed some of it because Maria was yelling again and I had to take her outside to calm her down.

"The speeches became famous. Spies, who was so white in skin color he looked like he had no blood in him, accused the State of wanting to hang the Martyrs of Chicago to break the back of the labor movement, but you couldn't stop labor now. The workers would never go back!

"When Gary asked Parsons if he had anything to say, Albert spoke for two days, eight straight hours in all. He told the tragedy of Capitalism and stipulated all the provocations the working class had suffered. Yes, it was enough to want to overthrow the government with dynamite bombs. And yet we were prudent, he insisted, we value life. We did not throw the bomb at the Haymarket. We are innocent.

"Lucy rose again from her seat, terrible in her anger and grief, and pronounced judgment. 'I give you to liberty, my husband.' Judge Gary grabbed for his gavel.

"Louis Lingg had not understood much of the proceedings. He had sat obliviously for two months, thumbing a book by Johan Most in German. Now like a coiled snake, he sprang from his chair to denounce the bosses' justice: 'I do not recognize your laws and I do not recognize the jurisdiction of this court. I say it now: I am a man who favors force. I will be happy to die for what I believe and when I am gone, it will be the people who throw the bombs that will bring down the Capitalist system. I detest you.'

"Judge Gary pushed back a yawn and set the execution date for December 3rd.

"After the trial, the men were moved to the Cook County jail and every morning their women would go to that terrible place and kiss them fondly through the stiff mesh wire that separated the Martyrs from their loved ones. A defense organization to save the lives of the Haymarket men was formed and an appeal filed to the Illinois Supreme Court and that stayed the death orders pending a hearing.

"That September, Lucy traveled to Ohio and Pennsylvania to plead for the lives of the Haymarket Martyrs. She went on to New England

and spoke in mill towns to the workers and educated the students at Yale University about the frame-up. In New York City, she talked at labor forums and defense rallies so often that one writer joked he was in favor of releasing her husband if only to give Mrs. Parsons a breather. Haymarket put Lucy Parsons on the road, preaching her husband's innocence, anarchism, socialism, and workers' solidarity, and ya, she did not get off that road for the next six decades of her life.

"Lucy was like a woman possessed now. She could not stop talking about it, not stop shouting out night after night her righteous indignation at the slave system that wanted to hang her husband.

"I couldn't take my eyes off her. I followed her everywhere. I went to every lecture and meeting. She was like my live wire to the revolution.

"Lucy liked having me around. I was big and could push back on the police. I was sort of like her bodyguard. But I was falling in love with her too.

"We went to St. Louis on the train. She had many speaking engagements there. We stayed in the same hotel together but in separate rooms. We stood in the hallway and she took me in her arms and knew that I loved her. But we didn't sleep together. She couldn't make love with another man until Albert had been hung. She was his slave until the State murdered him and released her from her obligation to stand at his side until Death do thee part.

"So I decided to stay on in St. Louis. Being around Lucy with all that feeling I had for her just hurt too much. She knew, she understood it. I put her on the train back up to Chicago and stood there until she was long out of the station. Then I went down to the carpenters' hall and got a job. I'm a good carpenter.

"Well, amigo, what do you think of my sob story so far? This could sell as one of those tell-all books. How do you feel about a screen treatment? Any chance of getting one of your Hollywood pals to give us a read?"

Loves of Ross

My first love came to me when I was a fumbling 17-year-old boy who could never unhook the stays of her brassiere without ripping it to shreds. Suzanne was already at university, Sarah Lawrence, where she became student-body president, their first black, an achiever. The year was 1955 and there was not a lot of black-white coupling going on in Leave It To Beaver America. Yet Suzanne McClain fit right into the anti-universe of my cockeyed family dynamic.

In the late 1940s, during a high-end vacation in Haiti, Mom had taken up with the Afro-American painter Harlan Jackson and, after a stormy disengagement from my biological father, packed up her mink coats and martini shaker and moved into his sparsely furnished loft on West Broadway, a decade before Soho became the art moguls' wet dream.

The loft was enormous, large enough to accommodate a regulation basketball hoop under the skylight. Harlan Jackson was a hoopster, having joined the Harlem Globetrotters' backup team after his discharge from the Navy. But his athletic skills were always sublimated to art, and when the G.I. Bill afforded him the opportunity, he enrolled at the California School of Fine Arts up above North Beach in San Francisco, studied with the Abstract Expressionist Clifford Styll, and won a Rosenberg Fellowship to live and paint in Haiti.

Harlan had a voodoo cross carved into his chest. He learned to summon the Houngans on skin drum and drive the dancers into ecstasy. He painted chiseled, earth-tone African mask–like canvases, and today is remembered as one of the very few blacks to show up for the almost exclusively caucasian art rebellion of the 1950s.

Like Pollock and Herman Cherry and other masters of that school, Harlan was a jazz aficionado whose tastes hovered between Jimmie Lunceford and Charlie Parker. He invited me downstairs to Birdland to catch the Basie band and uptown to Minton's Playhouse where bop was born. We caught Billie Holiday and a Joel McCrea shoot-em-up at the Apollo Theater. Harlan was a Western-movie junkie although he always rooted for the Indians (he claimed Cherokee blood.) Harlan Jackson was the perfect family to bring Suzanne McClain on home to.

As with all first loves, delirium reigned and the breakup was like delicately shattered glass. Sue fell for one of Harlan's running partners, an aging bon vivant who probably saw her as the end of the cornucopia of young women thrown up on his doorstep in the course of a debauched life. I know the syndrome now that I have rambled through the tunnel of love for 65 years myself. But my heart was broken for the first time and the first time is forever.

There has indeed been a crazy-quilt parade of heartbreakers ever since. Some of the drum majorettes became wives, others stayed lovers and some have even become friends.

Norma was a bad-talking Beat groupie when we teamed up in the East Village in the late '50s, a Catholic schoolgirl who got radical and cruised the bars for sex. Her clique never liked me much. "She used to be pretty before she met John Ross," they would cluck. We ran off to Mexico and had kids, some of whom are still alive. She suffered me as an arrogant, blitzed young man wild to become the white Rimbaud (Bob Kaufman was already the black one), and I treated her very badly.

Ellen was a child of the Mayflower, the scion of Cambridge Brahmans who shared the rich blue blood of the British Churchills.

Her true first name was Lucretia Ellen, after her great-grandmother Lucretia Mott, the first suffragette, but I think it was a burden to her. She was a golden-haired S.D.S. naif and I a jaded class warrior when destiny hooked us together in the most tumultuous moments of the 1960s. But she took to the barricades as if they were her natural habitat, and has spent the rest of her life on them. When last spotted, she was driving the #14 bus up San Francisco's Mission Street, still entertaining the possibility that the revolution could begin at the next intersection.

I treated Ellen as badly as I did Norma.

You can see the pattern by now. I shall not bother you with the names, dates, or details of these soap operas. I did not begin this soliloquy to apologize for past misdeeds and miscalculations. But the bruisings of the heart have not all been one-way. When a man loves a woman he will sleep out in the rain and it has often been a hard one.

Irma was a poor girl from the Nuevo Laredo desert who had scratched her way up through the Texas educational system and hid a trail of pain and *desgraciada pobreza* beneath an eternally beautiful masque that only a pact with the devil could have guaranteed. She came for me and I was dazzled in the way old men are after their love life has faded to black and I never even noticed that she was married although she wore all the appropriate rings. We made furtive and frequent love in dozens of hotel rooms from Hollywood to Havana. The champagne flowed at midnight and the flamingoes flocked in the first rays of the rosy-fingered dawn. *Ay Que Rico, verdad?*

Then she got the brilliant idea of divorcing Joe, her husband, a working stiff on the midnight shift back home in Houston, Texas, and I guess she divorced me too, leaving me waiting in a Mexico City hotel room for a knock that would never come again. Sure, it was a whirl—*suave danzon* on the *pista* in Veracruz puerto and the lush strawberries we gobbled on the windy back road to Santa Barbara California. But in the end she got even for all my past sins and treated me as badly as I had treated all the others.

"Are you done with your whining?" a moss-green voice sneered.

Did you say you wanted more wine, Eddie?

"Pour it on me, brother. Man-o-Manichewitz!" Schnaubelt licked the bones where his lips used to be. "Hey, do you think I could continue with my story now? I'm coming to the crucial part."

"Take it away, Comrade Schnaubie. After all, it's your life."

Death of the Martyrs

"The Illinois Supreme Court turned down the Martyrs' appeal in September of '87 and set a November 11th date with the hangman.

"Time was running out and I knew I had to go back to Chicago for the end if only to stand with Lucy.

"Lucy's lecture tours on behalf of the defendants had raised enough funds to make one last appeal to the United States Supreme Court and a young company lawyer named Clarence Darrow volunteered to take the case without a fee. But the outlook was bleak. The bosses had the country by the throat and the labor movement was paralyzed, divided, and dispirited. No matter how hard we pushed, we could not turn back the juggernaut of bourgeois justice.

"I went to see Lucy and she was in a frenzy. Now she wanted that the State should hang all four of them together, Lula and Junior too—it was a craziness that Parsons himself had endorsed. There was within them both a wish to die in public. Only then could they sleep the deep sleep that successful martyrs achieve and be at peace. Both of them were real Americans martyrs.

"Three of the defendants, my brother-in-law Schwab, Fielden, and August Spies had appealed to Governor Oglesby for leniency and a commutation of their death warrants. Albert and Lucy would not hear of such a thing and demanded that all seven should swing from the gallows as one—a position seconded by Fischer, Engels, and Lingg. Young Oscar Neebe, who had received only 15 years for his part of the "conspiracy," demanded that he be strung up with all the rest.

"I began to see how badly Lucy needed her husband and the rest to hang. Only when the Martyrs were finally swinging in their nooses would she be freed from the slavery of keeping them alive. Only then when Albert was finally gone could she remake his memory into hers and own it for all of time.

"As November came on and the weather grew grim, the workmen began to build the gibbet in the courtyard of the jail. The women could hear the *tack-tack* of their hammers when they went to visit their men and it put a chill on their hearts. On November 2nd, the Supreme

Court "justices" informed Darrow that they would not listen to the Haymarket appeal. Commutation was still a possibility for Fielden, Schwab, and Spies but for the rest, their doom was sealed.

"'SEVEN NOOSES DANGLE FOR DYNAMITE FIENDS'! the newsboys hollered. Rich folks was wearing little gold gallows pins. Talk about your Rosenbergs. This was a bonafide lynching.

"Then, on November 7th, during a routine search of Louis Lingg's cell, four bombs were found hidden inside some hollowed-out oranges. Lucy thought that Lingg's fiancée, Eda Miller, had smuggled the bomb parts in her bustle and joked to the jailers that they didn't have to be afraid of her because she didn't need a bustle.

"Lingg was taken to a solitary cell and kept under heavy surveillance but he was not done yet. With his steel-gray eyes and muscular build, he was like a bomb himself. 'The rest of the defendants say they reject force' he had spat at the court, 'they do not belong on trial with me. I do not pretend to be innocent. Force is the only arbiter. We will use our dynamite against you!' Lingg was determined to die but the State would never kill him.

"Three mornings later, on the eve of the Haymarket hanging, Louis Lingg made good on his word and blew off his face with a dynamite blasting cap inside the surveillance cell. How he got ahold of the blasting cap remained a great mystery and some of us suspected the cops had done the job to prejudice the rest of the defendants who now, as the end neared, were at last gaining sympathy among the working class of people.

"On the very day that Lingg was blown up in Cook County jail, downstate in Springfield, Governor Oglesby commuted Professor Schwab's and Fielden's sentence to life imprisonment but let stand the hanging of Spies and the rest of the Germans. Parsons, the only American in the lot, was said to have been offered commutation too but turned down the governor flat.

"Whoever you figure murdered Lingg, his last minute dynamiting had cheated the hangman and put the city into a panic. On the night before the death day, thousands of police and militia surrounded the jail and no sympathetic citizen could get within blocks of the gibbet. Only a select audience had been invited by the State to witness the hanging, and the families were not on the guest list. When Lucy went in the morning for her last minutes with Mr. Parsons, there was a ruckus.

"The coppers took Lucy and the kids and Lizzie Holmes to Central Station and threw them in a cell and ordered them to strip to see if they were carrying bombs—even the kids. It was the most terrible humiliation. While the state of Illinois was hanging Albert Parsons, his wife and his children were huddled stark naked in a freezing jail cell just a few blocks away.

"So Capitalist justice in its blind stupidity hung them. The trap was sprung one by one and all were strung up like strange, twisted fruit. Their executioners had tried to muzzle the men under black-leather hoods but the Martyrs of the Haymarket would not be silenced then and are shouting still. "The day will come when our silence will be more powerful than the voices you are throttling today," Spies thundered in the darkness. "Hurrah for Anarchism!" Adolph Fischer whooped. "This is the happiest day of my life!"

The Life After Death of the Haymarket Martyrs

"Sunday was just for the dead. The day dawned dead and stayed that way into dusk, slate-gray dead, dull frozen dead.

"I went over to Milwaukee Avenue and stood with the crowd there. No one said a word while we waited for the cortege to come by. You could feel the sadness on your skin and it cushioned us from the cold.

"Then we began to hear the feet, many feet, slapping slowly against the paving stones. And soon their steps became a dead tramp, ponderous with sorrow, and the workers removed their hats and the women softly sobbed as the bodies of the Martyrs inched by. The city had decreed that the men could not be buried within the city limits, security precautions in case they might be carrying concealed bombs into the grave. So the Haymarket Dead would be interred instead in the German cemetery Waldheim south of the Chicago line, even Parsons. the native son. Their surviving comrades were determined to accompany these heroes through the length of Chicago to show the world the unspeakable crimes of the bosses.

"They say there were 125,000 working people gathered along the route that drear dead Sunday, some dressed up in their only suit, the one in which they had been married and would themselves be buried in. Others proudly wore their overhauls and leather aprons and their tattered rags. It did not much matter how you came—there was no dress code. Farmers journeyed from the prairies in dung-stained boots and sailors in yellow slickers from off the Great Lakes and the coal-blackened miners from the pits of Ohio and Pennsylvania, they all came. But mostly who was there was the grimy industrial army that was crushed under the iron heel down in the river wards. They marched that day muzzled like the hanged men, and the voices of their silence, as Spies had foretold, shouted out for justice.

"The Mayor would permit no workers' anthems to be sung and so the masses' battered shoes sang out 'Les Marseilles' and 'Solidarity Forever' for them. Mayor Richardson too had ordered that no flags be flown, but Lingg's coffin was defiantly cloaked in a brilliant red banner.

"Lucy sat ramrod straight behind double veils in the first carriage of the cortege, her children—'anarchist sucklings' the *Tribune* had savagely called them—wrapped around her in grief. The wind blew in frigid gusts off the icefields of the Lake, boding a bad winter.

"Over the open grave down at Waldheim by the Desplaines River, the German anarchist writer Robert Reitzel cursed those who had murdered the Martyrs of Chicago: "We have loved too long. Now it has become time to hate." Mrs. Lucy Parsons had to be restrained from leaping into her husband's grave.

"The winter of 1887–88 was a bad one and Mama Rebeka gave out and died on us in her 49th year for want of enough coal to keep warm. Rudolph was never coming home and my sisters were all married. So now it was finally time for me to move on. I would take Henry, he was but 16 and sorely missed his poor ma, and we would head for California to see if there might be some of those gold nuggets left lying around on the ground.

"I went over to see Lucy to ask her for her blessing. She had already taken up with that no good Martin Lacher. Later he broke up all her furniture and she took him to court. Can you imagine! Lucy Parsons taking someone to the ruling-class court!

"We looked at each other from afar. 'Good luck, Eddie,' she held out a long, black hand, 'maybe we'll meet each other again on the picket line or down at the meeting hall but if we don't, never forget that we are the many and they the few and we are going to win our freedom from this terrible slavery.'

"And I turned away and traveled west with her words still in my hand and in my heart. A few months later, I learned that her little Lula had succumbed to scarlet fever and I broke right down and cried for the hurt it must have caused Lucy.

I wrote her a letter but thought it would be a rainy day in hell before she ever answered me.

"So the Martyrs of the Haymarket were dead but of course they never died. They rise up every May 1st and beg to be remembered. Some of you do and come and lay red roses on my grave and I hope they do the same for Mrs. Lucy Parsons. And for her husband. And for all the martyrs of the world."

Schnaubelt sounded like he was choking back a sob.

"The bosses, of course, did their damnedest to erase our memory. *The Chicago Tribune,* which thought it owned the town and probably did, announced it would erect a statue to honor Degman and the other dead cops. They held a contest for the best design, and the sculptor Gellert was contracted. He took as his model a beefy Irish cop named Birmingham who he saw directing traffic every day in the Loop and posed him with his large arm upraised, as if he were protecting the innocents of the city from the evil, bomb-throwing anarchists.

"But Birmingham was a poor subject and was often too drunk to pose. Later he was tossed off the force for fencing stolen property and it was nosed around that he wound up on skid row. Emma Goldman, who wearied of political connivance and became a nurse, always claimed to have seen him dead at the county hospital of cirrhosis of the liver.

"Birmingham's likeness was installed near the Haymarket and it too suffered its fill of vexations. Someone tried to bomb the statue in April of 1890 but only succeeded in knocking the cop off his pedestal. On May 4th, 1926, the 40th anniversary of the Haymarket bombing, a streetcar motorman named O'Neil deliberately smashed his trolley into the monument. He was sick of seeing it there every morning, the motorman confessed. So Birmingham the Cop was moved to Chicago Civic Center for its own protection."

Can I pick up the story from here, *compañero*?

"Well, you know it as good as I do. . . ."

During the 1968 so-called "Democratic" convention in Chicago, protesters pummeled the statue with spray paint and rotten tomatoes and it became a symbol of oppression all over again. Then on October 6th, 1969, two members of what would soon become the Weather Underground, Bill Ayers and Terry Robbins (later blown to bits in the Greenwich Village townhouse blast), took off Birmingham's head—it was the first official Weather bombing.

Mayor Daley, as the script indicated, went ballistic and vowed revenge at this treasonous deed. The FBI threw up a dragnet and a patriotic Chicago disc jockey raised funds to repair the damage. By May 4th, 1970, Birmingham the Cop was back in business with a 24-hour police escort posted nearby. Notwithstanding, on October 6th, 1970, exactly one year to the day they had blown the cop's cap off, the Weather Underground struck again, reducing the much-damaged officer to shards of scrap. The remains are said to be held behind glass in the lobby of the Chicago Police Academy, an arcane trophy in the class war.

"Ya, you told them right, Johnny. Those Weather boys were good boys. A Toast! A toast to the Weather Underground!"

Book Two

Belly of the Beast

A Matter of Life and Death

So how did you like Seattle? You said you were there, right?

"I've been there before. Seattle. Let's see. It was a radical town in my day—Red Seattle they called it because so many Wobblies and Reds congregated there. I was working in the woods organizing loggers against the timber barons and against McKinley's war out there in the Philippines. We'd come into Seattle for the marches and to hear radical speakers. I heard Lucy speak there for the Anti-Imperialist League—it must have been the tail end of the 1890s."

Eddie, what I was referring to was the huge demonstration against the World Trade Organization in Seattle just three weeks ago, You said you were there—or at least your spirit was.

We were standing side-by-side up in the graveyard, or rather I was standing side-by-side with the old-timer's cenotaph, and a thick ocean mist was soaking all my surfaces. It was almost high noon on the day before a new millennium would dawn.

"If I said I was at Seattle, I was there all right. I didn't see you. I'm a lot of things but I'm not a liar," Schnaubelt snapped irritably.

It was a demonstration against globalization. Sixty thousand people came to protest how the World Trade Organization was taking over our lives. It is the first of many. In the spring, we will go to Washington D.C. and march against the World Bank and the International Monetary Fund. The battle will soon spread to many cities: Prague and

Quebec City and Genoa and Barcelona, Cancun, and even to Cincinnati. It is like the new International! What do you think about all this? About the corporate globalization of the planet earth? Can we stop it?

"I think that I seen it all before."

You mean you saw the environmentalists costumed up like butterflies and dolphins, the stiltwalkers and the steelworkers in their hard hats, the farmers and the feminists in overhauls, the rainbow banners and the red and black flags, the rabbis with their whiskers and the nuns in their wimples, the anarchists cloaked in dangerous black raincoats, all of them singing at the top of their lungs about how another world is possible?

"You left out the cops and the tear gas and the National Guard and the curfew. This 'globalization'—where did they get such a fancy name for Imperialism? That's what we called it back when I was your age. You kids all think you invented the dictionary."

Eddie, this is a new monster. The world has changed since you've been dead. There were still countries when you were breathing. Now the nations are going out of business. Governments are just commercial agents for the transnational corporations and the World Bank, and the 500 biggest billionaires in the universe. Globalization concentrates all the wealth in the wallets of the few. The poor of the earth set up their cardboard huts outside the gates of the factories and sink deeper every day in the mud and the market. They lose their histories and their languages and their corn and their forests and when they fight back, Bubba Clinton or whoever the president happens to be hollers that they are terrorists and sends in the stealth bombers. I tell you man, it's a matter of life and death.

"I seen it all before I repeat." And Schnaubelt began making this weird sound with the hollows of his cheekbones. Name that tune! I realized that he was tootling "From the Halls of Montezuma." This guy should have been on the *Ed Sullivan Show*.

The mist had become a drenching rain as North Coast mists are prone to do, and I was not waterproofed. Schnaubelt instructed me to sit down, usually a preamble to a long afternoon of narrative. I declined. What I needed was an umbrella.

"You know, I was around when they invented this stuff."

What stuff are you talking about, Ed?

"Imperialism. It was invented by William McKinley in 1898. He was the president then. You know who McKinley is, don't you—that guy trapped inside the statue down in the Arcata Plaza?"

Ummm *compañero,* I think it was more like the Persians or the Egyptians who invented imperialism. Empires go back a ways.

"Hell, boy, I'm talking about good old Yanqui Imperialism! Hey, you got a snort of something to keep out the cold?"

Who are you calling boy, you stinking mummy! I roared back into the rain. I produced a flask of ersatz Kentucky sipping whiskey, poured a thimbleful into the streaming grass and knocked back a shot myself.

"Of course McKinley didn't exactly invent imperialism all by himself. If ever there was a puppet president, it was William McKinley. Just give him 20 cigars a day, slap a silk topper on his thick skull, and send him out to meet the people. The party bosses like Mark Hanna pulled his strings and Wall Street shuffled him like a deck of cards. When John D. 'Stick-em-up' Rockefeller and his gang said they wanted markets, cheap resources, slaves, new trade routes, expansion, their own empire, William McKinley jumped like a monkey on a wire. Some days, they called it 'Manifest Destiny,' 'Enlightened Colonialism,' 'God is on our side,' 'Free Enterprise,' 'Democracy,' whatever they could dream up to justify their plunder. But it was always Yanqui Imperialism to the rest of the world.

"First, they killed all their own Indians, stole their land, took half of Mexico, and were on their way to Panama. It was Westward Ho! and Southward Ho! and Any Which Way Ho! Wherever the U.S. Navy could tie up its ships. It all belonged to Uncle Sam.

"Cuba was God's personal gift to the White House. 'Every rock on that island, every grain of sand, was drifted and flushed from the Mississippi river—it's all American soil!' You know who said that?

Abraham Lincoln's secretary of state, that's who, the Great Emancipator. You could look it up.

"McKinley and Honest Abe shared the same bullet and they shared old John Hay who served in both their cabinets. Both of them dreamed of a Yanqui Empire—Lincoln wanted free trade with Juarez in Mexico. By McKinley's day and age, Imperialism was booming. The White House saw the Spanish empire was crumbling, went to war against 'em, and put a blockade around Cuba. . . ."

. . . Just like Washington did to Fidel Castro a half century later.

"You noticed. Then, in cahoots with Hearst, the king of the yellow press, Big Mac blows up his own battleship, the U.S.S *Maine*, kills 250 swabbies, blames it on the Spaniards, and 'liberates' Cuba. Ha! Before you can even whistle 'Yankee Doodle Dandy,' Teddy Roosevelt is planting Old Glory on the beach to claim the island for Uncle Sam."

. . . Just like LBJ at the Tonkin Gulf, attacking his own aircraft destroyer so he could get on with bombing Vietnam back to the stone age.

"You're learning quick boy.

"Now, this McKinley he was no hundred-watt lightbulb but he did know what side his toast was buttered on and he mouthed the words for the bosses' class. He was a corpulent grifter from Canton, Ohio who twice bribed his way into the governor's mansion in Columbus before Hanna took him national. He played the politician to the max. When he put on that frock coat and top hat, you didn't have to call casting for a president.

"McKinley ran in '96 for the Republicans against William Jennings Bryan, a useless fool from Nebraska. As the candidate of Wall Street, McKinley promised boom times and labor peace but it was the boom of the bombs and the peace of the graveyard. The country had been torn apart by the big strikes, many of them against McKinley's moneybags. First there was the Pullman strike that blew up Chicago all over again in '92. Grover Cleveland was president and he sent in the federal troops although Governor Pete Altgeld, a labor Democrat, fiercely resisted him. They dragged Gene Debs out of his shack down there in the railroad yards and put him in Joliet on a sedition charge.

Dozens was killed at Homstead Steel in 1894 when Berkman shot Frick, a McKinley man. Dozens more died in the coal fields of Pennsylvania but out in Colorado and Idaho, Haywood's miners had dynamite and they were generous with it. I tell you—those were dangerous days.

"Now McKinley, he didn't win the election of '96—the working class just gave it away on a silver platter. Sure, I'm a damn old anarchist and I don't vote. To me, voting is a bourgeois joke. But if the Democratic Party is supposed to be the party of the working man and woman, they sure picked a lily-livered windbag to go up against the bosses and the trusts. I suppose the problem was that Pete Altgeld should have been the candidate but he had pardoned the surviving Haymarket Martyrs in '94—Neebe and Fielden and my brother-in-law, Professor Schwab—and the tycoons and their bought-for-a-lousy-dollar press had carved him up pretty good and made his name scum to the lace-curtain types. Pete just didn't want to take any more abuse. So that creep from prairie with the wavy locks, Jennings Bryan, bamboozled the convention with his bullcrap about silver coinage. Why, he crucified the Democratic Party on that cross of gold and split the working class right down the middle."

It was getting bone-quick cold and I gulped down a splash of sipping whiskey and threw another one down on the ground.

Were you there in Chicago with Altgeld at the convention, Eddie? I had read about it in Howard Fast's book.

"*Merci,* comrade. Nah, I was out here in the rain and the raw, cutting down the trees, and trying to get the lumberjacks to wake up. I'll get to that part soon enough. But I read about what happened in the newspapers and heard about it in the working men's saloons. I couldn't get enough of it.

"Even with Wall Street's millions and the working class dazed and confused, McKinley still did not have his landslide. So on election day, they closed the factories and sent the workers home early and put up a big sign telling them not to come back if Bryan won because the factories were going to be closed for good. This happened all across the country, from Patterson, New Jersey to Portland, Oregon. It was a conspiracy to steal the election, but who was going to start a revolution over that stink-breathed Jennings Bryan? And they did put the military into the street anyway just to make sure the election stayed stolen."

It doesn't sound too different from Tricky Dick or LBJ. America just keeps repeating itself, don't you think?

"Like I said before, I seen it all a dozen times. . . ."

The rain was finally slackening but my clothes were drenched through. I wanted to go home and squeeze them out before I came up with triple pneumonia on New Year's Eve but Schnaubelt down there in his snug little cubbyhole grew irate.

"Listen, boy, this is history I'm telling you, the real deal. You said you wanted to have this palaver about globalization and imperialism in the book—it was even in the outline."

Eddie, just who do you keep calling "boy"? I'm 62 years old, four years older than you when you started pushing up daisies.

"The dead have seniority. Sit down, son. . . ."

Wet as the grass was, I plunked myself down.

"So McKinley got himself elected by fraud and flimflam and now he needed a war to fill Rockefeller's pockets and get the flags fluttering so that they could keep the workers down and divided. He sent the troops into Cuba through Siboney and Daiquiri and Santiago down there at the end of the island. The bugles sounded and the blood flowed and Teddy Roosevelt charged up San Juan Hill. Both sides dropped like flies under the tropical sun. Roosevelt had a lot of black troops under him in the Rough Riders and they turned yellow with the fever. But God was on his side and the victory secured Teddy a spot on McKinley's re-election ticket. So that was Yanqui Imperialism at work, boy.

"McKinley, he was a fat man. He had a big appetite. Gobbling up Cuba was just the first course. Then he went and snatched Puerto Rico like it was a golden *cuchifrito* floating out there in the blue Atlantic and promised the Borinquines their freedom and they are still slaves today, chained to the U.S. I hear about it. I see Don Pedro Albizu

Campos down here now and again. Well, maybe I don't exactly see him but I feel his spirit.

"Then McKinley slid his ships out there to Hawaii and took Queen Lillukalani hostage and installed the sugar king Spreckels in her place and Hawaii too is still bound up on McKinley's watch chain.

"The U.S. Empire was a-building big now. The Yanquis had a head of steam. Wherever they threw their darts, well, that was theirs. McKinley grabbed off Guam and American Samoa. Taught them how to play American football. But the Philippine Islands were the prize plum. The Philippinos were not Christian enough for Reverend Bill. He was going to Methodize those Papist heathens. 'I walked the floor of the White House night after night,' he preached to the Methodist Episcopal Counsel in March of '98, 'and I'm not ashamed to say that I went down on my knees and prayed and then it came to me, I know not how, but that there was nothing left to do then but to take them all and educate the Philippinos and uplift them and civilize and Christianize them and then I went to sleep and I slept soundly.'

"Next morning, the Big Man calls in the engineers from the War Department and tells them to put the Philippines on the U.S. map, where they stayed for the next 50 years."

This is excellent stuff, Professor Schnaubelt. I don't think I've ever heard the machinations of Yanqui Imperialism described better.

There wasn't but a few sips left in the jug to keep our teeth from chattering but we split it down the middle. Somewhere out in the grass, I dimly recalled having stashed an emergency pint of Tequila.

So then what happened? I asked admiringly.

"Same as usually does. Admiral Dewey sailed into Manila Bay and made a big to-do about raising the Stars and Stripes. Five thousand were killed the first few months, most of them Philippinos. Aguinaldo, their president, built a guerrilla army and they went into the hills and cut down the marines for the next three years. After McKinley was assassinated, Roosevelt came on board and sent 50,000 paid Yanqui assassins into Luzon. But they were not all Gary Coopers and many an

American boy died a miserable death from dysentery and jungle fevers and poisoned punji sticks.

"Though they lost a lot of young men, at last the Americanos prevailed and the Philippines became the Yanquis' base of operations to control the Far East and its markets during the 20th century. Yanqui Imperialism would never have succeeded without the Philippines."

You're right on the money there, Ed. During Vietnam it was B-52s cruising in from Clark to bomb the Cong in their spiderholes. Westmoreland figured he could soften up the NLF with the big bombs and then send in the ground troops to finish them off. It worked just about the same. A lot of soldiers got shot or shot themselves or their commanding officers. Finally, the VC and the anti-war movement right here inside the belly of the beast sent the U.S. home with its tail between its legs, the first big defeat for Yanqui Imperialism and I was proud to be a part of it. You won't find Vietnam on any U.S. map today.

I cleared my throat cautiously. You know, I went to jail instead of going to Vietnam. . . .

"Ya, you told me that one."

When I was in jail, I got letters and Christmas cards from the National Liberation Front, congratulating me for choosing prison. They said it was just like Uncle Ho.

"'Hell No! We won't go!' I could hear you kids up here."

That war just about drove me crazy. No matter what we did we couldn't stop Vietnam from bleeding. We threw bombs at the war, blew ourselves up, took massive amounts of drugs to obliterate it from our brains. Nothing worked except the determination of the people of Vietnam.

"Don't feel so bad about it. A lot of good Americans have been driven mad by imperialist wars. McKinley's war pushed Lucy over the brink. There she was speechifying up and down the country—that's when I saw her up in Seattle. 'I appeal to you young men not to enlist in this imperialist war to rivet the chains of slavery upon the Philippino people,' she would scold from her pulpit.

"But then Albert Jr., the only son of Albert Parsons, the Martyr of all Martyrs, signed up for McKinley's war. Maybe he just wanted to get his mother's attention or get back at her for hauling him along to too many meetings. Maybe he really wanted the glory of being a Rough Rider, I'll never know."

The taste of remembered bile rose to my tongue.

Eddie, did I ever tell you that my eldest daughter, the one named after the wild Welsh poet Dylan Thomas, who went to Cuba on the second Venceremos Brigade trip to cut Fidel's sugarcane when she was 14-years-old. She joined the U.S. Navy and got sent down to Roosevelt Roads in Ceiba, Puerto Rico where she bombed the living shit out of the island of Vieques for 14 years. I never could understood it. My own daughter bombing Vieques. What had I done wrong? I was so upset I got drunk for five months straight after she joined the Yanqui Navy.

"Well, Lucy didn't drink but she flipped just the same. Junior was only 18, not yet of age and still her property, she insisted. He'd lost his senses, she told the court, and had him committed to the Northern Illinois Hospital for the Insane, which destroyed what was left of the boy. The other inmates taunted him and called him an anarchist. He got violent and fought back and they put him in a padded cell, where he went catatonic. Lucy kept him in the crazy house for 19 years until he died of the influenza and then she went out there and took his ashes to be buried with her at Albert's feet in Waldheim."

What a sad story! Seems like everyone who gets born in America winds up being digested in the belly of the beast.

"Shit, I wasn't born here," Schnaubelt rued, "I'm just buried here. You can read all about it on my tombstone. Still, Capitalism had me for lunch."

Life of Schnaubelt (cont.)

"We came across this country riding on top of boxcars, ox carts, with mule trains or on our own four feet. The country was wide and still wild. When we ran out of steam, we signed on to a railroad crew and laid ties and they would give us grub and a free ride further west. We came into California walking the track and smelling the Pacific Ocean. Henry was a strong, quiet kid and I never knew what he was thinking.

"We took our time getting out here but we knew many people along the way, hard-rock miners and jack-leg preachers, outlaws and gun-runners, buffalo skinners and Jack Mormons with ten wives. I met my first Indian out in Nevada, a Shoshone, Everett Last Eagle. He packed a big buck knife—a scalper he called it—and his people were still at war with the paleface devils but for some reason he took a liking to us and explained what America was all about and how it was really a big turtle and we were riding along on its back. We had to take care of that turtle if we were going to make it.

"We got to San Francisco and saw many a working man sleeping in the doorways. We went up to the Barbary Coast and Henry had his first fancy woman. It was getting to be the Spring of 1890 and I still had the wanderlust. In a barbershop, we heard about a logging camp that was hiring near Santa Rosa out on the coast so I dragged Henry up there to learn a logger's trade. Growing up in Chicago, I had never thought much about trees but now I wanted to know them, to be with them. I figured if he were riding around on this turtle we might as well hitch up to the part under the trees.

"Sure, I cut down a lot of trees in my time but it didn't seem like the forest would ever end back then. I know better about that now.

"Logging in the old days was all muscle and sawteeth, steam engines and bull teams. There wasn't much science to it. The axes chopped down the trees and the saw bucked them into logs and the logs got hauled off to the mill. I signed on as a donkey puncher and they put me to minding and mending the machines seeing I was already a journeyman machinist. Henry got sent out in the woods and he didn't like it one bit. First day he was out there, he saw a tree limb come down and crush a poor logger and it spooked him. He took his first paycheck and lit out back to the Barbary Coast without even telling me. That made me real mad.

"Later he got on the police force in San Francisco and changed his name to Snowball so he wouldn't be connected up to the infamous anarchist Schnaubelts, I suppose. He was a big kid and I bet he beat up a lot of strikers down on the waterfront. He was even promoted to be a detective—Detective Snowball! Ha! Can you imagine? The crooks must have burst out laughing when they heard his name. I wouldn't have anything to do with him by then. After I was dead and stinking, Tina came and told me Henry had got mixed up in the investigation of the Preparedness Day parade bombing and helped to frame poor Tom Mooney and Warren Billings.

"Now, logging was not a folklore tale like Paul Bunyan and Babe the Blue Ox. It was dangerous, back-splitting work and we had no guarantees or protections. The timber barons owned the West Coast all the way up past Vancouver. A long time back, they had staked claims with the land trusts and taken choice pieces of the great forest here and there. Then they signed up all their relatives and stooges for tracts and pretty soon, they had stolen the whole goddamn thing.

"The timber barons built great mansions in Eureka and Portland and Seattle high up on the hills looking over Puget Sound and they never went into the woods again. Big Lagoon Brizzard got himself a department store and ruled Arcata. George Zehndner, an old Indian killer, was boss of Uniontown, which he renamed McKinleyville. They were millionaires and McKinley men. They owned the banks and they lorded it over the smaller operators, squeezed them dry, and took their mills.

"The little guys had to highball it all the time just to keep the banks from foreclosing and it was every man for himself out in the woods. When the price of timber was high, you ran full blast from dawn to dark even in the dry season, when one spark could burn up tens of thousands of acres. I didn't ever have much use for fires. We'd have to go in after they had burnt off and I'd see the charred bodies of the loggers that had been caught up in there. The old-timers told us the forests would come back but the men were gone forever.

"All the camps highballed and Meeker's camp was no exception. You could hear the whistle punk laying on the tootsie all day—five blasts meant that a man was down. Whole trees would fall on them or they'd lose a limb in the sawhouse. The choker setters and the chasers ran through the rolling logs and someone would get his brains bashed out every other shift. The cables got real taut and could cut off your head if you weren't looking sharp—I saw it happen once. That poor logger's head didn't stop rolling until it hit my caulked boots.

"The highballers didn't have time to shut down the operation. If a man was killed or hurt, you just carried him off to the side of the skid road and lay him out in the shade so he wouldn't get trampled by the mule teams and pray he would still be alive at the end of the shift so you could get him to a sawbones. Every day, loggers were murdered by Capitalism.

"Although Captain Meeker drove his men to their death, it was the banks that had the blood on their hands. Loggers were worth a lot less than a tree and those bastards measured human life in boardfeet. In a good year, the highballers gambled every penny they had but it was the bankers that took home the jackpot. I got to see how it worked real good up there at Meeker's camp. This logging wasn't much different from busting your back pounding railroad ties or being stooped over one of McCormick's lathes for ten hours a day back home in Chicago. I learned a lesson in economics up there I never would forget. The workers were just the lowest insects in the food chain.

"Pretty soon, a bunch of us were getting together to talk about how we were in a class war and what could we do so that we wouldn't keep losing all the time. Too many of our brothers were getting mauled and Captain Meeker just kept speeding up. We demanded a slowdown and then we just slowed it down ourselves. We got Meeker his timber but at our own pace, not his. Old bastard couldn't abide that and fired the whole crew, every last man but we refused to leave until he paid us our full wages right there and then—which he did but reluctantly. Then me and Red Jake went to work. We got ahold of some dynamite and blew up the sawhouse. I jiggered the donkey engine so that it would never work again. We used our wooden shoes. It was the most terrific weapon the working class had—sabotage!

"Red Jake was a Jew from Manhattan. Rabinowitz was his full name and he was the son of a rabbi. He wasn't red because of his politics so much as the color of his hair—but he was a pretty radical kid too. When he found out that I was the notorious Rudolph Schnaubelt's brother, he buddied up to me and we traveled all around the North Woods organizing the loggers for the Industrial League of America out of Seattle—we were regular Wobblies before there was even an IWW.

"We'd go into the bunkhouse with whiskey in a jar and pass the hooch around and tell the men how the bosses' class and the workers' class had nothing in common. We'd sign on for a week and, sure enough, some poor logger would get killed and then we'd wildcat the men out until the company promised to stop highballing. The county sheriff would deputize all the low-life trash in the villages and there would be big trouble. One time up near Bellingham, Jake and I liberated a whole camp of Siwash Indians that were being worked like slaves in a log camp there and they took us home and made us honorary chiefs.

"And one time in Thunderbird County, the goons caught us out on a railroad trestle. There were ten of us and thirty of them and right away, I could see this wasn't going to have a happy ending. Three of our comrades went over the side into the ravine and we never saw them again. The rest of us got laid out with clubs and they broke my arm in three places and fractured my skull. My old bones still ache from that beating.

"Red Jake and I would come into the big cities for anarchist and socialist meetings, and to help out in the marches and the strikes. We'd grub up in the soup kitchens and hobo up and down California. We traveled all the way to San Pedro to shake hands with Joe Hillstrum who was organizing the dock workers there, and later the seaman during the West Coast steamship strike. He became the great working-class songwriter, Joe Hill. Joe asked us to stick around and help him sign up the stevedores but I couldn't get used to all those palm trees—it didn't seem like it was still America down there.

"We met Big Bill Haywood in Portland during the railroad strike in '92. He was just getting the Western Federation of Miners on its feet but he already had plans for One Big Union. And we went to see Emma Goldman when she came to San Francisco. I thought she was stuck up on herself and Jake called her a 'yenta' because she never stopped giving out her opinions and bossing everyone around. I heard that Emma Goldman wrote her autobiography and it was more than a thousand pages long!

"A few years later up in Seattle who did I bump into but Mrs. Lucy Parsons. Now it was '98 and she was preaching against McKinley's war for the Anti-Imperialist League. She still carried herself straight as a Nubian queen but there were worry lines around her eyes. I said that I was glad to see her, really glad. She said you're a logger now—she saw me in my tin pants. She took me out to meet her anarchist friends on San Juan Island but they were more like Social Democrats to me and when they heard I was that awful Rudolph Schnaubelt's brother they looked at me like my fly was open and got all snooty. I told Lucy good-bye and caught the first ferry back to town. 'You're married now, big boy' she told me—I guess she must have noticed the ring on my finger. That's too bad. . . .'

"Lucy was right—I had just gotten hitched up. I met Tina in San Francisco and we got married two weeks later at City Hall there, just like you only in my caulked boots. She was an Italian girl from a family of Italian anarchists. We were sitting next to each other at a meeting at Fugazi Hall one night. The speaker was Malatesta, the great anarchist writer. She had the deepest, darkest Italian eyes that I ever fell down into and I invited her out to a restaurant but I didn't have enough money to pay for us both. 'That's O.K. I'm a socialist,' she told me, 'we'll just go Dutch.' It was love at first sight.

"She took me home to meet her family and they offered me grappa. When she told them that I was the brother of the anarchist who had thrown the bomb at the Haymarket, her uncles embraced me and we drank all night to the revolution—they weren't like Lucy's snooty friends in Seattle at all. Tina had a big heart and a big family—her niece was also named Tina and she became an actress and even posed for nude pictures. Then she learned how to take pictures herself and went off to photograph the Mexican Revolution.

"Red Jake knew that after I got hitched we wouldn't be making so many trips to the camps anymore though we did gallivant around some. Tina would come along—she loved to bum around with the rough boys then—but it got between Jake and me and one night he disappeared off into the woods. Years later, I heard he became a Wobbly and got killed by troopers when he sailed into Everett, Washington on the *Verona* to help out in the shingle-weavers' strike there. The shinglemen had been out for months and they had no more food so the Wobblies came to the rescue. Four were shot and killed and they went down singing hard: 'Hold the fort for we are coming!'

"So Tina and I set out to make our own way in the world. There was talk of a gold rush up on the Trinity River in '99 and we went up there and built a cabin. I panned at it for half a year—Charlie Ming, the last Chinaman on the river, showed me how to go about sifting for nuggets but I never struck it rich. By then, the whites had strung up and run off most of the Chinese in California.

"Later, we took a lot by the Klamath, almost to Oregon, and I logged it out myself. But by now, I had my dream of building my own shingle mill. It would be a good mill with no highballing. I would do it different. I would hand-tool all the machinery myself and others would work out in the woods. All the workers would share the profits together. It would be an anarcho-syndicalist mill.

"Tina was already big with Henry when we moved down here to Trinidad and I got a job at Houda's mill to build up a grub stake and see what was the lay of the land. So that's where I was on the day William McKinley got shot, September 6th, 1901. I remember it like it was last night's bad dream. . . .

"We were just coming off shift at Houda's when we were told the news that the president had been shot by an anarchist in Buffalo and my heart jumped a beat to hear it. 'The dastardly act' had been committed by Leon Czolgocz, who confessed that Emma Goldman had incited him to do the deed. That's how the Arcata paper told it.

"I was with some pretty radical comrades and this kid Sven Toomer who we called 'Haywire' because he could sing all the Joe Hill tunes in the right key, began to shout 'Whoopie! I'm glad the old buzzard got what was coming to him!' Some of the mill hands got all patriotic and there was a ruckus. We had to haul young Haywire out of there if ever he was going to sing again—later he became a member of our anarcho-syndicalist mill.

"Here is what it said about that incident in the *Arcata Union* the next week. Hold on, I've got the clip right here some place. Hmmm. There sure ain't much light down in this hole:

'When news that the president had been shot reached us here, we felt a sorrow like we had never felt before and a feeling of vengeance for his assassin took possession of us. A young employee at Houda's mill who upon hearing of the shooting, expressed that he was pleased, was not so pleased a few minutes later, when his fellow workers gave him a well-merited thrashing. If it had not been for cooler heads who ought

to be ashamed of themselves, this young man would never have been capable of expressing such sentiments again.

The feeling of the neighbors here in Trinidad is that all such scoundrels should be hanged by the neck or banished from the country, preferably the first.

"Czolgocz claimed to be an anarchist and that Emma Goldman had set him on fire. *The Arcata Union* yapped about 'The Anarchist Menace' and pinned the blame on Governor Pete Altgeld because he had pardoned Schwab and Neebe and Fielden. 'These fiends in human shape are gloating that President McKinley lies dying.'

"I was real glad that McKinley got shot myself—he was a damned imperialist and he deserved his fate. But Czolgocz got a raw deal. He got the electric chair while Emma who had put him up to it, reigned over the jail for the few days she was locked up and the Democratic ward bosses in Chicago, who hated McKinley because he was a Republican, sent her hampers of champagne and flowers.

"From what I know, which wasn't really that much, Emma used her feminine charms to manipulate young Leon into bumping off McKinley as revenge for the government's torture of her companion Sasha Berkman, then doing 20 years for shooting the steel magnate Frick during the Homstead strike back in '94. They had him locked down in solitary in Alleghany City just outside Pittsburgh and Emma couldn't see him. When she tried to visit, the guards told her that Sasha was going blind and they had put him in a straightjacket.

"Leon worshipped Emma and would have done anything she told him without questioning it. Anything at all. He had first met her at a Liberal Club lecture in Cleveland in May 1901 and followed her everywhere that summer. The next month, he heard that she was in Chicago so Leon, who had been reading Emma's pamphlets, went out there to ask her about all this free-love stuff. By then Emma was in her 30's, a mature woman with countless lovers. Leon was a curly-haired virgin with dreamy blue eyes and she took him to bed for a lark although her friends at *Free Society* magazine didn't much approve and wrote that he was a spy. Some would say Leon sacrificed himself on the altar of Emma Goldman's big, beautiful tush.

"In late July, Emma and Leon rendezvoused in Buffalo where the Pan-American International Exposition had just opened its gates. The Exposition was supposed to show how much McKinley loved his Latin American *amigos*. They strolled the fairgrounds and she told Leon that Sasha was in a straightjacket and she wanted McKinley to hear about it when he came to the Exposition in September. Leon bashfully promised to do his best.

"But when Emma returned to Rochester where she was staying for the season with her family, she found a letter from Berkman saying he had been released from solitary confinement and there was even talk of commuting his sentence.

"So Emma rushed off to Pittsburgh and there she was finally able to see her companion. From what she wrote in her diaries, Sasha just kept staring at her with his dark, haunted eyes and would not say one word. Although Berkman's condition had improved, so far as I know Emma never again contacted Czolgocz to call off the assassination of McKinley.

"It was only after McKinley was dead that Emma was stricken with remorse and cried out to save Czolgocz from the electric chair but it was too late. She said he had been driven mad by Capitalism and pitied him in public. 'I never wanted the president dead,' she said, 'Leon must have misunderstood.'

"After the assassination of McKinley, it was the Red Scare of the Haymarket days all over again. Emma and her comrades were rounded up and taken to the Harrison Street station in Chicago where the Haymarket Martyrs had once been held and she claimed to be communing with their ghosts through the prison walls. The usual flags unfurled and anyone who didn't wave one was suspected of treason. 'Anarchists' were jailed and lynched from Pittsburgh to Omaha to Arcata, California, although no one much knew what an anarchist looked like except maybe they had a bushy beard and carried a big black bomb in their overcoat pocket.

"Right here down in Arcata they had a preacher who told his congregation that anarchists were like mad dogs and had to be chased from hole to hole and shot dead. The rumor went around that two loggers had gotten drunk at Robert's saloon on the plaza and made rude remarks about McKinley so the reverend marched his Christians down to the Arcata Hotel, where the men was staying. They brought a rope with them but settled for tar-and-feathering the sinners. *The Arcata Union* reported that the Ladies Sewing Circle sat there the whole time embroidering 'Nearer My God To Thee' which was supposed to be McKinley's favorite hymn, on their doilies.

"So what do I think about all this? The way I see it William McKinley burned up little Philippino babies and deserved what he got and it was a good thing that he was shot. Czolgocz should have been declared a national hero."

The Death of Bougainvilla Vallena Palanan

"I was born here in the free territory of Palanan in Isabela province in the north of the island of Luzon on the 17th of May, 1884. I died here April 1st, 1901, burned alive by the Americanos and their hired killers, under the command of Major Frederick Funston who had been sent by your president William McKinley to punish us for not wanting to be his kind of slaves.

"We were five sisters. Our mother, Flor del Campo Palanan, loved her garden and named us all after the flowers she grew in it. Our names were Flor Dahlia Lilia, the baby, Flor Jacaranda, Flor Amapola, Flor Orquidia, and myself, the oldest, Flor Bougainvillia Vallena Palanan. We were each born one year apart and so were very close both in age and spirit. With our long glossy hair and bright clothes, you could not tell one of us from the other and the flower sisters were considered the most beautiful girls on the peninsula.

"My father was Crispillo Vallena Palanan, a farmer. Although his Spanish family name means 'the whale,' it was sort of a joke because he was a very slight man. My mother Flor was more like the whale, or rather, like a lovely plump pig.

"My father tilled the rich earth of Palanan and filled our home full of grains and fruit. We are lucky here on the northern coast of the island where we are protected from drought and bad weather by the mountains of the Igorots, a fierce people who they say take the heads of their enemies.

"'Palanan is our paradise,' my mother would laugh, 'we have plenty to eat here and we do not have to work so hard for it.' Father grew sweet potatoes and rice, maize and coconuts, and because the Spaniards had become our masters, tobacco for fine cigars that rivaled even those of Havana, Cuba. The sea was filled with fish and, of course, we kept many fine pigs.

"Father had no use for the Spaniards, who he called 'imperialists' because they made us speak their language and accept their gods and swear allegiance to their king. We were Christians now but we spoke our Tagalog in the home and reserved Castilian for the *principales* of the town who we knew reported to the Spanish authorities.

"When Aguinaldo rose against the Crown in 1896, Crispillo was the first here to declare for him but soon the whole of Palanan was in *El Presidente's* favor. The few Spaniards that were left up here quickly closed up their plantations and ran to the city for protection.

"It was then that we heard there had been a war between Spain and the *Americanos* and the *Americano* president McKinley had claimed us as his subjects. 'Now we will have to fight the *Americanos,*' my father told us.

"Our troubles began when McKinley's ships sailed into Manila Bay and Aguinaldo was forced to go into the countryside to organize the resistance. McKinley ordered a reward for his capture and the Yanqui troops pursued him from village to village brutalizing the people. We were far away here in Palanan but we heard the horrible stories they told about General Jacob Smith and Bell and Funston and the others. How they set the villages and the crops on fire and forced the townspeople into camps they called 'strategic hamlets.' Frightened travelers told us of men hanging from the trees or crucified along the roads and we grew fearful.

"Late in the year when the new century began, Emilio Aguinaldo, *El Presidente,* came to Palanan seeking sanctuary from the *Americanos* and we were only too happy to receive him. The poor man had lost his whole army—when he came to us, there were only 12 men left. They had climbed into the mountains from the Cayacana Valley on the east of the island and wandered for months in the forest. Their mules had stumbled over giant tree roots and fallen into ravines. Great boulders fell on the men and smashed them, and others perished from the stings of insects and the malaria and poisonous snakes—but the Igorots never took their heads.

"Although Aguinaldo would not say that this was his name, we all knew it was *El Presidente* and we honored him as such. He was still young, in his early 30's I would think, and he seemed trim and dashing to us. Father joked that he would make a good catch for the flower sisters.

"*El Presidente* set up his camp at an old tobacco plantation out beyond the fields where the jungle begins, and we did not see him often—but he would smile and wave to us at the fiestas. Well, girls can dream, can't they?

"In March of 1901, the news came to us that Major Funston had advanced to the Cayacana Valley, just a few days away, and we were put in panic. They said the *Americanos* had hired the Macabebes to come and kill us, black devils who hated the Tagalag people, and we prayed in the church that the Igorots would take their heads when they crossed the mountains. But they did not.

"At the end of March, *El Presidente* rode into town on a silver-colored horse and ordered us to evacuate before the *Americanos* fell on Palanan, but father refused. 'I am Palanan,' he said, 'my name is Palanan. My land is Palanan. My lovely pigs are Palanan and I am not going to leave them here for the *Americano* McKinley's lunch. I will stay.' The neighbors heard his little speech and said he had gone crazy.

"So they came in their wide-brimmed hats that made them look like cowboys. They were all very tall and their slaves, the Macabebes, were short and dark like ants on the shit pile. They went from house to house and set them each on fire. When they pushed through our front gate, Crispillo grabbed his homemade patik pistol and began firing but the cowboys just laughed. They threw him down on the ground and beat him with their rifle butts when he would not say where Aguinaldo was hiding. They pulled open his mouth and poured gallons of filthy water down his throat and when he was filled to bursting, they punched him with their rifle butts again and his stomach burst apart before our very eyes.

"We watched in horror from inside our *nipa* hut. The *Americanos* ordered us to come out but we would not. So the Macabebes set the hut on fire. The baby Dahlia Lilia was the first to be seared by the flames and when she ran out, the cowboys skewered her on their bayonets and raped her. One by one, my sisters fled the flaming hutch, Amapola and Orquidia and Jacaranda who I dearly loved, and then my dear mother, Flor del Campo, and each was raped and murdered in their turn. Only I, Flor Bougainvilla Vallena Palanan, among the five flower sisters and their mother, would not allow myself to be violated by the *Americanos* and so I was burnt alive and I died a free woman.

"At my funeral many days later, I heard that Aguinaldo had been captured by the invaders and had sworn allegiance to McKinley. This made my whole family very sad and angry—I cannot tell you how angry! Even today, a hundred years after this treachery, we are still angry about it."

The Death of McKinley

The pistol fires,
McKinley falls
Doc says McKinley,
I can't find that ball,
In Buffalo, In Buffalo

"I confess! I confess! Only I beg you to stop this torture! Oh, my God, I can take no more!

"I confess that I was a bastard but I was America's bastard. I confess that I am the Father of Yanqui Imperialism. Is that the kind of thing you want to hear?

"Ooooo, I am bursting apart at the seams. Yes, Yes, I confess that I ordered the U.S.S. *Maine* blown to smithereens to justify the war with Spain and get William Randolph Hearst off my back. It was a matter of national security. The blood of 250 young Americans is on my hands. Yes, Yes, I confess to burning up the Philippino babies and forcing myself upon the fair Liliukalani, the last Queen of Hawaii, and all other acts of collateral damage.

"No more! No more! I confess to being the stooge of Wall Street, the tool of Free Enterprise, and the running-dog lackey of Savage Capitalism! Oh stop, Lord! It is like being boiled in oil from the inside out. Is there no Human Rights Commission here in Hell?

"Yes, I sent the army to quell the strikes and strikers were maimed and killed. I am sorry for that and will pay compensation for each worker so long as their families present the proper identification. Only just stop whatever you're doing to me down there! Yes, I claimed to be a Christian while starving Americans expired at my feet. Yes, I bribed my way into office and stole elections and became a millionaire many times over by fleecing the public treasury.

"The bullet burrows into my intestines and I can feel the gangrene spreading. Yes, my sins are dark and closeted. Yes, I confess that I derived sexual gratification from Ida's fits of epilepsy and that I once fornicated with a sheep but only once and it was a female sheep too and I did not reach climax. May I go to heaven now?"

Czolgocz, Czolgocz,
You done him wrong,
Shot Mister McKinley
While he was walking along,
In Buffalo, In Buffalo.

"Oh, this bullet that now sears my belly was not unexpected. Hanna warned me that the assassins were on their way. Infernal machines arrived at the White House one a day by parcel post. They got King Humberto in Italy just last year and the Empress Elizabeth, the most beautiful monarch in all Europe, the year before that. The

Secret Service showed us intelligence reports that there were contracts out on Czar Nicolas, Queen Victoria, The Pope, The German Kaiser, and myself. Pretty elite company for a bumpkin from Ohio like me, don't you think? And yet when the bullet was fired into me, the Secret Service took a powder. I have no doubt that it was anarchist scum and foreign buggers who pulled the trigger but behind Czolgocz and Goldman, more sinister hands were orchestrating this tragic shadow show. It could not be more obvious.

"Oh no, not again! I am filled up. I can take no more!"

Roosevelt in the White House
He's doing his best,
McKinley in the graveyard
He's taking a rest.
And he'll be gone
a good long time.

"I was the president of these United States for four years nine months and six days and I am still the president wherever I go next. My people loved me and I loved them, all of them, the white and the black, the yellow and the red. Even as I lay dying there in the Temple of Music at the Pan-American Exposition I had so innocently inaugurated only hours before, Buffalo Bill Cody and a band of war-painted Indians came and prayed over me. Oh Great White Feather—that's just what they called me—if you die the spirit will go out of the land.

"Now as I writhe here in deathbed agony, I think back upon the magnificent fireworks we viewed on the evening before they put this bullet in me. The red, white, and blue bombs bursting in air into the shapes of Puerto Rico and the Philippines and then the scrolled gold letters that read and I quote: 'God Bless America and William McKinley—the Chief of Our State and of Our Empire!' It makes me blush to recall that long ago moment—or was it just last night?

"And it was not just my people who loved me but the people of the whole world, even the Philippinos who I uplifted. The spics and the greasers worshipped me. They came to the Pan-American Exposition and licked my behind, especially those darkies from Cuba to whom I had falsely promised their liberty. When I was shot, the Mexican ambassador threw himself at my feet, yapping like a little Chihuahua. It was so funny that I wanted to burst out laughing but it hurt too much to laugh.

"I was so popular and now I am dying in ignominy. I was the president and now I am lying here with a brass bullet inside my belly and a rubber tube up my arse and it is a shame because it is humiliating and wounds not only my inflated pride but that of the nation which I governed so benevolently.

"I was the president and I had secretaries and under-secretaries, a whole cabinet of them. I had generals at my side! Statesmen! Congress and the press were in my pocket. Valets and chauffeurs, footmen and barbers, did my bidding! And now no one can save me and I just want to say good-bye to all of my fellow Americans out there—but first can anyone tell me what all this is doing to the stock market? Ooooo.

Roosevelt in the White House
Drinking from a silver cup,
McKinley in the bone house
But he'll never get up.
And he'll be gone
A good long time.

"What saddens me most sorely about all of this assassination stuff is that that perverted little twirp Teddy Roosevelt is going to reap my reward, sleep in my four-poster bed, and smoke all my fine cigars. He was a two-faced hypocrite and never my ally. He told Mark Hanna that I had the backbone of a chocolate eclair and Mark Hanna put him on the ticket. The two were in cahoots! It's plain as the nose on my face if I still have a face! I need to get this story out there. Where is my press secretary when I need him? Hold the front page!

"'He's getting too excited. I ought to pump some more chloral up him' I heard the doctor mutter.

"'William, do you know me?' Hanna was sobbing at the foot of the bed. Sure I know you, you slimy traitor I tried to call back but suddenly there was a great clap of thunder and I could hear the flapping of black wings above the gabled mansion and I knew the fatal moment was nigh and tried one last time to put myself right with the Lord by singing him a chorus or two of 'Nearer My God To Thee' but the words choked in my throat and I died and gave up the ghost. Arrrghhhh!

"'He's gone' the doctor said and Hanna wiped away his crocodile tears and closed my eyes. Downstairs they were already swearing Roosevelt in. I could hear it through the floorboards. Then the screen went black.

"Several years later, I woke up here on this pedestal and there was a KEEP OFF THE GRASS! VIOLATORS WILL BE PROSECUTED! sign at my feet and I thought I must be in heaven at last. . . ."

The Death of Czolgocz

"I did it for the people. Only for the people. It did not matter that the people did not care. I did it for the American people and for the workers of the world. That's what I told the detectives when they grilled me and gave me the third degree. I did not want to involve Emma in any of this.

"They said, 'She doesn't care a fart for you boy, you better confess.' They beat me on the head with rubber hoses. The detectives threatened to sodomize and castrate me if I didn't give them Emma. They said they would make me swallow live rats and take my heart out through my back but I would only say that I did it for the people because I am an anarchist.

"We are anarchists. We believe in the annihilation of all authority. We will only be free when we have assassinated all the rulers. My inspiration was not Emma Goldman at all but a simple silk worker, Gaetano Breschi. You do not know him?

"When Breschi decided that it was his duty to assassinate King Humberto, he went to his comrades in Patterson, New Jersey and asked them to pay back the money he had lent to them for their anarchist newspaper. They called him a miser and a cheapskate to his face and it wounded Gaetano but he would not tell them what he needed the money for. Only when he had done his brave deed and been shot down like a dog in the street for it, were his comrades ashamed. It taught them a good lesson and I would only hope that my own humble 'propaganda of the deed' has taught those class traitors at *Free Society* magazine a similar lesson.

"When they published that I was a dangerous spy and that I asked too many questions, it hurt me and I cried. I was naïve and only asked so many questions because I wanted to find out what it meant to be an anarchist. Then Emma came to my defense and said that I was a good boy, a little queer—but a good boy. I was a good boy too. I did everything she asked me to do.

"My little atentat was held up as a shining example in many anarchist circles. The Spaniards and the Italians celebrated the act and in Patterson, it was said that Breschi's comrades drank to my name so often that they become quite drunk and nearly burned their hall down.

"I do not care what Sasha Berkman wrote from prison—that I was a madman and acted rashly. Everyone knew he was insanely jealous of Emma and me. At least after I was done with McKinley, he was dead. But Frick was still alive to torment his workers.

"My stepmother called me crazy too and said I was not normal. Well, I'm not crazy not even one bit. The proof is that I did what I set out to do. McKinley had all the power and we were nothing. This is why I told the police my name was Fred Nieman. Fred No Man. I am not a man but part of the people and the people spoke through my hand under the white handkerchief that fated day in the Temple of Music with the Brahms music ringing in my ears. In Buffalo. In Buffalo.

"It was not easy to shoot the president. I could not just walk up to him and say, 'This is what you deserve.' We had to wait in line and the summer sun beat through to my brain but I was cool and determined not to blurt out my intentions. Then the Secret Service grabbed a swarthy Italian-looking man out of the line and roughed him up and I knew it would be fine now because I was blonde and white and did not fit the racial profile.

"When my turn came, I shot the president twice and would have shot him again only my Johston pistol got too hot. The Brahms sonata was like musical accompaniment. It made it all seem as if I was a character in a spooky melodrama. I saw myself fire the gun. I saw myself gazing at the blue smoke as it curled from the barrel. I felt proud. I had shot the president. Me. Mister No Man.

"They fell upon me as one. They threw me to the floor and beat my head against the marble. The big buck Negro who had been in line behind me tried to gouge my eyes out. McKinley sat there blubbering in his chair like a stuck pig. 'Go easy on him, boys,' he kept repeating but they only beat me worse.

"The honest truth is that doing the deed was worth the beating. The more they hurt me, the better I felt. McKinley was a bad man. He shot down workers and burned up Philippino babies. I did justice for the people.

"My only regret is that my gun was no good. The first bullet bounced off a thick speech McKinley had placed in his breast pocket and the second got lost in all his fat and it took him a week to die. Still, that was positive too because he had a lot of time to lie there and think about the evil he had done in his life. My only other regret is that my name was too complicated for the American people to pronounce.

"The detectives beat me so badly about the head with the rubber hoses that I could not distinguish between what I was thinking and what I was saying. Even down here in Guantanamo, the tropical paradise where my brain is kept under lock and key, I still have a hard time figuring it all out.

"It got so bad that at first they would not take me to the court for fear the judge would notice something was wrong. But even when I went with my head all swathed up in bandages, the judge never said a word.

"By now, I just wanted the beatings to end and I yelled out to the judge that I would plead guilty. I did it, I told his honor. I did it for the American people, but the judge said no way, I was going to have to stand trial because this was America, the land of the brave and the home of the free, and justice must triumph. I was so dizzy I almost fell over in my chair.

"The judge—I never even knew his name— assigned me not one but two lawyers and some scientists came and measured my brain. Even before I had been convicted, Cornell University requested my skull be sent to them for experiments. The scientists all said that I was sane. Why did you do it, one of the professors asked? I did my duty to the working class, I told him, it was not fair that McKinley and his kind should have everything and the rest of us who are the majority have nothing. 'That sounds pretty logical,' the professor said.

"It was a real kangaroo court. My lawyers would not let me speak out and threatened to gag me if I did. They referred to me as 'this wretched man' and when they spoke of McKinley it was all how he was such a gentleman and a great patriot and how much he loved his wife. The lawyers even apologized for defending me and pleaded with their colleagues that it wouldn't stain their reputations.

"The jury did not take but 15 minutes to convict me. Judge whatever his name was anyway said there was going to be no appeal so he might as well get it over with right there. Did I have something to say before he pronounced sentence on me?

"I had everything to say: how the working class and the ruling class have nothing in common. How William McKinley burned up the Philippino babies and shot down the strikers in cold blood. How they had Sasha Berkman tied up in a straitjacket. And how when I was 12, they put me in a factory and chained me to the punch machine so I wouldn't run away.

"But I wouldn't give them the satisfaction of knowing all that. All I told that court was that I did it for the people. That was enough. The judge wanted to get rid of me anyway. 'Take him to the death house down in Auburn and have him electrocuted this October 29th,' he ordered and the bailiffs dragged me out.

"Now its October 29th and I have no more time to give to the people. I looked out the high window in my cell today and I saw that the leaves were all golden and falling. The air felt cool upon my cheek. When they brought me here a month ago, it was so warm I could barely breath. Everything has changed so suddenly. It seems that I have lived many lifetimes since I shot the president. Me. Mister No Man.

"I think it is ironic that I am being electrocuted. I believe electricity is a great invention and it will change the course of history. In Buffalo, I would go every day to the Exposition to sit in the Temple of Light where a million light bulbs burned at once. In its center was this incandescent figure, the Goddess of Light, and I burned to make free love with her.

"Now I am going to be the first presidential assassin ever to be electrocuted! I feel as if Thomas Alva Edison himself will pull the switch! Do you know that the electric chair was invented by a Negro? I feel honored to sit in it.

"The leather straps are new and smell good. They have shaved my head and clamped this metal cap to my scalp. It feels scientific and modern.

"I have asked the warden to put sulfuric acid over my body when it is dead so that I will disappear entirely from everywhere. It is my last request.

"The warden pleads with me one last time to confess that Emma put me up to assassinating McKinley, but I refuse. Emma has suffered enough for my foolishness. Her father lost his furniture business and they threw him out of the synagogue. So I told him what I always say. The official line: I did it for the people.

"Wait! One last thing, my last words. Emma has said that I was a queer boy with queer ideas, that I read queer books and did queer things and that I died in a queer way. I just want to make it perfectly clear that I am not gay."

The Life After Death of William McKinley

"Now I'm going to tell you the story behind the story, the inside story of William McKinley's well-merited demise. I never told it to anyone before. Consider it a bonus for our book, an exclusive, a scoop!"

I'm flattered, Eddie. Let me hook up the tape recorder.

I fetched the machine from my shoulder pack and set it up by the cenotaph. A dim little red light popped up.

"Is it ready?

O.K., you're on . . .

"McKinley never really died!"

You mean like Joe Hill and the Haymarket Martyrs? How they inspired and became part of the struggle for class justice?

"Well, not exactly comrade. It's more like William McKinley got trapped between life and death by a biochemical conundrum and he never graduated from limbo.

"Let me explain this part as delicately as I can. You see, during the seven days it took for the president to give up the gaggle, the doctors administered many infusions of bromides and stimulants right up the old fundament. Some were virulently toxic and when they came in contact with the brass bullet Czolgocz had lodged in McKinley's guts, a weird gastric alchemy must have been triggered. I'm not a metallurgist and much less an M.D. but what seemed to happen was that McKinley's insides started to bronze. Pretty soon, the metal casting had seeped through to the surface of his dermas. By the time McKinley was officially certified to be dead, he weighed five tons and more resembled a monument than a human cadaver.

"The doctors put down the cause of death was 'gangrene of the pancreas' but that was just to cover up the tone the president was turning. The presidential morticians, all of whom were sworn to secrecy, hired a crane and winched him up into his big plush casket. They dressed him up in his president's duds and slapped a pound of pancake makeup and rouge to his face so he would look halfway mortal to the mobs of mourners.

"McKinley's death train lurched from Buffalo to Washington and then to Ohio. At every stop, there was heavy weeping but no one seemed to notice the dead president's strange demeanor. Back home in Canton, Ida and the kids locked up the late president in the family mausoleum and tried not to think about him too much. . . ."

Tried-not-to-think-about-him-too-much. My tape recorder had malfunctioned and I was scribbling frantically. That was Canton, Ohio, not China, I assume?

"Yup. After that, Teddy Roosevelt got up in his bully pulpit and sent 50,000 more *Americanos* to burn up the Philippinos in Luzon and people around here began to let McKinley slip out of their memory. The government put his mug on the $500 bill in memorium but not a lot of working stiffs ever got to see one of those.

"Now we come up to '05 and McKinley's heirs had just about squandered the family fortune. Ida's medical bills were piling up. So the family decided to put the president on the market as a statue of himself. Those were patriotic times and there was a lot of demand for public statues, especially those of the dead presidents, Lincoln and Garfield as well.

"They listed him with a private dealer in Cleveland and a sleazy Armenian reporter named Patigian at the *Examiner,* the Hearst paper in San Francisco, got wind of it and wanted to be cut in. The family offered him a commission if he could find them a buyer.

"Right about that time, George Zehndner, the lumber baron and dairy queen, was campaigning to change the name of Uniontown to McKinleyville. Zehndner was a German fellow who had come out here following the Forty Niners, the gold miners, not the football team. He lived through the Indian troubles and he took his share of scalps. Later, he got religion and joined the Republican Party—he was their Daddy Warbucks up here on the North Coast. He loved McKinley and believed in Manifest Destiny and Christianizing the Philippino babies to which cause he pledged a good part of his fortune. He hated the anarchists but he had them all mixed up with Jews because of Emma Goldman. After Czolgocz shot his idol, Zehndner got up a posse and ran all the Jews out of Humboldt County, just like he'd done with the Indians and the Chinese before that.

"A couple of years later, he convinced the city fathers in Arcata to put up a statue of McKinley in the town plaza. Zehndner had bought every seat on the city council, and his pal Brizzard owned the plaza outright.

"They heard about Haig Patigian through the hot-statue grapevine and haggled the Armenian down to $15,000 delivered to the door step. Zehndner gave the reporter half up front and Brizzard agreed to help out with the rest. The McKinley deal made Patigian's reputation and he later placed Abe Lincoln in front of San Francisco City Hall and Herbert Hoover out in Golden Gate Park."

Eddie, just where are we going with this? This has all the earmarks of a shaggy statute story to me.

A profoundly wounded silence ensued.

"What is it? You don't believe me? You could look all of this up, you know."

Later, I did. Some of it could be found in the *Arcata Union*, the resource of record for that era. Some of it could not.

"Zehndner told the *Union* that McKinley would be installed on May 1st, 1906 to commemorate the 50th anniversary of his Moose lodge. May 1st! This alarmed us. We anarcho-syndicalists could not permit such sacrilege to come to pass! McKinley, the father of U.S. Imperialism, the fiend that put the soldiers on the strikers and burned up the little Philippino babies, was to be put up there on International Working Men and Women's Day? The day set aside to mark the struggle for the eight-hour day and mourn the Haymarket Martyrs? Over my dead body!

"Just about then we got word that the president had arrived in Frisco from Cleveland on a train and Patigian was warehousing him at a foundry south of the slot. We sent a spy to scout it out and to hear what the comrades down there had to say about it. Tom Mooney was at the meeting. He explained that he had plenty of dynamite and volunteered to take care of it for us. No problem.

"But we didn't hear from him for a few weeks and it was getting closer to the first of May. I was really in a sweat. Then, before dawn on April 18th, a stupendous blast shook San Francisco to the bedrock. Many were killed and buried beneath the rubble and there was widespread panic. A great fire raged out of control through the downtown. The bourgeois press described the blast as an earthquake.

"By the time Patigian got down to First and Howard, the foundry had been gutted. The embers were still red-hot. McKinley was gone. It took the Armenian hours to locate him, stretched out there in the street with his finger pointed towards heaven. He must have stumbled out of the building looking like the Hulk on fire, and then lay down to cool off. It took five days for McKinley to cool down. Passersby shook his hand or spat in his face, depending on their class orientation.

"So McKinley was saved and we were some glum monkeys. Patigian who was a clever chap and knew how to work all the angles, crated up the president and, to beat the freight charges, wrote on the crate 'Return To Zehndner' and—

Ufff! You shameless son of a boss! Edward Bernhart Schnaubelt Born 1855 Died 1913 Murdered by Capitalism, you just sucker-punched me before all our readers. Shame! Shame! Shame! I whooped, sounding a little like Gladys Knight and the Pips. Well, maybe only the Pips.

"I repeat—you could look it up. Yogi Berra said that."

I'll bet your lying ass $50 it was Casey Stengal . . .

"Just let me finish, O.K.? So they dragged William McKinley on board the packet boat *Pomona* and put him off in Eureka port. Zehndner sent dray horses to haul the president ten miles north to Arcata and they hoisted him up on his pedestal—they had to put a chain around his neck to raise him up and the workmen joked that it was a public hanging. Zehndner didn't like that kind of talk around his hero and he fired the whole damn crew.

"The Frisco comrades had helped to delay McKinley's installation but now the inauguration was arranged for July 4th. So we called a meeting to decide what to do about it. Some of the more extreme elements just wanted to blow the living crap out of the president before the official unveiling. But some of us got to thinking, what if this really was McKinley sealed up inside the statue of himself forever? Wouldn't that be just retribution for all the deaths of the strikers and the Philippino babies? Anarchist justice!

"I went down to Arcata to investigate the truth of the matter and I saw him up there with that big speech that had stopped Czolgocz's bullet, scrolled up under his arm, and his outstretched hand pointing westwards into the Pacific towards Hawaii and Samoa and the Philippinos . . ."

And Vietnam. Don't forget Vietnam.

"And Vietnam. And I asked him, 'Are you really Mister McKinley in there, and after awhile I heard a sigh and McKinley cleared his throat and began to declaim: 'I walked the floor of the White House night after night and I'm not ashamed to say that I got down on my knees and prayed and then it came to me I know not how but that there was nothing to do for them but to take them all up.' It went on a lot longer but I couldn't listen to any more. Now I knew it was him all right, the president himself. Sure, you think I was hallucinating, but I'll tell you what, young man. Why don't you go down to Arcata and hear it for yourself. I guarantee you'll come back a believer."

By now, Schnaubie was adrift in a sea of nostalgia.

"July 4th, 1906 was the big day. Brizzard decked out the whole town in red, white, and blue bunting and George Zehndner shelled out for the victuals. It was an all-American hoedown. There was a pie-eating contest and potato-sack races and fat men's races. The Volunteer Fire Department dressed up in ladies' lingerie and had a hose fight. Near a ton of barbecue was set out, a whole hillside of coleslaw, and a hundred kegs of beer, which got the Women's Christian Temperance Union all sore and huffy.

"A preacher gave the benediction and called William McKinley 'a genuine American holy man' and said that the anarchists should be trampled down underfoot like vipers and snakes. Then the Grand Army of the Republic band struck up a Souza march and little Henry woke up. He began bawling so loud Tina had to take him to the back.

"George Zehndner was exultant up there on the bandstand. 'William McKinley is not dead!' he proclaimed to the joyous crowd. 'He will live right here in our hearts and in our plaza for all of time!'

"When he said that I swear I heard a pitiful sob arise from inside the statue of the assassinated president."

• • •

Now I wouldn't have swallowed Schnaubelt's cockeyed tale if I hadn't known better. Long before, way back when I was still an unrepentant boozer, I had my own run-in with McKinley's statue although I always chalked it up to acute delirium tremors.

By the 1970s, no one much knew what McKinley meant anymore. Although his barbarous behavior in the Philippines was a precursor of Vietnam, history is not a North American strong suit and McKinley had become a kind of public shape to hang one's hat on. The Optimists' Club dressed him up as Santa Claus every Christmas and the high-school teams used him as their mascot on big game weekends. The Deadheads who camped out in the plaza back then thought it was hilarious to wedge a fat reefer in the president's bronze mitt, and drunks from the multiple bars around the square had been pissing without remorse upon his pedestal long after midnight for several generations.

One evening, after a shift on my favorite bar stool at the old Jambalaya Club, I tottered out to the plaza and added my piddle to the puddle, zippered, and slumped down on a concrete bench. A patrol car swung nosily around the square and skidded off south in search of convenience-store holdups. Stars twinkled. The whole town snoozed. Then I too heard it, a hollow metallic mutter at first until the words became a distinguishable patter, a malignant sort of rap: 'I-walked-the-floor-of-the-White-House-night-after-night-and-I-am-not-ashamed-to-say-that-I-got-down-on-my-knees-and-prayed-for-light-and-then-it-came-to-me-there-was-nothing-to-do-but-take-them-all-UP!'

'Shut your trap, you imperialist bastard!' I bellowed and scratched my way up the pedestal to McKinley's knees. I just wanted to get my hands around his thick bronze throat and throttle the infernal lies out of him but just then the patrol car swung back into the plaza, its turret lights flashing red, white, and blue. The cops did not immediately bail out of their vehicle, just sat there and used the loudspeaker instead. 'Come down off McKinley with your hands up and you will not be hurt,' one of the officers arfed gruffly. They met me at the base of the pedestal with drawn guns. The plastic handcuffs cut off the circulation in my wrists.

I was charged with being drunk and disorderly in public and released from county jail on my own recognizance the next morning. Later, I was sentenced to a hundred hours of community service in lieu of a fine. The judge assigned me to shine up McKinley every Saturday for six months but the Big Man never said another word at least so long as I was rubbing on him.

Schnaubelt's story explained the whole thing.

"Speaking of drunk and disorderly in public, how about another slurp of fake sipping whiskey?"

I inspected the jug but it was bone-dry.

I knew I had a pint of Jose Cuervo stashed somewhere in the grass but just where was a mystery. I excused myself to rummage among the tombstone and sure enough, there it was hiding out with the Nortons.

'Salud old comrade,' I toasted, sprinkling my co-author's grave with the cactus juice. We sat there in silence sucking up the Joe Crow and reflecting upon the moral lessons of McKinley's life after death.

And I recalled what old Issac Bashevis Singer once wrote in a book called *Gimpel the Fool:* "Whatever doesn't happen to one, happens to another. Whatever doesn't happen during the day, happens at night in dreams. What difference can it make?"

"I'll drink to that, comrade," Schnaubelt said.

The Lives of the Assassins

Leon Czolgocz!
"Live like him!"
Charles Guidreau!
"Live Like Him!"
Lee Harvey Oswald!
"Live Like Him!"
Ramon Mercador!
"Who?"
The guy who got Trotsky!
"Live Like Him!"
Gaetano Breschi!
"Live Like Him!"
Muhamet Ali-Agca! (He plugged the Pope.)
"Live Like Him!"
"Nicolo Clavillo!
"You're losing me"
Sarajevo. Archduke Ferdinand.
"Live Like Him!"

It was long after cemetery curfew but no one had come to lock up. "Glen Saunders" must have been away for the weekend. As usual, it was just me and the dead.

You know Eddie, I have dreamed of assassinating every U.S. president who has occupied the White House in my lifetime. Well, perhaps not all of them. Franklin Delano Roosevelt saved the Capitalist class's ass but he was a paraplegic and I could never shoot a man when he was sitting down. Besides, my poor grandmother, the tiny Mamie Zief (Ellis Island for "Jew") Applebaum worshipped FDR and huddled by the radio to warm herself at his fireside chats. 'You have nothing to fear but fear itself,' she would say whenever I told her that dead fish scared me, echoing his stern warning.

"Eat your fish or I'll have to wrap it up and send it to the starving children of Poland," she would always threaten, although I could never figure out what the Polish kids would do with the remains of my mackerel. Out of respect for my poor grandma, I will not fix FDR in the zoom scope of my Italian Carcano.

But Harry Truman is another story: A mass murderer who dropped the Big One at Hiroshima and Nagasaki, incinerating 200,000 human beings on impact alone and a million more from cancers ever since, just to show Joe Stalin that the U.S. was Number One.

Oscar Collazo and Gracelino Torresola were two of my childhood heroes. You probably don't remember them. One day, the 3rd of October, 1950, in the name of the independence of the free people of Puerto Rico, they opened fire on the Blair House, where Truman was lounging about while the White House was being remodeled—the first-ever assassination attempt with automatic weapons. Torresola and two of the president's Secret Service guards fell dead but Give-'em-Hell Harry survived, at least for a few years.

The guy who pulled the trigger, Oscar Collazo, lived to be an old man. Jimmy Carter commuted his sentence in 1979 and he went home to Puerto Rico as a peoples' hero. Jimmy Carter is another president I'd probably pardon. Although he was a candycorn Christian with lust in his heart, he was the most harmless of the lot. But all the rest are on the hit list.

Eisenhower fried the Rosenbergs and he should have been fried right back, dipped in sizzling fat, battered to a pulp, and served up in the basket at a Norman Rockwell church picnic.

JFK came next. Howard Hunt and Frank Sturgis picked him off from the grassy knoll under orders from Santos Traficante—but who gave Traficante his orders? Whoopie and L'chaim! Jack was a bad guy in my book, as much a Yanqui Imperialist as ever was Willie McKinley. He sent the CIA and their *gusanos* up against Fidel at Playa Giron and did his damnedest to jump-start World War III over the so-called Cuban missiles.

You want to know where I was when JFK got whacked? Am I under oath or something? Where were you, Eddie? I have an air-tight alibi. I didn't do it.

The morning was cool, the air transparent. From my hillside, I watched the *campesinos* of Santa Cruz Tanaco, the state of Michoacan and the Republic of Mexico, as they readied their ox teams on the valley floor below. Tanaco, a Purepecha Indian village near the top of the Meseta Tarasca, was at the peak of the corn harvest and there were fiestas every night now. I felt sad to be leaving in this bountiful season but it was my turn to bring home the Yanqui bacon. We were broke, selling what corn we could glean when our neighbors invited us to put on the *tchundi* basket and help wrest the big ears from the trampled stalks. Norma had already gone up twice to the Other Side and now she and Dylan would stay and take care of the goats.

I had not been up to Yanquilandia for three years now and didn't consider myself much of a North American anymore.

I bent to dust off my new Mexican loafers. We would walk the dirt road out to the highway and I would catch the bus first to Zamora and Guadalajara and the border and soon I would be in San Francisco, a city I did not yet know. It looked so easy when you studied the map. I was scared shitless.

I flicked on the purloined Zenith Transoceanic shortwave radio that had kept us abreast of the rest of the world for so many years. The president has been shot in the head in Dallas, Texas, it said. Later, he was dead on arrival at Parkland Memorial Hospital. I will always keep that instant in freeze frame: Norma and Dylan jumping the fence at the top of the property carrying water buckets back from the town well. Kennedy dead in Dallas.

So that was it. I unpacked. I'm not going anywhere. Kennedy was a bastard anyway. We returned to the harvest and it wasn't so bad.

Fidel Castro came on Radio Havana that night to defend the Cuban revolution from imminent attack. Washington was already trying to pin the hit on Fidel and he spent three hours meticulously analyzing the evidence and concluding that Oswald's rifle could not have put that many bullets into Kennedy and Connolly in so short a time. We all know that now.

Then Pancho Merced, a young *bracero,* serendipitously returned home from El Norte with the first ever television set to come to Tanaco and we got it hooked up to a car battery and fixed it to an antenna just in time to watch Jack Ruby plug Oswald. We watched it happen over and over again all that Sunday—by then Pancho was charging a *toston* at the door just to see the reruns and there was a line of Indians down the street waiting their turn. Everyone in Tanaco was positive that LBJ was behind it all.

So that's my alibi. I watched the whole thing on television with Purepecha Indians in the mountains of Michoacan. I have signed affidavits.

Assassination is a haphazard sport. Why no one ever took out Johnson or Richard Nixon, the most despicable presidents of all time, is a modern tragedy. I sighted them up in the crosshairs of my imagination every day of their bloody war, my finger squeezing off cyanide-tipped dumdum bullets. I would become a human bomb and hurl myself at the Secret Service, smear napalm on the White House walls like it was strawberry jam, and burn Amerikkka down!

But no one ever knocked them off. One poor schmuck flew a hijacked jumbo jet around and around the Nixon White House but the FBIs lured him down with a tub of counterfeit bills.

Instead, two uppity women—Squeaky Fromme and Sara Jane Moore, took back-to-back potshots at Gerald Fucking Ford during a West Coast swing in 1975. Both of them missed by a mile—maybe they thought they were on *Saturday Night Live* and the Prez was really Chevy Chase. Ford was a joke but he made my list the day he pardoned that scumbag Nixon.

"There comes a time when the only worthwhile political act is to pick up the gun," Sara Jane, a Mission girl, later told the cops.

It goes without saying that Ronald Reagan is on the shoot-to-kill docket. Although he committed multiple crimes against the people of the world, the mutilated corpses that showed up at the El Playon garbage dump in Salvador each morning most merit his deconstruction. I was so pissed off when that asshole John Hinckley went and ruined any hope for peoples' justice with his pitiful "I-did-it-for-Jodie Foster" bullshit. Anyway, Hinckley was just a Mark Chapman wannabe.

"You know son, Americans seem to kill their presidents for a lot of different reasons—I don't see much of a pattern," Schnaubelt puzzled.

"For example, there was the Italian bricklayer Giovanni Zagara. He tried to kill the president because his stomach told him to. It actually said to kill Herbert Hoover, but by the time he got close enough, the president was Franklin Roosevelt. He missed anyway and killed the mayor of Chicago instead. His stomach wouldn't let him alone."

Squeaky Fromme fired at Ford to liberate Charles Manson. Sirhan Sirhan cut down Bobby Kennedy to liberate Palestine. Americans think they can change their political system by blowing away their presidents. Arthur Bremer saw how Sirhan had altered the presidential succession and he went gunning for a candidate, any candidate. He stalked McGovern for months before he settled on George Wallace in a Maryland shopping center. But it doesn't work very well. Politicians are like mushrooms. You shoot one down and another pops up to take his or her place.

"Ya, give me those old-time assassins any day. They were dogged. Old John Neputnick Schrunk was a man who never gave up. McKinley had come to him in a dream and pointed a finger at Teddy Roosevelt.

'There is my murderer' he said, 'you must avenge me.' But every time John Neputnick Schrunk drew a bead, some fool would jump up in front of him. It took him years to finally plug Teddy—he caught up with him in Milwaukee in 1912 when Roosevelt was running for president as a Bull Moose. Just like McKinley, a 30-page speech folded in his breast pocket deflected the bullet. 'It takes more than one bullet to bring down a Bull Moose,' Teddy cracked, but he was grievously wounded and never the same after that.

"The difference between failure and success, history or ignominy, is often just a few millimeters, in the assassination business. The way I see it, John Wilkes Booth was an amateur who got off a lucky shot—his Derringer only permitted him one anyway.

"I had much more respect for Charles Guidreau, who shot James Garfield in the back in Union Station in Washington, July 1881. The bullet got stuck in Garfield's spine and it took the president two months to expire—Czolcocz's bullet only took a week to do its heroic work. I suppose that is progress.

"Guidreau claimed that what he had done to Garfield was really a mercy killing: 'If he is a Christian like me than James Garfield will be happier in Paradise.' Guidreau had been kicked out of the free-love commune in Oneida, New York and never recovered from the rejection. He is usually described as a 'frustrated office seeker' but there is a lot more to this story than meets the eye. For example, Charles Guidreau once wrote a book, "Truth—Or the Alternative to the Bible," and someone unknown printed up a whole new edition just before he gunned down Garfield. Who was that person and what did he or she know?

"Another thing: Guidreau shot Garfield with a beautiful ivory-handled English Bulldog pistol. He thought it would look swell in a museum someday or fetch a fortune at auction. But Charles Guidreau was penniless, a raving maniac who did not even wear socks. Who paid for that pistol and why is history so silent about it?"

Eddie, you know you can't have an assassination without a conspiracy. It's in the rules and regulations. Like Oswald could not have flattened Kennedy just because Kennedy was a rich Yanqui prick. Or James Earl Ray, a racist nut, couldn't take out King on his own just because he hated niggers. People do not think that one man's fury can do the job. It always has to be a plot.

But you are right on target about today's assassins. That the first George Bush got off scotfree is proof that they don't make American assassins like they used to do. Daddy Bush deserved to be thrown alive on the pyre, payback for the hundreds of women and children his smart bombs carbonized in the Almariya shelter, Baghdad, Valentine's Day, 1991!

Bill Clinton is another shyster who should have been drug out of the big house by the homeless he cut off welfare and roasted at the stake in Lafayette Park, if just for his piggish yuppie smugness. And while we're at it, bring out Hillary too! Let's make this a his and hers auto-da-fé.

(This is a legal disclaimer: Let it be known that the author of these words is really a peaceable fellow, crotchety and nearly blind, but non-violent—or at least he has never been convicted of a violent crime.)

That is true. I have only fired a gun twice in my life, sir, two Saturdays running at the Coyote Point shooting range in the summer of '67. We were warming up to off a pig but we never did. In fact, I missed the target every time.

I am also a real klutz around bombs. You would not want to take me along on your next terrorist act.

"Do you really think all this talk about assassination will help sell the book? Maybe we should take nommes de plume?" Schnaubelt was whispering just in case "Glen Saunders" had arrived home on the other side of the fence, "If you really did assassinate a president, its best that you don't tell me anyway. They could charge me with conspiracy. Under Clinton's 1995 anti-terrorism act, the dead can now be charged as co-conspirators. A lawyer named Robert Kogan came up here and warned me about that. But don't worry, my lips are sealed."

Life of Ross (cont.)

Now I'm going to tell them my side of the story, Eddie. Is that copacetic with you?

"No problem—but try and stick to radical politics. That's what we advertised this book to be all about."

I'll try.

Well, for starters, my story is not that distinct from *On The Road*. But where does that road begin?

How about West 4th Street, the stroll from Sheridan Square across 6th Avenue, cut through the park and zigzag around NYU into the Lower East Side where Monk and Coltrane wailed every night of the summer of '57 at the Five Spot Cafe on the Bowery. Miles Davis was often at the Bohemia on Barrow Street back in the West Village and Charles Mingus carried on farther west yet at the Half Note over on Hudson. Sheilah Jordan, the outside bop singer, warbled nightly at the Front Page off Seventh Avenue South, and it could be anybody and his uncle—Babs Gonzalez and John Cage, Professor Irwin Corey or Sonny Rollins (I was Sonny's bandboy-publicist for one hellish month in '57) downstairs at Max Gordon's Village Vanguard.

All along the route, I off-loaded New York Nickels, Dimes, and O-Zees of Chicago Light Green to musicians of renown and their retinues. Perhaps the apex of my career as a drug dealer to the luminaries of the Jazz World was the night I sold Dizzy Gillespie a zee under the stage at Town Hall. "Don't tell Lorraine" (his wife) Diz giggled and slipped me a crisp twenty-dollar bill. I was 18 years old and too hip.

Off hours I hung out with the competition on the steps of Pandora's Box, a smoky 4th Street coffeehouse—dealers with sub-titles like Jimmy Dash and Heavy Lewis and Mezz Mezzrow Jr. (the son of the original Muggles man)—or else juiced it up at Johnny Romero's on Minetta Lane, which was truly "no place to be somebody" as Charles Gordone later pointed out in a Pulitzer Prize–winning drama.

Halfway through my teens, I gravitated to a devious role model and guru. I first knew Jacques B. Longini while he was "working" at Sam Goody's 48th street record palace, boosting customized jazz collections for exclusive customers. A sophisticated con artist and extortionist who looked uncannily like the Zigzag Man (he sometimes affected a fez), Longini also sold exotic narcotics to the heirs of major American fortunes and pimped classy call girls on the side. 'Round any given midnight, Miles Davis might be seated at a table at Longini's hidden Hell's Kitchen carriagehouse. Chinese bit actors, unscrupulous Latino painters, and down-at-the-mouth trombone players lounged around on the living room sofas stoned on mescaline and throwing the I Ching.

Longini's eclectically assembled library was full of Sartre and Beckett, Robbe-Grillet and other esoteric French literateurs. I first read Nietzsche and Aleister Crowley there, Luigi Pirandelo, Ionesco, de Ropp's pioneering *Drugs And The Mind*. D. H. Lawrence's "The Plumed Serpent" whetted my thirst for Mexican adventure.

An annoying fit of fake coughing erupted from the grave. "Sorry to interrupt, friend," Eddie Schnaubelt interjected in a sepulchral tone, "but this doesn't have much to do with politics. Its just not what we promised the readers."

Excuse me, buddy, but I let you ramble on for years. Give me a break. Besides, I'm getting to a political part.

Sure, I admit that bebop, not politics, was at the top of my adolescent agenda but I wasn't unaware of revolution in the Americas. On the weekends, we bought joints in the Columbus Avenue Cubano bars, the profits from which were said to flow to the mythical Fidel Castro and his band of sainted *guerrilleros* up in the Sierra Maestro.

Jazz was not the only art that propelled me through my teens. The Village was aswirl with Abstract Expressionist painting in the mid-1950s. Harlan studied with Hans Hoffman on West 8th, and the Cedar Tavern, an asylum for exploding visionaries, was just down the street. In our paint-spattered loft, my stepfather anguished over his art. Figures had begun to emerge from his once starkly abstract canvasses, and every Tuesday, Gertrude, a Rubenesque model, would perch nude on the bureau to provoke his muse. On such days, I would hurry home from the far-off Bronx High School of Science and "sketch" the human figure—actually the sketch pad conveniently covered up my tumescent adolescent hard-on.

Summers we spent out in the Hamptons where De Kooning and Klein were already homesteading and Larry Rivers headed up the house band at the Amagansett Inn. One day we walked down Three Mile Island Road to Jackson Pollock's studio and Lee Krasner let Harlan and I mount the balcony and watch the mad master fling paint at his canvas.

We had first set up in the Hamptons—actually closer to Sag Harbor—because it was a relatively easy area for black-white couples to rent a bungalow back then. Two black middle-class summer home enclaves—Azurest and Sag Harbor Hills—had coexisted with that one-time historic whaling port for many years. We played softball on the beach with a teenage Colin Powell and I first came to know Q. R. Hand, the oracular black poet with whom I've been hanging out for 50 years now, knock on wood, and to whom this memoir is dedicated.

Q and I, Billy Pickens, Janet Martin, who else, Kent Drake, Butch Parks, the Clovers on the box. We are driving through eastern Long Island potato fields. As usual, I'm the only white kid in the crew. My friends are taunting migrant pickers, all of whom are black. Every little bit, Billy slows down and pretends to stop and offer the men a ride to town but when the poor guys dash for the car, he cruelly guns the gas. "Look at those fool niggers" the sons and daughters of the

E. Franklin Frazer's Black Bourgeoisie are cackling. I suppose that's how I first learned race was really a class thing.

Back in the city, the jazz world sucks me up. After high school, I enroll at the University of Pennsylvania, but that doesn't last a month although I stay on in Philly and live the vibrant jazz life there. Harlan's niece, Jeanne Dixon ("Here comes the Dragon Lady" is how the boys in Basie's band would greet her) takes me out to Pep's and the Showboat and the Blue Note. Pretty soon, I'm managing a band of hot young local boppers headed up by Jimmy DePriest, Marian Anderson's nephew, and pretty soon after that, I am back in the Village hanging posters for the eccentric impresario Bob Reisner's two clubs, the Open Door and the Pad. I do the advance on a Billie Holiday midnight concert at the Loew's Sheraton moviehouse for the fledgling *Village Voice,* and am backstage when Lady stomps in hours late. Her sister Irma is right behind her, carrying Billie's tiny Chihuahua dog and she tosses it to me like I'm Stagedoor Johnny.

The night I caught Billie Holiday's Chihuahua.

Poetry reared its twisted beautiful head in the midst of my adolescent confusion and I begin to scribble and declaim. Dylan Thomas was then touring America, puking from the lecterns of prestigious universities between drunken bouts at the White Horse Tavern.

Another culprit who exposes me to this precarious craft is a street poet named Harvey. I am scooting down West Fourth one Saturday afternoon and he is shouting and waving his arms and selling his poems, a quarter a sheet. I'm thrilled to buy one and I take it home to my mom to prove that I am not alone in my delirium. "Wonderful," Mom clucks reprovingly, "but does he make a living at it?"

Actually Mom, he made a great living at it. Harvey became a Frenchman named Jack Micheline, a Beat luminary, obstreperous poet, prolific painter, and obsessive horse player, who died one day on the train to Golden Gate fields beyond Berkeley to play a hunch on the exacta. Whenever I pass the Curtis Hotel on Valencia Street near 16th in the Mission where Jack bunked for years, I always wave hello.

Man, did we dress funny in those bygone days. When I first

descended the Birdland stairs at age 14, a crudely altered selective-service card in my callow paw, I featured powder-blue pegged pants with white saddle stitching down the side seam, a long suede jacket that made it look like I finally had obtained shoulders, Mister B roll collar curling on my chubby neck. But a few years later, I exuded Ivy League cool, battened down in my four-button green tweed suit with leather patches on the elbows. I looked at the cosmos through deep dark shades—'Shades' indeed had become my *nomme d'street.* All this is to say we were hipsters. The only Beats we knew were the short, incisive jolts Philly Joe or A.T. (Arthur Taylor) kicked in behind Miles's bluest splats.

Then I began to tarry at the Half Note on Monday nights when Mingus would let the poets on stage to jam. I did my riff, all jazz and junk, fuck that chump Eisenhower, balling chicks in East Village pads and walking the Brooklyn Bridge into the new dawn, and Charles Mingus did not throw me off the stage.

The Beats were still a West Coast crowd but the celebrated Six Gallery "Howl" bust in '55 had put them on the map and they were beginning to leak east. Rexroth brought poetry and jazz to the Five Spot (I can't remember who backed him up) and so did Kerouac who read a poem titled "Stanley Gould, Don't Go To Florida" for the round-shouldered Village junkie of the same name, sometimes my roommate. The New Orleans clique, Bob Cass (who put out *Climax* magazine, an early Beat journal) came to New York too and took home some of my poems and I became a younger Beat poet.

On The Road hit the bookstores to great critical acclaim in the fall of '57 and Max Gordon asked me, "Johnny, could you please find Kerouac and bring him to the Vanguard to headline for a week." Norma, the complicated Catholic Worker Beat lady with whom I had taken up residence, had been Henri Cru's lover (Rene Bontemps' in *On The Road* and Kerouac's oldest friend) and we ran down Jack at his mother's in Orlando.

Kerouac's week at the Vanguard at Christmastime '57 was an unqualified disaster. Drunk on the exuberant reviews, not to mention the expensive booze he used to mitigate his fear of fame, Jack Kerouac was positively dangerous. Assigned to keep an eye out for him backstage, I was a 19-year-old greenhorn with no hope of controlling this berserk prince of the Beats. When the union rep from AGVA (American Guild of Variety Artists) showed up and demanded that Kerouac join, Jack pasted the poor schmo on the schnoz, grabbed a long-necked bottle of liquor from off the back bar, and chased me around the room seeking to club me into the checkered floor as if I were some hipster baby harp seal.

My mom, who had done the Vanguard publicity since Max moved in, called out *Life* photographers to record Kerouac's catastrophe and the mag ran a spread entitled something like "*Life* Goes To A Beatnik Party," which was the death knell for the Beat Generation.

So it was time to get my own self on the road. My mom presented me with a hardcover copy of the famous volume and I hit it. I was dying to get out beyond the skyscrapers and know the land all the way to the Pacific Ocean. I had to see Mexico and learn how they did things there. I had already figured out that was where the good weed grew.

But wait, here's another political part. Just before I split, I committed what became my first political crime. Now it was the spring of '58 and Dwight D. Eisenhower had sent the marines into Lebanon, an obscure Yanqui aggression, but it got my blood to roaring. In a fit of fury, I ripped my draft card into a hundred tiny pieces and shipped them back to the Selective Service board.

When I finally hit the road, *Downbeat,* The bible of the jazz world, ran a squib: "John Ross has gone to Mexico to write a novel." I did too.

"I dunno . . ."

What don't you know, Eddie?

"This second book was supposed to be all about Yanqui Imperialism and you're taking it somewhere else. . . ."

Well, I can't tell that part of the story unless I tell this part first.

"You know what I think comrade?"

What Eddie?

"I think we need an editor."

I hopped the Hound for Chicago and went looking for my proposed travel partner, a flame-haired stripper who billed herself as Bonny Bubbles. She had run the New York scene with Longini (who by now had split for Ibiza), booking orgies for some perverse shuck called "The Kingdom of Karista." In one wee hour of the morning, I had rhapsodized my Mexican dreams to Bonnie Bubbles and she surprised me when she asked if I would take her with me when I got ready to hit the road. But Bonny was busy just now. She had been schtooping an elderly Hasid who, with his nine brothers, owned a tulip-bulb company and Bonny Bubbles had recently been promoted from receptionist to their Chief Executive Officer.

The CEO put me in touch instead with one Oliver Jones who was in the process of dissolving his record-store partnership with Schatzi Youngblood, Longini's ex, and was about to skip out to L.A. with the entire inventory stashed in the stern of his station wagon.

Although I proclaimed myself a younger Beat poet and was now at last on the road, I had never learned how to drive a fucking automobile. Nonetheless, I would be overjoyed to pay the gas all the way to California. Oliver Jones thought that was cool and I climbed into the co-pilot's seat and began to take notes.

Barreling down the Interstate was still a dangerous game for black-white drive-aways in June of 1958. Roadside restaurants rudely refused us service and at some stops, there were still separate restrooms. "What are you doing with that nigger in your car?" a prototypical peckerwood asked me on the east side of Texas. I started to explain that it was his car but clammed up when I remembered that we were packing a wagonful of hot merchandise.

Our modus operandi for the motels was that I checked in at the desk after dark and got the room key and Oliver would slip in when the coast was clear. But my man was mightily attached to his music and inevitably trundled in the hi-fi and a few choice Dinah Washington sides. Remember "TV Is The Thing This Year"?

"You be playin' nigger music in there, boy. You got a nigger in there, don't you?" The clerk would come pounding and we'd be on the road again.

When we crossed into Arizona on Route 66, I had had just about enough of racist Amerikkkana and bailed. "California's just one state west," I encouraged Oliver, who understandably did not like to drive this country alone.

So I caught the bus to Tucson and then down to the border at Nogales, Mingus's hometown, crossed over to the other Nogales, sat down on a bench in a little park and snorkeled up a cold Carta Blanca. It was Sunday and a brass band was playing up in the kiosk. I drew a deep breath out of the turquoise-blue sky and realized I was really on the road.

I caught a train overflowing with *braceros* through the Sonoran Desert sweet with sage, rumbling further south through Sinaloa and Nayarit into the heartland towards Guadalajara. I don't think I have ever felt so free before or since in my life.

Many lurid chapters in Beat history were written in Mexico. William Burroughs plugged his spouse Joan right between the eyes, playing William Tell in their Mexico City Colonia Roma apartment in 1950. Kerouac wrote *Tristessa* and "Mexico City Blues" in a little rooftop room there. Neil Cassidy, the Dean Moriarty of *On The Road*, and, later, Benzedrine-chomping chauffeur to the stars on Ken Kesey's Merry Pranksters excursions, was found dead along the railroad tracks in San Miguel, Allende, circa 1969, putting a macabre Mexican coda on the book of the Beats.

The road I was on took me west from Guadalajara out to Lake Chapala where Lawrence had set *The Plumed Serpent*. I kept staring at the dark surface, waiting for Quetzalcoatl to suddenly surge up from Chapala's turgid, ancient depths.

Alex Trocchi, Scotland's most accomplished junkie decades before *Trainspotting*, and a fellow barge captain whose *Cain's Book* was one of Barney Rosset's first titles at Evergreen, was hiding out in Ajijic. I bunked with Ned Polsky whose quibblings with Norman Mailer and his "White Negro" thesis were well-published on the Left. But heroin is a lethargic drug and weighty words did not spark much adventure. Ajijic, packed with dissipated gringos, seemed to me a kind of leper colony and I soon bid it *adios* and grabbed the puddle-jumper down to Puerto Vallarta, still a coastal backwater before Burton & Taylor filmed *Night of the Iguana* there, and caught a sail canoe out to the legendary Beatnik colony near the south cape of the bay at Yelapa.

Yep, Yelapa was the place. A lush paradise with bone-white beaches and crystalline waterfalls. Whales frolicked at the mouth of the cove and manta rays catapulted out of the sea. But paradise had fallen on tough times. The year before I showed up, Bryce Wilson, the one-time manager of the all-star junkie trumpet player Chet Baker, had built a beach-side hotel for Beat visitors where substance abuse had been generous and when the *federales* showed up everyone ran off into the jungle. Now the Feds were gone but the hotel was padlocked. Bryce had sneaked back in from the bush and taken up residence on a hill with a bird's-eye view of the bay. I rented a thatched *palapa* in a coconut grove down below where the river curled into the shining beach to form an emerald-hued lagoon. The next time I went into Vallarta, I telegrammed Norma and Dylan and urged them to fly down.

The party on the hill at the Wilsons never abated. Bryce had discovered colorful opium poppy plantations back in the hills near Tuito which added a potent ingredient to the general debauchery. The cast of characters was forever remaking itself. I hung out with Jimmy Hines—he had another name then, a bank robber whose mug shot graced post-office walls all over the southwest—and Jungle Jim Dunn, direct from the Coexistence Bagel Shop on Grant Avenue in San Francisco's North Beach, who claimed intimacy with the original Beats.

The rains came in sudden white sheets, and after the rain came insects that sucked your blood and scorpions that could sting you into palsy. And after the insects, came the invasion of land crabs, millions of them, deftly scissoring through all our remaining clothes, eating their way through the roof of our house, leaving us naked before the world. Through it all, I sat there, pen over paper as I sit here still, trying to figure out how to write a novel.

"I'm not trying to criticize but this part is really self-indulgent. You writers are all alike. All you can write about are yourselves and how you write. What was happening to the world? Who was winning the class war?"

Pipe down, comrade, here comes your goddamn politics.

Comandante Fidel Castro and the Cuban Miracle finally rode triumphantly into Havana at New Year's, 1959. The news dawned dimly in the drugged haze of Yelapa but by the next year, the bucks had run dry and we were back on the Lower East Side. I was working out on the barges and we were putting together a stake to go back to Mexico. The figure of Fidel loomed large.

That fall, he and Che Guevara came to the U.N. and you remember the story—how the Lexington Hotel evicted the comandantes because the roosters for the Santeria sacrifices kept waking up the more civilized guests. So the *barbudos* moved up to the Hotel Teresa, 125th Street and Seventh Avenue, the vortex of the Harlem whirlpool. Mr. Nikita Khrushchev came to meet with Fidel there and we stood in the street in front of the Teresa, chanting *"Cuba Si! Yanqui No!"* all night long.

By Christmas, we had our boodle together and I kited a mess of checks and embezzled a Zenith Transoceanic shortwave radio that would keep us in listening range for the next four years, and the next thing you knew, we were crossing the big river at Laredo. First stop was San Luis Potosi where the glittery little vials in the all-night *farmacias* kept inviting me back for more. We had outgrown the stoned gringos of Yelapa and wanted to live with Mexicans now.

From San Luis, we bussed it south to Cuernavaca where Dylan and Norma, already six months pregnant, would hunker down with a transplanted New York painter, and I stepped down to the Oaxaca coast to hunt out a new sanctuary.

I walked the Oaxaca coast for a month, from La Ventosa on the isthmus to Puerto Escondido, then just a few thatched huts in the sand. The Zapotec Indians who lived in the villages through which I passed had never seen an American before and took me for a gypsy. I did not disappoint them, tracing love lines in callused palms and predicting the imminent arrival of handsome strangers, in exchange for coffee and tortillas. I met up with armed bandits and was knocked out cold by the amateur middleweight champion of Oaxaca in a hut filled with bananas. I sailed on the *Margarita* hauling a load of hibiscus leaves up to Acapulco with a raspy-voiced old *bracero* named "Chicago." I had many adventures but I never found the sanctuary I had set out to discover: a shrouded inlet named Chacahua where black people raised crocodiles.

We traveled west out to Michoacan and expatriate U.S. communists, Bundy (Mike "Jews Without Money" Gold's niece) and Walter Ilsley, a civil engineer who purportedly had worked with Mao in China, told us about a Purepecha village up in the meseta, Santa Cruz Tanaco. There was an American living there, they warned, Don Federico Esmith, "The Maestro," who collected *pirecuas* (Purepecha folk songs) and taught townspeople how to read music, in exchange for friendship and strong drink. Federico Esmith had been a resident radical at the conservatory in Mexico City and apprenticed with the U.S. avant-gardist Conlin Nancarrow, also in political exile.

We hiked into Tanaco in March, 1961. The road was chokingly dusty and ran eight kilometers off the Uruapan highway. Norma was big with Tristram. It had been a troublesome pregnancy and she was very tired. I just wanted to get off the road for a while and write my book. Dylan, then six, skipped ahead and urged us on.

We asked for "The Maestro," Federico Esmith at the bottom of town and small boys escorted us to the house of Pablo Augustin, the leader of one of Tanaco's two famous brass bands. The Maestro was perched in the patio, a storklike figure in a florid *gavan* and crushed sombrero. He was very drunk, his eyes rolled up way in the back of his head, but he didn't seem unhappy to see us. I explained how we had been on the road for a while and Norma needed to lie down and gather her strength back for the baby, and me, I just wanted to write this novel I had in my mind, but if he didn't want us here, well, we'd move on.

"It's yours!" he hiccuped with a sweeping flourish that took in the thickly forested mountains soaring above us, "all yours!" He was going to Cuba to see the revolution for himself. And in a week he had packed up and flown off to Havana to join Fidel and Che.

"Well, it's about time. At last, someone with politics!"

The Maestro never looked back. A few years later, during the Cuban missile crisis, we made up a petition and sent it to Kennedy demanding that not one thin hair on the head of Federico Esmith, maestro of this place, should be harmed.

So we raised our house on the edge of town above the *barranca Ker-Cuaro,* "where the devil lives." I danced in the mud to make the adobes that built up its walls. The carpenters fashioned me a wondrous writing room, a cool mossy den that hung over the side of the ravine. I set up rough pine-plank bookshelves and alphabetized the titles I had on permanent loan from the New York Public Library to stock its new Santa Cruz Tanaco branch, 60 volumes from the Bible and the Ancients through James Joyce and *Journey to the End of Night.* Over the years, I would read each one front to back. They became my formal education.

In April, we went down to Uruapan where we had settled on a midwife but while we were waiting for Tristram to arrive, Kennedy and his Worms sailed into the appropriately named Bay of Pigs and Fidel's *muchachos* on the beach at Playa Giron picked them off one by one. We heard the Comandante read the names of the bourgeois pirates that had been captured, on Radio Havana on our stolen radio.

By 1961, Fidel and Che's audacious revolution had struck a thunderous chord from Tijuana to Tierra del Fuego—and particularly so out in Michoacan where the beloved ex-president Lazaro Cardenas, a native son, was, at that very moment, flying off to Havana to defend the island from the Yanqui invaders. The news broadcasts squalled from every stall in the market and the vendors did not gaze upon us with much kindness in their eyes.

At night, I stood in the shadows off the plaza while young men threw furniture out in the street and set fire to the North American Cultural Institute, a rumored CIA front. "Que Mueran los Gringos," they were singing, that the gringos should die. Oh my. I suddenly understood that they meant me.

Mexico was still a literary experience for me then. I had been on the road and now I was going to write the *real On The Road* in the mossy den above the deep ravine. I looked at Mexico from the wrong end of my binoculars—if I looked at it at all. I was not engaged.

Then my infant son died in his sleep in his first month of life under a crabbed *Tejocote* tree on a muddy hillside in the Purepecha hamlet of Santa Cruz Tanaco. His small bones are buried there yet.

I can never erase that moment. Even now, it remains a burnished pain upon my heart. Tristram blue in his wicker cradle, his mother grabbing for him frantically, trying to breath life back into his tiny lungs, to give him to God before there was no god anymore. She was still a Catholic then.

The news spread like lightning that the gringos' baby had died and our neighbors came running to offer solace. Doña Teresa Garcia took charge right away. She counseled us that there was much to be done and that it was better to stay busy. She had organized many funerals. "You had better go see about the coffin," she instructed me and I went to talk to Tata Trinidad, the town carpenter, and haggle over the price of the box. The Doña comforted Norma and Dylan and put all the women to work gathering flowers and hauling water to prepare Tristram for the grave.

Today, at 91, Doña Tere is still my comadre, a strong old woman who tends her own cornfields at the foot of Marihuata mountain and slaps out warm tortillas over her kitchen fire in the cool nights.

Tristram's death was a turning point in a life that has never wanted for twists and turns. I was 21 and a tenderfoot at life—death had never touched me yet except for two old grandparents I barely knew. Death happened in Dylan Thomas poems or at the movies or to others, not to your first-born son. Nana Teresa, Tata Goyo, Tata Santiago, all the others, taught me about death—and about life. That was 43 years ago last month and we are all still tied to each other by the remembrance of our dead children.

As the weeks wore on following Tristram's funeral, I begin to understand that each family in Tanaco had lost many children to the cold and the mud, malnutrition, the absence of a doctor or even a road to transport the sick to the nearest clinic, 20 miles away. Santiago had lost six brothers and sisters, and when he was born, his father, Tata Candido, would not pay for one more birth certificate because this baby would not do any better than the others. "I suppose I fooled him," Santiago whispered sheepishly the night we sat up with the dead baby.

In the late spring of 1961, not long after we buried Tristram, I heard Fidel Castro pronounce the Second Declaration of Havana on the stolen Zenith in our too-quiet home above the *barranca Ker Cuaro* and came to understand the terrible dimensions of infant mortality in Latin America. My personal tragedy became a continent-size one. I became engaged.

"That was very moving, comrade." Muffled clapping, like the snapping of brittle bones, rippled from Schnaubelt's bier. "We need to tug the old heartstrings if we're going to sell this property. Is it my turn now?"

Eddie's crass outburst stung like a slap in the face.

Listen, old man, this is my story. Show it the same respect with which I listened to yours, I muttered when I had recovered my breath. This is my story, about how I escaped the belly of the beast and came to know Yanqui Imperialism firsthand, and I'm going to tell it until it is done!

"Don't get me wrong now. This is really a literary experience. I don't mean that in a bad way. This literary stuff is fine, it's going to help us sell the book—although I'm still partial to a screenplay."

Eddie, you're becoming a complete mercenary asshole. All you can talk about is the money. But we're not writing this book for the money, remember? This is about history, our real history, in case you've forgotten.

Schnaubelt saw quickly that he had overstepped the limits of our friendship and actually said he was sorry. "I really am. It won't happen again. Next time, I'll bite my tongue—if only I had a tongue to bite." He encouraged me to continue. I poured two fingers of Cuervo by way of shaking hands, and picked up the thread.

We camped out on that hillside in the house above *Ker Cuaro* for three, nearly four, more years. Many things happened. We had many adventures. We got to know our neighbors well and they us. The seasons turned round and round. Each December, the new crop of *xungapiti* would come in and I saw it was the same herb we sold in New York under the brand-name "Chicago Light Green." Much of this is described in an unpublished manuscript, *The Marijuanos of Zapicho—A Beat Adventure in Mexico*. I used to read it in the Arcata bars with a Norteña *conjunto* band—Ruben Jaramillo and his clip-joint *orquestra*. All the musicians worked at the mill. Maybe you heard us?

"Nah, I don't get downtown much anymore" Eddie sighed. "Hey listen, I'm really sorry about what I said before. . . ."

The outside world talked to us through the famous Zenith. I confess on this page that I listened religiously each afternoon to the Voice of America—but only the *Jazz Hour* with your host Willis Conover, a gray flannel-mouthed moldy fig but what other option did I have?

Mostly, we stayed tuned to Radio Havana 24/7 and the news of a continent on fire crackled in our little kitchen. We heard of the epic struggles of the landless peasants of northern Brazil, of the guerrilla fighters Hugo Blanco in Peru and Douglas Bravo in Venezuela (years later, I met them both at a Zapatista conference in the Lacandon jungle.) We heard too of the Colombian priest Camilo Torres who had risen in arms against his government and the Guatemalans Luis Turcios and Yon Sosa and a Chilean socialist named Allende. In Mexico, Lazaro Cardenas was organizing the *Movimiento de Liberación Nacional* and the Left thumbed its nose at Kennedy and his two-faced "Alliance for Progress" Listen Yanqui! Here in the south, there was a continuum of resistance and it gave one hope.

We also heard of a land called Vietnam and of Uncle Ho and General Giap and how they had run the French out of their country at Dien Bien Phu in '54 and now first Eisenhower and then Kennedy had landed Yanqui troops there to keep the Vietnamese in their place. There were just a few hundred "advisers" on the Indochina peninsula in 1962 but a million more were in the chute.

The missile crisis that October kept us glued to the dial and we got an earful from Radio Havana, Free Territory of America. Kennedy had thrown up a Naval "quarantine" around the island and every incoming Russian ship was to be stopped and frisked for "offensive weapons." One afternoon, Fidel took to the airwaves to advise the world that one of those Russian ships was reportedly transporting a famous Moscow circus to Havana. Was a bear to be considered an offensive weapon?

And later we heard the Cubans' wounded indignation when the Soviets backed down, withdrew the rockets, and left the fledgling revolution to swim for itself. I was already a doubter of the revisionist Soviets and their CP-USA stooges and Khrushchev's treachery only confirmed my suspicions.

One afternoon I had been rummaging through Maestro Federico Esmith's abandoned little hut—the Purepechas call them *trojes*—and embedded in the mud floor, discovered a pamphlet by Mao Zedong, *On Practice* which I just about had memorized now. Mao preached Doing It, turning theory into deeds—"The only way to know a peach, is to taste it."

Tata Santiago received both the *Peking Review* and *URSS*, the monthly magazine the Soviet embassy sent out with color photos of hydroelecric dams and women in babushkas. We sat in his front room leafing the pages and made up our minds to become Maoists.

At the apex of the missile crisis, with Kennedy and Khrushchev eyeball-to-eyeball and nuclear cataclysm just over the horizon, I warned my *compañero* Marcelino Velazquez, a grizzled *bracero* who had laid track in the frozen Montana tundra during World War II and never tired of telling me the tale, that the world as we knew it might very well be coming to an end. How much time did he have, Don Marsa wanted to know? There was some primo *xungapiti* down in Cheran and he needed to get down there quick if we were going to die happy. . . .

Koff Koff. Koff Koff. Schnaubie was making like he was chugging on some boss underground spliff himself.

Yah, Eddie, what's up?

"Now, I don't want to get you upset all over again but don't you think there's a little too much marijuana smoking in your story? What with the War on Drugs and all, the industry isn't buying dope books anymore. An agent told me this."

I was flabbergasted. You have an agent?

"Well, actually I read about it in *Editor & Publisher* or one of the trades."

Look Fast Eddie, I repeat, this part is my story. I'm not changing it for any editor. Besides, we don't even have an editor, let alone a publisher, yet.

"O.K. O.K. Let's just drop it. You obviously don't want to talk business."

Not now, man. This is important.

What the Zenith broadcast just as loud and as clearly as the Venceremoses from Havana were the "We Shall Overcomes" from Alabama. Black voices had begun to bleed through the ether and we tracked the civil-rights marches each night from city to city, Montgomery; Albany, Georgia; Jackson, Mississippi; Birmingham. . . . We heard of the dogs and the whips and the waterhoses. We kept count of the arrests and the deaths and learned the words of the freedom songs. We followed the route of the Freedom Riders from one mob beating to the next, the SNCC workers waiting to be served at the Kress lunch counter in Greensboro, North Carolina. George Wallace ordered out the National Guard and stood in the school house door to keep Miss Arthurine Lucy from attending the University. We tuned into the Oxford, Mississippi riots the night a fascist retired general Edwin Walker led the Klan up against James Meredith when he sought to enroll at Ol' Miss.

And we did not miss Dr. King's towering sermon that August day in 1963 by the Washington monument wading pool. A great summer storm had just blown up over the Meseta, a *tormenton,* when blue stones fall from the sky, and I held the fading radio close to my ear as MLK's dreams streamed through the static.

Someone up north had sent us that summer *Negroes With Guns,* Truman Nelson's stirring account of Robert Williams' battles with the

Klan in Monroe, North Carolina. Armed self-defense began to make more and more sense after Bull Connor turned loose the dogs.

We sat in the smoky kitchen all that sad September Sunday in 1963 when four little girls were blown up to heaven by KKK bombs in Birmingham. "I've got to go back," I said after a while to Norma, "I can't take this any longer."

So that's where I was headed the day that Kennedy got what he had coming. To El Norte and into the struggle. But instead, we stayed on and worked in the harvest and Dylan even got a few toys for Christmas and the Day of the Kings.

To while away the time, I had gotten myself chin deep in a scrape to stop timber goons from taking Tanaco's fine pine forests. It was my first environmental battle, I suppose. The clique that ran the town back then, the Bravo clan, were all PRI-istas, the ruling party, and they had been paid off by a slimeball politico from Zamora, Maximo Iturbide. Now his men were cutting skid roads into the mountains. They set up a mill just below town and the whine of the saws was driving me nuts.

In those days, if an Indian hacked a few shingles from a downed tree to roof his hut, the *federales* would throw him in jail and toss away the key. I wrote an outraged front-page article for *La Voz de Michoacan*, the statewide paper, my first published piece anywhere on the planet outside of my high school paper (of which I was the editor.)

Then Iturbide's sawmill abruptly went up in flames. I had nothing to do with it. I repeat, I had absolutely nothing to do with it but whether I did or not, the Bravos did not much appreciate my published comments and one Sunday that December a man with a long gun yelled "pinche gringo" at us from the top of the hill and put a dozen bullets in our front door. . . .

"Hold on, partner. Your story is starting to bear a strange resemblance to my story. . . ."

Well, there are certain commonalties. Trees, for example.

Just then, Walter Illsly, the commie from Uruapan, showed up out by the *baranca Ker Cuaro* and handed me $200 to leave town. He warned me that some folks in Tanaco did not feel I was going to live too long if I stayed around. Tensions were running high. Santiago and I and a few of the *compas* had invited the National Liberation Movement to help us stop the logging.

So I took Walter's money. I didn't have a whole lot of options. It was time to get back on the road anyway. I would bus it up to San Francisco, find a job, and send the money orders home like any self-respecting whiteback. Norma and Dylan would stay out by *Ker Cuaro* and my surrogate grandfather, Tata Gregorio Alvarez Zalpa—I have to tell you about Tata Goyo when we have more time—would watch over them in the dark, his breach-loader Mauser tamped and ready to put a blast of buckshot up the *culo* of any intruder.

I crossed the border between Mexico and the United States of North America, Tijuana to San Ysidro, California, on January 14th, 1964 and caught the Big Dog to San Fran. Ten days later, a warrant was sworn out in the Southern District of New York for my arrest on charges of refusal to report for induction into the United States Army, and the manhunt was on. I just want to point out here on these pages that the only person besides Norma, Dylan, and a few select neighbors to know where I was going and when I would get there, was the Uruapan gringo commie Walter Illsley.

The next year, the students in Uruapan were scrawling accusations on the walls of that city that Walter Illsley was a CIA agent and should be thrown out of Mexico—which he was for a short time. Did he fink me out? You can draw your own conclusions.

Like many recently arrived immigrants from Mexico, I got to know San Francisco and its environs from the bottom up. I watched my new Mexican loafers melt in the January rain on Market Street. I wolfed down the slop the good Dominican brothers doled out to the down-trodden on the conga line at St. Anthony's dining room. I sold girlie magazines in the Mexican barbershops on Saturdays and shook down suckers for the "California Missionary Army," a scam run by two Detroit slicksters out of a Mission Street boiler room. When my money ran out, I slept in doorways hard by the Minna Alley office of Manpower Inc., so I could be the first to shape up for the morning call to unload boxcars at below below the minimum wage.

I got a room at the Holland Hotel, a fleabag on Stockton in North Beach where the Beat flame was flickering out, and from there moved to a grim flophouse under the freeway on the Waterfront. On payday, thugs rampaged through the hallways with baseball bats. Then I bumped into Barton Stone, the Wobbly, who took me home to a Bernal Heights Zen compound on Mullen Street, where I met my first hippies. By '64, the next bohemian wave was about to wash over the city.

I joined the struggle. I joined the Wobblies, the Ad Hoc Committee Against Discrimination with 18-year-old dynamo Tracy Simms leading the charge. I joined CORE and the Committee for NonViolent Action, the May 2nd Coalition—a Progressive Labor-organized front that was the first group to focus on the evisceration of Vietnam, and I joined the Progressive Labor Movement—it was not yet a party but it was already on the road to revolution.

I did not miss a picket line anywhere in town and sometimes made my own—such as at the Brazilian consulate on Market Street after the coup of the gorillas that year. I was dragged off by the gendarmes at the Sheraton Palace Hotel, sitting in to win jobs for black chambermaids, and at Kronenberg Cadillac on what used to be Van Ness Avenue Auto Row, throwing my hide on the turntables to back up demands for the employment of black Cadillac salespersons ("we can buy 'em but we can't sell 'em").

I walked on one picket line around City Hall that we promised would never end until justice returned to San Francisco or forever! We marched 24 hours a day and it got to be quite a social scene after the bars closed. Then the CORE leader whose arrest we were protesting walked through the line without so much as a "Right On!" and we all went home.

We marched around the city singing "This Little Light of Mine," "We Shall Not Be Moved," "Paul and Silas Bound in Jail," and "We Shall Overcome," only I could not carry a tune and Roy and Willie

Ballard came to me and warned that if I kept on trying, I would not be allowed to go to jail with them next time we sat-in.

The FBI computers worked like they were powered by molasses back in 1964 and it was a wonder they ever got their man. Finally, in April, the brownshoes surrounded the pad up on Mullen Street and knocked politely. Barton's wife Marti answered the door. She was nursing the baby and agent Ralph J. Fink (that's right, Fink!) was embarrassed and said he'd wait outside for me.

They took me down to the FBI headquarters for the obligatory grilling. Cool, I laughed, you can drive me to work—I had caught on with a subcontractor janitoring at the old Federal Building where I wiped off the local Bureau's transoms every night. Jimmy, a little Muslim cat, and I had been systematically sabotaging the fortresslike premises, taking down the portraits of LBJ and scrawling "Viva Fidel!" in red crayon on the back. We had emptied the building of those annoying yellow and black nuclear attack shelter signs. Jeez, I do hope the statute of limitations has run out. . . .

"I wouldn't count on it, son. Remember, the Feds are still looking for Rudolph. . . ."

They locked me up at the so-called Hall of Justice for 36 days in a tiny cell with a Black Muslim maniac who repeatedly attempted to stab me in the jugular vein with a sharpened pencil—I must have told Wilbur I was a writer. Norma and Dylan arrived from Mexico and I welcomed them on the jailhouse telephone and waved through a thick glass window. My mom, from whom I'd been estranged since I hit the road, came through with the five-figure bail and hired one of Vince Hallinan's stable of able attorneys to accompany me through the legal labyrinth. Thanks, Mom.

My bust was one of the first Vietnam draft beefs in the Bay Area. Even though my original objection to the draft had been Ike's 1958 invasion of Lebanon to sustain the fascist Christian Falange in power, that incursion did not ring many bells by '64. The geography didn't much matter anymore. I was not going to fight in any U.S. imperialist war no matter where they were staged.

• • •

The army had no idea who it was dealing with and cheerfully offered me one last chance to sign up to fight for the Free World against Godless Communism although I was now 26 and past draft age and the father of a family. I told them to go fuck themselves and applied to Julian Bond at SNCC in Atlanta for a job that would be truly in the national interest. But General Lewis Hershey, LBJ's hoary head of Selective Service, refused to go along with the scheme. In the end, I pled nolo to refusing induction—I was proud of what I was doing and did not want to say I was not guilty. But I wasn't a pacifist—I fancied I would pick up the gun when it came to self defense or national liberation. . . .

"Good for you, comrade. I hate that squirrely non-violent scum myself," Schnaubelt enthused.

Well, I guess I just wasn't going to let myself wind up a dead pigeon for the Capitalist class. . . .

My sentencing was set for the end of July so I had a few months to make trouble before they sent me off to the big house. We stomped around the Bank of America, demanding black bankers. We flung ourselves at the turnstiles out at the Cow Palace when the Republican National Convention nominated the troglodyte Barry Goldwater. Rodney Fletcher from Freedom House and I chained ourselves to the Mississippi delegation's cars way in the back of the darkened parking lot but the crackers never showed up and after a few hours, Rodney unlocked me and we went home, free at last.

I rode with the Ballard brothers and their Jewish girlfriends in a Volkswagen bug all the way to Greenville, Mississippi for the Freedom Election. It was really cramped and the Mississippi Highway Patrol gave Roy and Willie a lot of grief. Back in San Francisco, we were dragged out of the U.S. Attorney's office, a black man named Cecil Poole who had once run with Harlan, after Schwerner, Cheney, and Goodman had been found dead under a dam in the Mississippi delta. It was an evil summer.

Despite the bad omens, Norma and I got married not once but twice—first at City Hall during a lull in the various trials of the Sheraton Palace defendants. We sang "If You Don't Find Me In The Back of the Bus" and "Deep In My Heart, I Do Believe" under the great rotunda and I pinned my CORE button on the nonplussed judge and Norma and I smooched to make it official but she was still a Catholic girl and we had to do it all over again the next week at Sacred Heart up in the Fillmore—Dylan was the flower girl.

I put on a big show at the sentencing. I read a statement in my broken *Purepecha* about how the Vietnamese were not my enemies. I drove the judge batty by howling a few stanzas of Bob Dylan's "Masters of War." I read the Brecht poem "To Posterity" (Ah what an age it is/when to write of a tree/is a crime/ because it is/a kind of silence/about injustice.) I did everything but tap-dance to get the judge's attention. Hizzoner, whose name has disappeared beneath the slagheap of trivia that calls itself my memory, wiped away a yawn and asked if I was done.

I caught two years, six months in the slammer and 18 months to be served working in the "national interest," not at SNCC but scrubbing baseboards at Mount Zion Hospital. The federal marshals snapped on the cuffs and chained me to a string of prisoners they were moving south. Whenever we got out of the car to piss along I-5, I rattled my chains energetically to the dangerous annoyance of my fellow convicts. I just wanted everyone to know I was a prisoner of LBJ's war. . . .

"This is all great stuff in here. Does it go on much longer?"

It goes on until I'm done, you old fart, I snapped. I did not much appreciate my erstwhile co-author's constant hectoring. It was downright irritating.

The big gate at Terminal Island Federal Penitentiary, San Pedro, California clanked shut behind me. The date was—are you ready for this? August 3rd, 1964, the night before Lyndon Baines Johnson faked the Gulf of Tonkin incident to justify bombing mainland North Vietnam. Although LBJ had to go to congress to rubber-stamp the big lie (only Ernest Gruening, once an editor at *The Nation,* and the maverick Republican Wayne Morse voted against the resolution), the Gulf of Tonkin is where the war began.

Despite its ominous name, Terminal Island was not really the end of the line. It was a medium-security pen near L.A. with its share of celebrity prisoners—the mobster Mickey Cohen was housed *in durance vile* and Billy Anderson, son of Rochester, Jack Benny's radio chauffeur, was a star running back on the prison football team. There were a handful of political prisoners too: the poet Maurice Ogden who the Feds framed for perjury when he signed a loyalty oath swearing he was not now nor had he ever been a member of the Communist Party (he hadn't been either); Blackie Campbell who had fought with the Canadian McKinzie-Papineau Brigade in Spain and was doing his third stretch for counterfeiting; and Ben D., a middle-class black drug runner who argued correctly that his had been a political crime. Together, we formed the nucleus of the Convicts Committee Against U.S. Intervention (Everywhere).

Blackie taught me how to print leaflets on a bed of illicit gelatin he had smuggled out of the kitchen and the leaflets were my Waterloo. It was a felony to use federal stationery (the only stationery in the Joint) to put out this garbage, the Warden bellowed at me. "I shed my blood for my country!" he frothed. "Well, I'm in your jail for mine," I counterpunched and they hammer-locked me off to the Hole, the jail inside the jail, for a week.

Isolation was hard time. They kept the lights on me day and night and I began to lose track of where I was. I stayed sort of sane by repeating that poem by Uncle Ho, the one that says, "being chained/is a luxury/for which to compete/the chained at least/have somewhere to sleep. . . ."

They took me back to the Hole again that fall after the Free Speech Movement exploded up at Berkeley. The guards had "information" that I was a pal of Mario Savio's and Jack Weinberg's—remember the guy in the police car?—which was untrue. To this day, I have never met either of these fine comrades although I may when I get up to rebel heaven. Should I sue for false arrest?

The day I hit Terminal Island, the parole officer, a bullet-headed skunk named Victor Urban, saw I had a civil-rights jacket and so for work detail, I was assigned to shine shoes up in the guards' quarters. Of course, I displaced a black prisoner name of Bernard from the job, which was one of the prime smuggling channels into the penitentiary and Victor Urban, who knew this, was setting me up to get shanked. So I went to Bernard and apologized. I told him I only had six months at most—I ran it to eight—and then he would have his job back again. He was an old-timer, a scag pusher off Central Avenue in L.A. who had run on the street with Dexter Gordon, the great tenor player, and jazz fixed it up between us.

As you might have figured, that asshole P.O. was my first customer up on the shoeshine stand and I really fucked up his shoes. But the next time he came, I was slapping and snapping, grinning and jeffing like any white-boy nigger worth his salt. Yessuh bossman, I be a shoeshinin' fool. One black guard, Captain Harry—jailhouse scuttlebutt was that he had been an army hangman in Germany—saw what I was up to and tipped me a dollar for my clowning. But the Jewish screw, Levinson, was ashamed of me because I refused to die for my country. To him, I was a traitor to the Jews too and he would never respond to my chatter while I was putting a high gloss on his Florsheims.

Now I'm going to tell you a story on myself.

"It seems like that's what you've been doing all afternoon. . . ."

The next year I'm out of the joint and mopping floors up in the terminal-cancer ward at Mount Zion Hospital when I run into Levinson. He's lost an awful lot of weight and is all gray like he's going to die tomorrow. "Ross," he yells at me and tries to get out of his chair, "Ross, don't you remember me? Officer Levinson from Terminal Island."

You know, Eddie, I just kept my head down and mopped right around that poor fool's slippers. It put a black mark on my karma.

Toward the end of my time at TI, I had these terrible toothaches. The prison dentist was a sadist who screamed that I was a yellow draft dodger and physically assaulted me. He yanked out six teeth he lied were bad. He wrestled me down to the floor and jammed his knee into my chest and wrenched out my wisdom teeth. That son-of-a-bitch broke my jaw and laughed that my time was too short to get false teeth. But I did get sent to the infirmary for a few weeks where there was Darvon on request and soothing jazz on the FM from L.A. The run-in cured me of dentists for good. I have never been to one since. People ask me—my own mother in fact—why I'm toothless. Well, that's why.

So my time got short and then it was done. I rolled up, laced on my free shoes, pocketed the Greyhound voucher north. The bullethead walked me out to the front gate. He didn't want to see me back there at Terminal Island. "Ross," he barked, "you never learned how to be a prisoner."

The Never-ending Life of Ross (cont.)

"When the prison gates open, the dragon will fly out." Ho Chi Minh knew his onions alright. In a few months on ice, I had been transformed from a half-cooked peacenik into an Anti-Imperialist, Pro-NLF Third World White Nigger Warrior. I had gone to jail just a middle of the road anti-Capitalist and emerged a full-blown Marxist Maoist Leninist-Stalinist revolutionary.

I came out of prison in February 1965 as if on jet propulsion pills and threw myself back into the struggle with abandon. Although virulent paranoia was then poisoning Progressive Labor circles, I refused to let it dampen my enthusiasm for making the revolution.

The paranoia was not unwarranted. The New York cadre had played a minor role in the June '64 Harlem riots, having printed up and circulated tens of thousands of WANTED FOR MURDER—GILLIGAN THE COP! posters after a New York pig by that Hibernian moniker gunned down the usual black teenager. The late Bill Epton, PL's entire Harlem section, linked arms with the black liberation lawyer Conrad Lynn and marched down Seventh Avenue to the 135th Street precinct in defiance of the police-state crackdown, and both were charged with violating the state's quaint "criminal syndicalist" law.

Conspiracy was alleged. Comrades were rounded up in classic predawn raids and dragged before grand juries and when they refused to spill the beans, were locked down for months in the Tombs and the old

Women's House of Detention for criminal contempt. Now Hoover's bloodhounds were dogging our offices on both coasts and everyone's phone was bugged (did the fuzz actually listen to all our drivel?).

To top off PL's troubles, a rich junkie with three names, Philip Abbot Luce, had turned Judas for 40 bags of scag and spilled his guts to the *Saturday Evening Post* of all possible gazettes, about how the Rockefellers (Amy) were funding the Maoists. The allegations of class collaboration made us all uneasy.

As a consequence of Luce's betrayal, the PL national convention held in New York in the spring of '65, at which the Progressive Labor movement officially declared itself the vanguard party of the downtrodden masses, proscribed all drug use under penalty of shunning and expulsion, thereby ensuring that the new party would be hopelessly out of step with the revolution for the rest of the 1960s. So long as I militated in its ranks, I brazenly violated that decree and never abandoned my affection for the devil weed—I had been smoking *mota* since I was 14 and found a fat roach in my stepfather's long

suede coat, and no Marxist-Leninist-Maoist-Stalinists were going to purge my urge now.

Hot upon my release, two events galvanized my energies. In early February, LBJ began daily bombing of North Vietnam after a NLF attack at the U.S. compound at Pleiku. That night, we marched out of the Wobbly hall south of Market with our fists clenched high and snakedanced through the city up in North Beach where we blocked traffic on the tawdry Broadway strip for hours, thoroughly alienating Carol Doda, her silicon sisters, and the mafiosos who ran the topless clubs.

The next afternoon, at a federal building protest organized by our despised rivals, the W.E.B. Dubois Club (Nixon once confused this CP youth formation with the Boys Clubs of America), we raised a homemade National Liberation Front flag on the esplanade pole. Although the banner only flew for about 20 seconds before GSA guards ripped it to the ground (the *Peking Review* bragged that it flew for 20 minutes), the stunt embarrassed liberal Dems like Willie Brown and John Burton who the CP-USA had hoodwinked into addressing the rally.

The incipient conflict at the Federal Building was a seed of later splits in the anti-war movement between those who championed Third World revolution and those who only wanted to bring the boys back home.

"Ho-Ho, Ho Chi Minh!" I could hear Eddie Schnaubelt muttering down below.

Then on February 21st, the other shoe dropped and Malcolm was gunned down at the Audobon Ballroom in Harlem by assassins who together had 26 X's annexed to their names. In spite of my blue-eyed-devil status, I whipped out a bloodcurdling leaflet fingering Elijah Mohammed for the hit and calling for retaliation in kind, and spread it around the Fillmore ghetto, to the consternation of my PL comrades. The party line made the assassination sound like a petty feud between bourgeois nationalists.

Malcolm's murder accentuated the growing divide between Dr. King and those who called for armed self-defense in the spirit of Robert Williams. The Freedom Now Party and later the Panthers and the

Black Liberation Army were expressions of the groundswell for Black Power in the Bay Area. The days of going to jail to win jobs for black chambermaids and black bankers and black Cadillac salespersons were numbered.

The August '65 uprising in Watts was an initial lesson in urban guerrilla warfare and seemed to confirm that King's dream was at least deferred. By the summer of '66, it was San Francisco's turn to burn, baby, burn. The fuse ignited according to the usual scenario after killer cops blasted a black teenager out in Hunters Point. When the Third Street Safeway went up in flames, National Guard troops took the city and a curfew was declared.

The Guard was bivouacked at the great armory on 14th and Mission, a neighborhood we had been organizing block-by-block, and we mobilized hundreds of locals to surround the mammoth building in solidarity with our brothers and sisters out at Hunters Point.

"Comrades, we can stop them!" I yodeled recklessly over the bullhorn as the steel armory doors rolled up and hard-eyed troops charged us with long bayonets drawn, puncturing several young protesters. "We can stop them!" I was still yowling when a comrade mercifully removed the bullhorn from my lips. "You are going to get us all killed," he admonished.

"Power to the People!" blared Schnaubie under the ground. "Eat the Rich!"

"You North Americans are so lucky. You fight the most important battle in the belly of the beast," Che cheered us on when we arrived for work in the Mission. Our idea, which was hardly unique, was to bring the beast down by boring into its abdomen from the inside out, an ulcer on the rotten underbelly of Amerikkka. Radical community organizing was afoot all over the land by the mid-60s, in Harlem and New Haven, Newark, Philly, Cleveland, Chicago, and Oakland just across the bay. Our slice of that belly was a few blocks of the Inner Mission, a tri-toned, bilingual neighborhood butt up against a freeway with a rich working class tradition.

We didn't have to bring the war home to the Mission. The flag-draped coffins were already stacked up on the Valencia Street sidewalk across from the poverty office outside of the funeral homes where New College now sits. Some of the caskets carried this disclaimer: "We are sorry that the circumstances of the decedent's death precludes restoring the remains to a viewable state.'

While the NLF took down the soldier boys, we would bring the mayhem back home. We started out on Shotwell Street banging door to door, hunting for rats and roaches and complaints about abusive landlords. "Bingo! I got one!" Comrade Max B. gave a holler one twilit night in the spring of '65. The tenant was Luis Melendez, a Puerto Rican nationalist, and his household pests opened the door to a two-year rent strike in the 16-unit building that became the cornerstone of the Mission Tenants Union.

In its salad days, the MTU threw dead rats at the homes of slumlords, confronted sheriff's deputies when they came to evict our members and carried their furniture back inside when it was already in the street, distributed cockroaches at the Board of Health, and demanded Rent Control Now! Norma "the cockroach lady" as she was called in urban activist circles, was a talented welfare organizer. Pretty soon, we had organized the kids to demand a minipark from the city, and established a neighborhood police watch patrol. Mariachis and soul bands played at our fiestas, including the Malibus, a Mission High combo featuring two teen-age brothers named Santana.

Our PL comrades critiqued us without pity for putting Band-Aids on a doomed system and not winning souls to Marxism-Maoism-Leninism-Stalinism and the vanguard party of the masses. They had good reason. I confess that I hid my politics every bit as much as had Dorothy and George during the Red Scare days, fearing that the mention of communism would drive our tenants away. Once when the FBI came knocking on the door of our star tenant to inform her of our true colors, I heard Luisa Diaz, the doña of Shotwell Street, ask the brown shoes, "but how could they be communists? They're such nice people."

We never slept. The mimeograph machine at our 16th Street offices ran day and night, splattering every inch of our lives with its thick black ink. We handed out our inflammatory screeds at the gates of high schools and shipyards, got busted time and again for posting them on streetpoles with thick wheat glue, and were forever raising bail money to spring ourselves from the Hall of Injustice. We pasted up scare headlines each month in *Spark-Chispa,* our own *Iskra* and hawked it at hectic street meetings. We were committed to lighting a prairie fire on the concrete plain of the Mission.

By '66, our base was growing and the neighborhood could taste its own empowerment. The main competition was Johnson's War on Poverty—our strength was such that we were red-zoned on the poverty-office block maps and their street workers warned to stay off our turf.

Determined to expose the War on Poverty as a Capitalist sham, we carried the fight to the local structure and ran several neighborhood teenagers for the Mission Economic Opportunity Council ("Elect us and you won't get your purse snatched.") After the kids won slots on the board, the Very Reverend Jesse James, a government interloper, turned on the poverty-fund spigot and co-opted Dickie Lucero and Money Ruiz into starting the Mission Rebels, in its time the city's hardest-edged youth group.

I myself got elected to the Mission EOC board along with other tenants-union reps, which was a great mistake. We were soon enmeshed in pitched battles between dark-skinned pressure groups for great amounts of government blood money. Bilious disciples of Saul Alinsky, most promiscuously Mike Miller, red-baited us at every opportunity. Still, we forged the first Mission Coalition against big-money development—but our battle to keep Bay Area Rapid Transit (BART) from penetrating the neighborhood ran aground.

Despite 24-hour-a-day immersion in the urban jungle, we were never more than a flick of the dial away from the wider war. Televised images of flaming Buddhists and the nightly body counts, the ack-ack of the free-fire zones, and Charlie hurtling into the abyss from the Yanqui helicopters flooded into our lives. Day by day, the war devoured our souls.

We ventured across the bay to the first Vietnam Day teach-in in the fall of '65 and then advanced on the Oakland army base. Allen Ginsberg, among other literary lights, was at the head of the line of march. At the Oakland city limits, Sonny Barger and the Hells Angels tried to turn us back. Country Joe McDonald was up on the flatbed truck belting out, "its one, two, three, four what are we fighting for? And its five, six, seven, eight, open up the pearly gates! I don't give a damn! Next stop is Vietnam!"

"Right On! Off the Pig!". . . .

Mesmerized by my own reminiscences, I had failed to notice that Eddie Schnaubelt was bawling like a frustrated banshee besides me.

What's the problem, comrade, you'll wake up the dead . . .

"Fuck the dead! I'm dead so I can say that about them."

Have I said something that upset you?

"Everything you say upsets me. You kids think you invented the revolution, that you were the first to fight the cops in the street, the first to make love not war. It makes me gag to hear about it!"

We were also the first to rush home from the demonstrations to watch ourselves on TV. . . .

"See, that's just what I mean. Step back! I'm going to barf big."

Jeez Eddie, I'm sorry if I've neglected you. The revolution wasn't going to stop to run the credits. Who had time to remember what came before? Who did what first when? What did it matter anyway, brother?

"Who are you calling brother? I'm not your brother. I'm old enough to be your grandfather!"

Uhhh, yah, I can get with that. Where was I now?

"Summer of '66 I believe—if anyone is still keeping track."

Thanks. Sixty-six was like *On The Road* redux. We rocketed coast to coast to a secret cadre training school in the Vermont woods, spent an hallucinatory week on the Lower East Side, marched on Sacramento with the farmworkers until Cesar Chavez excommunicated the reds. We jumped out of a driveaway in Berkeley into a roomful of radical students who had just been subpoenad by HUAC for having donated their blood to the enemy Vietnamese. Jerry Rubin was there dressed up in a heavy serge George Washington wannabe suit in which he was determined to take the stand. It was August and he had ferocious prickly heat.

"No memoir of the '60s would be complete without such details."

I confess I was out of place in Berkeley. We went there to stop troop trains and dance at the Steppenwolf but my roots were more nitty gritty inner city. The Last Poets rapping and snapping up on the roof and the Impressions "kept on pushin." When Dylan copped out and said he didn't mean what he said, that a hard rain was *not* going to fall and the times they were *not* changing, I wasn't listening anymore.

"I am so sick of the '60s. Everyone wants a piece of the action. Everyone comes up here to blab me their '60s stories and sing me their '60s songs. It's like a fucking disease. Or a bunco racket. Boy, the '60s don't matter anymore to anyone except you."

The war criminals—McNamara, Maxwell Taylor, Dean Rusk, Westmoreland, LBJ , Old Scratch himself, came to the Nob Hill hotels to spread their lies and raise lucre for their filthy genocide and I learned how a billiard ball can bring down a police horse. I even got close enough to spit on one of the Bundys but I can't remember which one.

Amid the clouds of tear gas, the days in jail, the never-ending boogaloo, the wall-to-wall criticism and self criticism sessions, and sectarian fractures, milestones stumbled by in my life—my son Dante was born in October 1965 and by the middle of 1966, Norma and I were splitsville after she busted me *in flagrante* with a poverty-program coed. I took up a yearlong residence on Comrade Max's couch and by the Summer of '67 melded with Ellen at the height of a melee with the San Francisco pigs.

You never know what kind of mischief you might uncover banging door-to-door in the Mission District. Behind Bayview Federal Savings Towers on Capp Street, I encountered two Mexican families who had roaches, lots of roaches. So many *cucarachas* that when Jose opened the drawer to show me the landlady's business card, they scurried up his arm. The business card indicated the landlady was a prominent

San Francisco attorney, none other than Beverly Axlerod, perhaps the most radical of the Bay Area civil-rights lawyers, who was always on the Bandung to Mississippi Express with overnight stop-offs in Tierra Amarilla, New Mexico to defend Reyes Tijerina, a movement hero who had dared to reclaim the communal land of his people at gunpoint.

We marched into Beverly's office above Vince Hallinan's on Franklin Street, caught the great lady flatfooted on film, and branded her as A Rad Slumlord on the front page of *Spark-Chispa-Iskra.* Thoroughly chastened, Beverly found the Mexicans a new apartment, even doled out a thou to cover the moving expenses, and we fashioned an understanding. Later, she would drive me down to the Deull-Soledad prison complex in Tracy to meet her most illustrious client, one Eldridge Cleaver.

Booted out of SNCC by Stokely Carmichel's edict to go work in your own damn communities (I was Stokely's senior at Bronx Science), white skin privilege radicals were floundering by 1966 in the rising magma of black power. When Eldridge came out of jail that New Year's, Beverly had a bash up at her Carmel Street digs. *Soul On Ice* was hot off the press and Cleaver installed himself in an imposing Huey chair and obligated all the white people in the house to crawl around on their hands and knees.

One of my first contacts with the Black Panther Party For Self-Defense was through Dante's godmother, Murry Lee Burton, whose nephew Otis had stood on the steps of the state capitol in Sacramento with an unloaded shotgun in the fall of 1965, thoroughly terrorizing the Caucasian population of California. The year before PL had handed Huey Newton a wad of bills to fly to Cuba on our annual trip to that tropical revolution, but instead he took the money and scrammed—maybe some of it made it to the gun fund before it went up his nose.

There was always bad blood between the Panthers and PL. We called them "petty bourgeois nationalists," a terrible curse in the Progressive Labor lexicon, and they dissed us as "Stalinist honkies."

The name-calling festered outside the 1971 anti-racism and fascism conference at the Oakland Arena. When Angela Davis and BPP lawyer Charles Garry pushed the button, a flying squad of Panthers burst out of the arena and gangbanged a PL contingent on the shores of Lake Merrit. Bones were broken and I finally realized I was not on the right side anymore.

But back in '67, Huey had just gone to jail for offing an Oakland pig and Eldridge was on the cover of *Ramparts* magazine. I was still a party honcho around the Bay Area. By then, us Maoists figured our community credentials were legitimate enough to run a candidate for the San Francisco Board of Supervisors and that candidate was going to be me. It took months for the comrades to brainwash me into believing this was my calling. We didn't really want to win, they argued, this was an educational campaign. We would teach the masses the folly of participating in the electoral process. I suppose we were not very clear on the concept.

All that summer, I ha-rangued the electorate at fiery street meetings on streetcorners along the Mission. We pasted my face on every light pole in the neighborhood until I grew sick of seeing myself in public. The warehouse strike boosted my working-class credentials and tenants-union members buttonholed their neighbors for a vote. Our slogans were "Rent Control Now!" and "Out of Vietnam!" and to my great embarrassment, the campaign had scratch down below.

Then, one Saturday in August, we put a baby-carriage parade of irate Latina mothers around the Mission pig station to protest an egregious incident of police brutality in the 'hood. That night, at a black anti-draft union benefit off Dolores Street, the coppers came down on us like the Cossacks in our grandfathers' nightmares.

August '67 was the most incandescent point in urban insurrection thus far in the war for the inner cities. Newark and Detroit were burning to the ground, and the San Francisco police had just been loaded up with Mace to control unruly blacks and Reds. They put their shoulder to the door and broke it down and emptied their canisters on us. Ten were arrested on a total of 70 felonies and I was beaten into steak tartar—the damage to my left eye set the stage for glaucoma and I eventually lost all vision in it.

The Battle of Dolores Street made banner headlines—11 COPS HURT IN MISSION BRAWL the *Chronicle* croaked. Another candidate named Ross read all about it, discovered I had done time for refusing to kill or be killed by my Vietnamese brothers and sisters, and had me stripped from the ballot because I was a convicted felon.

Undaunted by such ruling-class flimflam, we made up little stickers

advertising my candidacy and asked our supporters to paste them into the write-in slots on those creaky old green voting machines the city used to feature. Election officials immediately declared this to be felony tampering and in November 1967, the *Chron* ran stories about John Ross followers being jailed for messing with the voting machinery. John Ross followers?

So that was how I soured on electoral politics.

"Dum de dum dum dum." Schnaubelt was humming Jack Webb's theme song. "I'm not going to say I told you so. . . ."

Although my eyesight is dimming, four photographs frame those times and will never fade from my vision. The images are familiar now, much-anthologized as evidence of this nation's moral blindness. Too many Americans glanced at them and just turned the page.

One is of a naked 11-year-old girl running in terror through a blasted rural landscape, smeared with jellied napalm, half her skin eaten away. "A continuous column of flaming gel can be projected with speed and accuracy to a small target 150 yards away," bragged Dow Chemical, a continuing criminal enterprise.

Another is of a 20-year-old suspected Viet Cong "terrorist" recoiling from a bullet fired point-blank into his temple by the chief of the South Vietnam police. A third depicts five grinning Green Berets kneeling in the highlands, the dried ears of their Vietcong kills spread on the ground before them.

The fourth photo, which ran often in *Spark-Chispa-Iskra,* shows tightly organized phalanxes of German citizens sieg heiling an enormous swastika. By 1968, the only ideological question to be asked was whether you spelled "America" with one k or three.

"Baloney! The real ideological question is when is this all going to end? I'm talking about the silliness of the '60s. You've given us thousands of words that add little to the torrent that has already been spewed about them, and there is no end in sight. No decade can possibly be this important. You're confusing your story with history. This is not going to have a happy ending."

Thank you for your critical input, Professor Schnaubelt. May I continue now?

1968, the Year of the Pig, really begins the previous autumn, on October 8th, 1967 to be exact, with the murder of Che Guevara by CIA proxies in the Bolivian outback. It is another photograph: Che propped up on a wooden slab, staring dead ahead at us, daring us to be like him. Twelve days later, on October 20th, the armies of the night laid siege to the Pentagon and shook LBJ right down to his shoes. It was as if Che's plasma was spreading everywhere, stiffening resistance, sewing spirit, and blossoming into one, two, three, many Vietnams. . . .

Events coincided and collided wildly. 1968 was born out of control, like crazed bumper cars at a global carnival of mayhem. In the first week of January, the U.S. government declared war on a whole generation by indicting the beloved Benjamin Spock, America's baby doctor, on charges of conspiracy to assist those he had whelped to avoid the draft.

In Vietnam, at the end of January, the NLF launched the startling Tet offensive, rising in 36 provincial cities, over-running the U.S. Embassy in Saigon, striking terror in the heart of the Pentagon, and putting the big lie to LBJ's rosy hype of an early victory.

1968 was an election year and by February, LBJ could see the handwriting in the driven snows of New Hampshire when a rookie, Clean Gene McCarthy, almost wrested the Democratic primary from an incumbent president.

Then on March 4th, even before breakfast, there was Lyndon Baines Johnson with his sad beagle-hound eyes on the tube drawling that he did not choose to run again. Ellen and I danced around our railroad flat down on Raush Street south of Market. All those furious years in the street, of tear gas and police batons, of wearing our shoes to a nub and our voices to a growl, of nonstop blood and ink, seemed finally to have made a dent.

But the euphoria only drove new atrocities into the shadows. Four days after Johnson pulled out of the election, Yanqui assassins led by Lieutenant Rusty Calley marched into My Lai, a village near Song

May in "VC-infested" Quang Nai province, "Pinkville" in "Indian Country" on their war maps, and murdered 128 women, children, and old men, spitting them on their bayonets, or mowing them down with round after round of blue machine-gun fire until the dead lay in piles of shattered cadavers—one GI reportedly forced a four-year-old girl to suck his cock while he pumped tracer bullets into the dying villagers. Then the Americanos pulled out their Zippos and erased My Lai from the earth. Calley and his commanding officer, Ernest Medina, were awarded Silver Medals for this heroic victory.

The madness did not stop at My Lai. Days later, on April 4th, Dr. King was executed outside a seedy motel in Memphis, Tennessee, an FBI-KKK plot to decapitate a civil-rights movement up in arms over the number of black deaths and rampant racism in 'Nam (the revolt of black prisoners at Long Binh was a fresh wound).

The mule-drawn hearse rolled slowly up the tree-lined avenue on the black and white screen to the dead boom of muffled drums. The national mourning had hardly begun when all hell blew loose and the warm, red glow of many ghettos burning in the night lit up the Amerikkkan skyline. Heavily armed troops, black battle slashes under their eyes, were called out to defend the Capitol of the United States from the vengeance of its people. I can't remember when this country has ever been so close to general insurrection.

"Pshaw! Who was going to overthrow the government? Black people on welfare? The Flower Children? A bunch of loony lumpens with Molotov cocktails? You need organization to make a revolution. You need the working class."

There were plenty of white workers ready to fight. . . .

"Pshaw again! How dare you call yourself a revolutionary! Why, you're nothing more than a fool poet who doesn't know how to end a story."

Well, Eddie, at least I'm a poet.

The timeclock punched into overdrive. At the end of April, Paris exploded. Auto workers and students threw up barricades in the streets for the first time since your mom was a kid, and came within a breath of toppling the De Gaulle government.

Everywhere that spring—in Prague and Tokyo and later in Mexico City, Che's blood kindled the flame of upheaval. Columbia University caught fire on the last day of April and hundreds of American universities would detonate like dominoes in its wake.

On May 9th, the Berrigan boys walked into the draft board in Catonsville Maryland, poured their blood on the floor, grabbed stacks of Selective Service files, and burned them to a crisp in the parking lot. They were not the only ones. By 1968, my own little act of refusing to fight in this atrocious war had been multiplied ten thousand times—1,500 men were now penned up in Amerikkkan prisons for refusing the draft, and 50,000 more had fled to Canada.

And just to twist the knot tighter, in June, Sirhan Sirhan took it upon himself to whack Bobby Kennedy at a Hollywood hotel on national television and threw the presidential election into total chaos. Events were moving too swiftly and I couldn't keep up. I began to do speed just to stay abreast. I didn't want to miss a minute of it. Sixty-eight was the closest I ever got to the revolution.

"It wasn't even close, bub," Schnaubelt hrrmphed. "It was mostly make-believe, a media hype. You guys smoked too much dope. It magnified your self-importance. The '60s were a happening, not a history. Capitalism survived, made a billion bucks on the war too, and now it's making another billion selling you back the memorabilia.

"And while we're talking numbers here, you need to know that your story now has 4,000 more words than my story and it's time to wrap it up."

I'm trying Ed, but the times just won't let me stop.

We didn't go to Chicago in August. Seven of us were on trial for the big brawl on Dolores Street the previous summer. It was a tense trial with a malevolent judge and the Battle of Chicago provided an appropriate backdrop.

One night after court, Ellen and I went to see *The Battle of Algiers* for the first time. Midway through the film, there is a freeze frame of a child licking an ice cream cone just before one of the women from the Casbah sets off a bomb in a European cafe. The moment sorely tests one's revolutionary commitment. I left the theater thinking these people are really serious. Maybe too serious.

PL excoriated the Yippies for showboating in Chicago—they definitely were not serious. I dissented. Abbie Hoffman was "antisolemne" just as they would write of the Zapatistas' Subcomandante Marcos 30 years later. His genius pranks—Pigasus the Porker who ran for president, the piss-in-the-polling-place concept, *Steal This Book*—stripped the system down to its BVDs and made you laugh out loud. So, it wasn't the revolution according to Marx, Mao, Lenin and Old Joe Stalin but the widescreen street theater did get the whole world watching.

Chicago split the left flank of the anti-war movement from the Mobes and the Moratoriums, which were still married to electoral politics. "Electoral politics are an inadequate response to the disaster that is America," my pal Frank Bardacke wrote in the *San Francisco Good Times* and in California, we lampooned the process by inventing the Peace & Freedom Party, qualifying it for the ballot, and then running Eldridge Cleaver, a soon-to-be fugitive from justice, self-proclaimed rapist, and well-known ne'er-do-well, for president. Only the Democrats and the Republicans outdid our sense of political satire by offering up the mummified Hubert Humphrey and spawning the mutant presidency of Richard Milhaus Nixon.

Although I shared its thirst for turning things upside-down, I was not a member of the Movement, upper case or lower. I may have been inside It and marched with It in the Mobilizations each spring and fall but I had already done my time. I was past 30 and not at all to be trusted. I didn't throw Frisbees or play hacky sak. We may have smoked dope together, a violation of the Marxist-Maoist-Leninist-Stalinist tabernacles, but I was always a Lenny Bruce–type outlaw furtively toking up in the alley and they were, uhh "altering their consciousnesses."

We did not agree on the music, either. I was still a bebopper to the bone. The suave flights of Bird and the bumptious runs of Monk still gladdened my heart. To my ear, the Dead and the Airplane and the million million-volt psychedelic bands that filled the Fillmore and the Family Dog night after night seemed to be acting out the hysteria of the moment and were often just plain musically inept.

Still I sneaked off to the Haight when I could ditch the revolutionary cadre and dropped Clear Light acid and sat with my old partner Tosh Angelos in the window of Bob Stubb's pioneer headshop and watched the whirled go by. I took my place at the Human Be-In with Allen G on harmonium and Jefferson Poland and the Sexual Freedom League fucking on the Golden Gate Park lawn.

"You know what this crap is? It's bourgeois garbage, Ross. That's what! Political pornography! I ought to kick you out of the book for this. You're just pandering to the nostalgia industry here. You, a hippie? You wouldn't know peace and love if it smacked you on the lips!"

O.K., O.K., I'm sorry. I don't know what came over me. It was like I had this cultural spasm. I'll get right back to war and revolution. Forgive me.

The war did not bend. The more we marched the worse it got. We tried to shut down the cities—No Business As Usual! But business went on as usual—the B-52s swooped in from the Philippines and carpet-bombed the villages and the cropdusters spread the Agent Orange cancers and millions—3,000,000 Vietnamese and 57,000 poor fool GIs were dead and dying. As usual in America's wars, the body count ran 20–1 in the Yanquis' favor.

On Mobe days, you'd get to the top of the big hill by the University of San Francisco and look back at the masses marching behind and in front of you—100,000 strong perhaps—and the terrible truth would dawn that not even this enormous swath of humanity could stop the madness. A half million marched on Washington in October '69 and maybe a million at May Day '71 and Nixon and Kissinger never flinched.

The numbers grew but the Movement was poisoned by paranoia and self-righteousness and the war just did not bend. There is no one way to stop it, Dianne di Prima warned as the Movement fragmented into many brittle shards.

The San Francisco State strike surged in the autumn of 1968 over open enrollment issues and lasted through the next spring. The cry of "On Strike! Shut It Down!" ricocheted throughout what Herb Caen used to call Baghdad by the Bay, and Mayor Joe Alioto mobilized his Brown Shirts. The battles on the S.F. State quad between the Swat Squad and the militants of the Third World Liberation Front were mythic, with S.I. Hayakawa, the semanticist-Führer, growling injunctions over the souped-up public address system from his leather-lined administration-building office. A lot of skulls got cracked at State and inevitably, the bombings began.

Ellen cut her radical teeth on the barricades at San Francisco State, facing off the pigs all day and organizing the next acts of resistance at night. Meanwhile, I had been shunted off to the industrial proletariat, sort of—a drug and sundries warehouse in Brisbane where my revolutionary strategies were pretty much focused on infiltrating the company softball team. I was shooting a lot of speed to make the job more interesting.

Much of my workday was spent trying to convince my fellow workers of the wrongness of the war. Fat John Gambini would listen to me tolerantly as we walked the aisles together, picking orders for Value Giant stores. He had a son who was a fighter pilot in 'Nam and he was proud of it but nonetheless he took my literature home with him. This went on for many months—uplifting the proletariat is slow and steady work. Then one day, Fat John brought me some literature himself. Oh boy, I trumpeted, I had finally engaged him. What he had brought me was a clipping about a company that was building split-level golf driving ranges in Japan. He was thinking about investing in it. Fat John had just wanted to share that with me.

In June 1969, Ellen stormed off to the Students for a Democratic Society showdown convention at the Chicago Coliseum, a wrestling arena. PL had swarmed all over SDS, sucking up whole chapters to forge our celebrated "worker-student alliances"—I forget which Leninist text this strategy was drawn from. Pitted against Progressive Labor was RYM, the Revolutionary Youth Movement with whom we bickered over who was most Maoist. The debate seemed to revolve around who could chant "Ho, Ho, Ho Chi Minh" louder and longer

(PL, which was already calling Uncle Ho a bourgeois nationalist, was at a distinct disadvantage).

One faction waiting in the wings kept insisting that you didn't need a weatherman to know which way the wind was blowing.

Ellen called each night to report on the ideological ebb and flow. The Panther (now congressman) Bobby Rush had reiterated Stokely's proclamation on the Woman Question: The only question about a woman's position in the Movement is whether it's prone or supine. I snickered reflexively and Ellen hung up on me.

So the convention worked its way to a split and what would become the Weather Underground by the end of the year walked out, and the rest is his and her story.

And not long after that, I read that Jack Kerouac had dropped dead in Florida, an aging drunk who spent his days cursing the demonstrators on the TV. It made me shudder. Something had died and it was not just Jack. . . .

"So that was the '60s for you son? Are you done?"

Well, not quite. The '60s, you see, really bled into the '70s. These timelines are never precise.

"Well, I'm not hanging around for any more of it."

Any more of what, Eddie?

"Of your interminably stupid life, that's what. You know what I think? I think you're using my life to tell your life story. This was your plan from the moment you proposed this collaboration and I don't want to be a part of it anymore."

That's bogus, man. I'm just trying to put stuff in context. To show how the U.S. Left is a seamless skein, a revolutionary continuum passed down from one generation to the next, our heritage.

"Bullshit! You've taken over this book and I quit. I'm going back to sleep. I don't know why I ever woke up in the first place . . ."

Life of Ross (without Schnaubelt)

Although in hindsight, I should have heeded E. B. Schnaubelt's threat to withdraw, I could not. My brain was on automatic pilot, garbage-picking through the rubbish fields of the '60s, and when at last I was done, I paid the price of dear departed Comrade Eddie's silence.

May 1st, 1969. Ten thousand protesters are gathered at the San Francisco Federal Building from where I had been sent to prison only five years earlier. It feels like a whole generation has passed before my eyes since that day.

Most of those gathered on the esplanade are black teenagers wearing black berets and black-leather Huey Newton jackets, a fashion statement. They are playing hooky from school—as I have noted, International Workers' Day is not a legal U.S. holiday. Huey has been in jail for nearly three years now and demands for his freedom have been voiced in every corner of the globe but fall forever on the deaf ears of his jailers.

What is unique about this rally is that the kids, instead of pumping their fists into the heavens when they shout "Free Huey!" and "Power to the People!," are each holding high a little red copy of Mao's little red book. By 1969, Mao Zedong was in the public domain.

Then word spreads through the crowd that a cop is down, out in the Mission on Alvarado Street, after a gun battle with young Latinos, and we split. When we get back to the *barrio,* the dragnet is out, the pigs are busting down doors and rousting *vatos* on the street. Helicopters black out the sky. A few days later, *Los Siete de La Raza* are run to ground in Santa Cruz but eventually they beat the rap and are enshrined in Betita Martinez's *500 Years of Chicano History.*

All over Amerikkka, brown people—the Brown Berets, Corky Gonzalez's Aztlan Nation, the Chicano Moratorium, the Young Lords on the sidewalks of New York, the FALN, Puerto Rican freedom fighters with real live bombs, were punching in for the revolution.

Later that spring, across the bay in Berkeley, white folks come to bat. Telegraph Avenue street people invade a university parking lot and turn it into a garden of Eden. When UC sends in its campus marines, students (and plenty of non-students) join the fray. "If they want a bloodbath, let's give them one," Ronald Reagan snickers. "We have a guerrilla war on our campuses and the solution to guerrilla war is to hunt and kill your enemy," the governor told a Sacramento press conference.

The National Guard is called out and martial law proclaimed. Light tanks roll up Telegraph and one demonstrator, James Rector, is killed. Helicopters spray C-2 gas on the populace and drench the city in an evil miasma.

Bad mojo was in the air over Amerikkka all that summer. As if it was a Haymarket rerun, Bobby Seale sat in a stifling Chicago courtroom, chained and gagged for the whole world to see. The rulers of Amerikkka just didn't care anymore about how bad it looked to the rest of the world. They want a bloodbath, we'll give them a bloodbath. . . .

COINTELPRO was working overtime to drive a stake through the Panther hierarchy, and the murderous feud between the Huey and Eldridge factions would soon bear its bitter, bloody fruit. By August, the Weathers were rampaging crazily up and down the beaches of Detroit, desperately trying to incite a youth rebellion—they were often thrashed for their efforts.

The Weathermen and ladies staged their Days of Rage in November in a frigid Chicago dripping with police, the ultimate in street-fighting chic. Then, on December 4th, Chicago pigs murdered Panther leaders Mark Clark and Fred Hampton, a last, last straw. At their council in Flint later in the month, Weather leaders declared war on the U.S. government and evaporated into the Amerikkkan underground. They had already blown up the Haymarket cop at least once. Now the password was "Bombs Away!"

No potluck or house party seemed complete that fall without spirited discussion about who and where we should bomb—although most of us did not have the foggiest notion of how to do the job. The Statue of Liberty was a favorite target, the Golden Gate Bridge, the General Motors boardroom, the White House (the Weather Underground dubbed it "the big top"), there was no World Trade Center yet. Someone did take out the Golden Gate Park police station and someone else walked into the Ingleside station and blew away a captain. I have it on good authority that the Black Liberation Army fired a homemade missile at the Mission pig house—and missed. Every bomb, every bullet, every riot and inner city insurrection brought the war home—but did not stop it. I don't think we wanted to stop it anymore.

Having the right analysis no longer counted for shit. I was 32 and I had never thrown a bomb.

On the night of March 6th, 1970, one of several young people who were assembling a large explosive device in the basement of a Greenwich Village townhouse owned by Kathy Wilkerson's father (she had been at Swathmore with Ellen) flubbed it badly and the whole world came tumbling down—three were killed and the explosion was so stupendous that no trace of Terry Robbins' DNA was ever located. One of those who fled 153 West 11th Street that night was Kathy Boudin, for whom as an adolescent on Fire Island, I used to baby-sit—our mothers had been lifelong friends and her father Leonard was Paul Robeson's lawyer.

The townhouse tragedy did not slow the bombers down.

Not a week later, on March 13th, mystery bombers blew up three corporate headquarters in midtown Manhattan. Maybe it was the remnants of the Up Against the Wall Motherfuckers, maybe the FALN, or maybe it was a tight little foco out of Portland, Maine that this time signed off as "Force-9"—the group would continue to bomb enemy targets into the early 1980s.

On March 30th, an inflamed student mob in Isla Vista California made front pages across the nation when it burned a Bank of America branch to the ground. Between the winter of '69 and the autumn of 1970, 40,000 bombings and attempted bombings were recorded by the U.S. Alcohol, Tobacco, and Firearms Bureau. Draft boards and Selective Service offices were regularly set ablaze. ROTC buildings at the University of Washington, the University of Oregon, and the University of California were torched by traveling firebugs that spring.

I watched much of the armed rebellion that gripped the U.S. in the first months of 1970 from a sickbed. The speed had finally caught up with me—it had gotten so bad that I was shooting up at demonstrations through the seat of my pants. I didn't mainline but mostly muscled off the methamphetimine instead and the rush drip dripped into my brain and kept it running at breakneck speed for hours. But sometimes I missed and the abscesses began to pulse deep under the skin, and festered for days. I was often unable to get out of bed and go to work.

The Kissinger–Nixon invasion of Cambodia at the end of April, 1970 was answered by a thunderous tidal wave of resistance in every nook and cranny of the nation. The firebombs brought out the National Guard and then there were four dead in Ohio and two more in Jackson, Mississippi. A witness to the carnage at Kent State had gotten to a phone booth and called KSAN in San Francisco, the hippest radio voice in the west, and hundreds of us rushed into the Board of Supervisors' chambers, demanding city condemnation of the massacre.

When I got home that night, Ellen was packing to go to the hospital—my youngest, Carla Carolina, was born the next night before my very eyes. Will miracles never cease?

This is the part of the story it wounds me to repeat. By September, Ellen had had it with my increasingly self-destructive lifestyle and kicked me out. I hit the streets the same night Janis Joplin was found dead with a spike in her arm in an L.A. motel. Sometimes it helps to connect up your personal tragedy with those of the rich and famous.

For months, I went homeless, couch-surfing on the sofas and davenports of comrades inside and out of the party. I spent my unemployment checks on drugs and did not eat. I had a writing doctor in a Sutter Street medical skyscraper who scribbled me script for Disoxyn, Codeine, and Nembutal, 60 each, every three weeks, 20 bucks cash and no questions asked. Pay at the desk. His waiting room was always packed to the rafters.

You took the Disoxyn home and put it under water until it turned piss yellow and shot it up. The jolt gave you a new life every time but the lifetimes kept getting shorter and shorter. By now I weighed about 130 pounds and wore two jackets and an overcoat when I visited Dr. Feelgood so he wouldn't notice how fabulously emaciated his miracle treatment had made me.

Somewhere in the middle of this black and endless night, I made contact with my ex-wife Norma and the kids, and they encouraged me to come east and clean up. I set off on a Greyhound ride to hell and emerged on the Lower East Side in February of '71. I signed into Phoenix House for a stretch and played the Game. It took a few months but I came out the other side feeling like a human being again and rode back to the West Coast speed-free.

Of course I didn't get out of the bus station without copping a bag of crank. I got a room way up at the top of Bernal Hill and spent my days prowling the Tenderloin hotels for the next fix. My man Little Bit and his partner, Nurse Lucy (she could raise a vein on the dead and always had a string of junkies lined up in the hall waiting for her steady hand) had me over to dinner often—although the table never featured much food.

In my murky, fearful mindset, politics became a distant death march. I heard the bomb go off Super Bowl Sunday in a U.S. Congress closet. I heard the manchild, Jonathan Jackson, walk into the Marin County Courthouse with a shotgun down his pants leg to rescue big brother George. I even got myself half together to cover the trial of Ruchel Magee, the only survivor of that suicidal adventure, and helped build his defense committee with Sandy Close. And I was listening in September '71 when George Jackson was murdered in the San Quentin Adjustment Center and six guards got their throats slit as payback. I was not unaware of the criminal atrocities committed by the New York state pigs at Attica penitentiary that summer. But I was not there.

Revolution had become a refrain in a Gil Scott Heron rap to me. Now I fancied myself a poet, albeit a revolutionary poet— after all, you couldn't have a revolution without poetry, no? I began to hang out at San Francisco readings where berserkers like H. David Moe and Cloudhouse Kush would rave and misbehave.

Drugs, poetry, and the fucking war roared through my veins. When Nixon mined Haiphong Harbor in the Spring of '72, the San Francisco poets went on the warpath. We rampaged out of Union

photo © Richard Gibson

Square, Roberto Vargas, who later fought with the Sandinistas on the southern front, on one wing, the Chicano bard Alejandro Murguia on the other. The city was remodeling downtown and there were bricks galore stacked up on the sidewalk. I picked one up and hurled it at Doubleday's—I'm a writer after all—and the brick just bounced off. At the corner of Geary and Market, some fat fuck yelled "God Bless America" and I scalped him. I wore the toupee on my belt all that day.

After dark, we called a poetry reading on the Kearny Street steps—Andre Codrescu was part of the crew. When the pigs showed up, we told them to just be cool and listen. They stood there dumbfounded for a few minutes. "This doesn't sound like poetry to me," I heard one oinker grunt and they closed in for the bust.

Yah, yah, I will try and make a long story short. I know my personal tragicomedy has you on the nod. I moved in with a jazz singer who liked to tweak—she could really riff on "Red Top." She kicked me out when a coke deal went sour and it looked like I was going to have to pay for it with my nose, took me back, kicked me out again. It wasn't a very stable relationship.

I spent the summer of '72 up in North Beach at the mercy of many dangerous drugs. One sun-flecked morning, I bumped into Q. R. Hand, my childhood sidekick, now a richly voiced jazz poet, and we declaimed at the Coffee Gallery on Grant, Minnie's Can-do up in the Fillmore, and the Ribeltad Vorden off Precita Park where I ran the readings. We'd sit in the Saloon or Vesuvio's from 6 AM on, sucking down bloody marys and Meyers 150s and sooner or later Bob Kaufman, America's Rimbaud, would come along to bum a smoke. I was a Beat poet all over again. It was like second childhood.

After Labor Day, I had a dumb urge to go back to work and bam! whaddya know, but I bust my leg under a pallet of Kitty Litter at the White Front store on 16th and Bryant. I got myself an attorney and thought, hey, at last I've struck it rich—but White Front filed for bankruptcy and I never saw so much as a thin dime.

I smoked and snorted and shot up my disability check and guzzled gallons of Boone's Farm apple wine to wash my sins away. Jazz lady had moved to Eureka and took me back yet again, the fool. I arrived on the Big Dog and J. J. Cale was purring "Magnolia, you sweet thing" in the beer bar next door to the depot. It was raining, a cold, dismal, big-drop North Coast Christmas rain.

Just out there across the Pacific, more bombs than ever in the history of the world, were crashing down from God's black heaven upon the people of Vietnam but I could hardly hear them fall.

So that's my story, friend. That is more or less how I got here to this ocean and these forests and this graveyard and how come I'm sitting by your side tonight.

Silence. Utter silence. I noticed that it had gotten quite dark. I couldn't even find my hands in front of my face let alone the dregs of the Joe Crow. When had this happened? How long had I been blabbing?

I said that's how I got here, Eddie. You wanted to know how it came out, didn't you?

Nothing.

I did it for the book, Eddie.

Eddie, I'm finished. It's your turn now . . .

Not a peep.

Eddie, you old fucker—speak to me!

By now I was beating on the cold ground and making a racket to wake up the yes, the dead.

The lights flicked on in "Glenn Saunders" All-Amerikkkan ranch house on the other side of the fence. I guess the big snoop must have come home.

It was all my doing. I had failed to take Schnaubelt's threat seriously. Now he had gone back to sleep or wherever it was he came from in the first place. He had withdrawn to the underground and our stories were left undone. Would we ever speak again?

Book Three

The Death of Dogma

The Cemetery

This is how you get there. First you must go to Chicago, a large industrial city on the shores of Lake Michigan more or less in the middle of the United States of North America. Then ask the nearest Chicagoan for directions to the Blue Line on the Metro rail system. If you jump on a Blue Line car headed towards O'Hare airport, you're going in the wrong direction. Walk across the platform and change to a train heading south under the Loop. Eventually, you will emerge on the Elevated. Stations with names like Pulaskie and Cicero, Al Caponc's old stop, will rumble by. Stay on until the end of the line at Forest Grovc just outside the Windy City's limits. If you've made arrangements, maybe Mark Rogovin, the son of the fine working-class photographer Milt "I focused on the poor—the rich had their own photographers" Rogovin will show up to take you on a guided tour. If not, walk the three blocks and plunge into Waldhcim (now Forest Home) Cemetery at your own speed. The admission is free.

Once inside the gilded gates, you will observe the large shiny tombs of the Rom community on your right. Likenesses of the defunct gypsies borrowed from old photographs have been rubbed into the Art Deco marble headstones. Poliaco Christo (1923–1980), "the man who saw it all and lived it all" and his Babe (1927–2000) who "did it her way" are tenants here. Drop by Roy (1921–1981) and Rosie (1930–1995) Bumbalo's and give my regards to poor Dianne Metlaw (no dates), who is in imminent danger of being dispossessed—a small orange sticker affixed to her dark marble marker advises that it "is scheduled to be removed for non-payment."

Mark says he finds jugs of wine and half-eaten birthday cakes out here—gypsies, like Mexicans, must leave whatever they bring with them to offer to the dead. Scavengers tempt potent curses.

Forest Home, like many North American cemeteries, is set atop an Indian burial ground. The bones of the Potawatani, of whom there are no more, enrich the flat suburban landscape. The cemetery is bisected by 12 lanes of the Eisenhower Freeway (thousands of peacefully resting citizens were moved for its construction) from which the whoosh of traffic reverberates day and night, undermining the stillness of the sanctuary. On the other hand, the Des Plaines River purls softly through the graveyard bottoms. Mark sees red fox here, white-tailed deer. Hawks and jumbo jets circle in the industrial heavens.

Down beyond the river, the Showpeople of America Inc. long ago bought their own section. Hundreds of victims of an Indiana circus-train wreck are interred there in tombs sculpted to look like elephants and ostriches. It is an egalitarian assembly, Mark reports, roustabouts and ringmasters are laid out side-by-side and the bearded lady lies down with the dog-faced boy.

Waldheim is home to various secret societies. The Oddfellows and the Druids (The Cambrian Benevolent Society) inhabit meditative alcoves demarcated by esoteric spires, the dead sewn in mystical circles, rubbing toes under the loam. African-American citizens and Jewish cigarmakers enjoy their own separate ghettoes here. A smattering of the semifamous are installed on the premises—Billy Sunday, an old-time ballplayer turned evangelical preacher, and Ernest Hemingway's parents—are three. But most pilgrims have come to Waldheim to worship at the Monument.

The Monument to the Haymarket Martyrs is a striking 15-foot marble altar featuring a majestic bronze woman in long, sweeping skirts that are eternally frozen in agitated motion. She is poised protectively over a beaten striker whose arm dangles lifelessly down to the monument's alabaster base. Her other hand is raised defiantly to fend off the unseen oppressor—one pictures a giant Officer Birmingham of Haymarket police statue infamy, about to swat her down.

The tableaux is deliberately reminiscent of the French Revolution as if to illustrate a verse from "*Les Marseillaise*" which the Martyrs sang in their cells on the eve of their hanging. The altar is inscribed with the last words of August Spies: "The day will come when our silence will be more powerful than the voices you throttle today," the very words I heard intoned on the 100th anniversary of International Labor Day in Santiago, Chile, amid the tear gas and fearsome water cannons of Pinochet's police.

The Monument was erected in 1893, six years after the hanging, by the Pioneer Aid & Support Society, which provided for the welfare and sustenance of the Haymarket widows and orphans, and was sculpted and cast by one Albert Weiner, of whom history seems to have little to report. It is a mindboggling turn of events that those whom the government once so cruelly martyred, now belong to the government—the Haymarket Altar was declared a national historical monument in 1997, and is now tended to by the U.S. National Park Service. Or so attests a nearby informational plaque that has been hand-decorated with the anarchist "A" circle and the words "We Will Win!" scrawled in blue marker.

The remains of the Martyrs lie under the altar—Spies, Parsons, Engels, Fischer, and the pieces of Lingg. Schwab, Fielden, and Neebe were added later. You will recall that the city of Chicago would not allow the Martyrs to be buried within the city limits for fear they would sew bombs in the earth, which is why Waldheim was selected as their final resting place.

The Haymarket Martyrs are hardly alone in the solitude of death. All around them sleep dozens of other martyrs of the U.S. Left, 69 of them according to a guide that Mark and Joe Powers once published, "The Day Will Come . . ." By my count, 27 of these moldering militants were charter members of the Communist Party USA and 27 others espoused anarchist causes. No Trotskyists are planted here. The 15 remaining stiffs were either freelance activists with no ideological preferences, or their political attachments were unclear. Mark claims that the tie between the anarchists and the Communists was scheduled to be broken on 9/11/01 with the reburial of perennial CPUSA presidential candidate Gus Hall but his executors took one look at the morning news and postponed interment until further notice.

Amongst this fieldful of left-wing luminaries, you cannot miss fellow worker Emma Goldman (1860–1940.) Her slab, as elaborate as the gypsy sarcophagi, is engraved with a strong portrait in stone by the eminent sculptor Jo Davidson, and the daring epitaph taken from her own words: "Liberty will not descend to a people—a people must rise up to liberty."

Although Emma dominates her row, the row itself is dominated by the Communists. By an odd fling of the dice, her closest neighbors to the right are black CP mavens Pettis Perry (1877–1967) and William Patterson (1890–1980.) Henry Winston (1911–1986) reposes next to Patterson but Claude Lightfoot (1920–1992), another black CP leader, lies several aisles removed. Also encamped in Emma's row are Elizabeth Gurley Flynn, "the Rebel Girl" (1890–1964) and Eugene Dennis (1904–1964), both of them jailed Smith Avenue defendants. William Z. Foster (1881–1964), the Stalinist commissar of the CP-USA, whose personal saga spans the convoluted history of that party, stands stoically four markers to the left.

Across the aisle clustered around the Monument, the anarchists abound. Among them is Irving Abrams (1894–1960) who inherited the Pioneer Aid & Support Society, and was its last surviving member. Irving is sort of the landlord of this section of Waldheim. Also over there, hiding shyly under a mulberry bush is Voltairine de Clyves (1866–1912), a legendary anarchist heroine. Dr. Ben Reitman (1890–1964), the King of the Hobos, and Harry Kelly (1891–1953), both of them Emma's part-time lovers, are right next door to Voltairine.

Out in the fields beyond, the ashes of Big Bill Hayward (1869–1928) blow in the breeze, as do the residues of Joe Hill (1884–1915) of which we shall soon hear more. So does the DNA of

Nina Van Zandt (died 1936) who married August Spies in prison and went mad when he was hung. So do the specks of Slim Brundage, once the bartender at the Dill Pickle Club (1908–1990) where a lot of these phantoms bent elbows. And likewise, Eddie Balchowsky (1916–1989), a one-armed barrelhouse piano player who lost his wing in the Spanish Civil War—Jack Micheline, my first role model as a poet, used to wax rhapsodic about Eddie's adventurous life. Balchowsky is out there somewhere across the access road around the chapel although the guidebook informs that the exact location of his bones "is unknown."

Most of the residents are former inmates of state and federal penal institutions, persecuted and incarcerated and sometimes executed for the political dogmas to which they were attached—if you laid the convicted end to end, these illustrious dead would probably have served a full century in the slammer. By my count, there are five women named Esther buried here, and nine African-Americans. The youngest resident is a 20-year-old Chicago youth organizer, Morton S. Shafner, who died of a heart attack while protesting the Vietnam War, and the oldest would appear to be an ancient, moss-covered stone laconically inscribed HEPP.

At the foot of the Haymarket Altar there is a small, loaf-size marker, gray granulated stone that has defused with age into a sort of granite pillow. Save for one freshly placed red rose, the marker is all business. "Lucy Parsons (1859–1942)" it announces. In the smoggy autumn industrial noon, I went down on my hands and knees and bent to kiss the stone and it was cold as death under my tongue.

"Oooo—do that again, big boy! That's just the way I love to be woken up—with a big wet smooch! Say, what's your game anyway? Are you some kind of kinky necrophiliac? Or just an unknown admirer?"

Jeez Mrs. Parsons, I didn't think that you were paying much attention, I apologized lamely, I meant no disrespect ma'am. It was more like a poetic gesture. You see, I'm a writer and a poet and a great fan of yours. . . .

"You talk like a poet, sonny boy. What is it you want with my old bones?"

Umm, its a long, strange story really. You see, I write books and I'm writing this book with an old comrade name of Eddie Schnaubelt—he says he knew you in the old days. We were about halfway through the book when Eddie just clammed up on me. I can't get him to speak up anymore so I came out here thinking that perhaps you might have some ideas about how to get his attention. He really liked you a lot.

"Now let me see—this is Rudolph or Eddie you're talking about? Which one threw the bomb at the Haymarket?"

Eddie always says it wasn't Rudolph. . . .

"Sure, Eddie Schnaubelt, the tall one with the ginger beard? Or was that Rudolph?"

He doesn't wear much of a beard anymore, ma'am but I believe he still has a jawbone.

"Lordy, I liked that big galoot. We went to St. Looie once on a train."

He's told me about it. It was a sad story.

"I haven't seen that guy in a coon's age. Is he still married?"

Mostly he's dead. He's been dead for 90 years now nearly. He was Murdered by Capitalism back in 1913.

"I lived a lot longer than that but Capitalism murdered me just the same. Capitalism murdered just about everyone in this damn cemetery, even the bearded lady and the dog-faced boy. That's the long and the short of it."

Testimony of Mrs. Lucy Parsons

"First thing I remember when I was dropped was the whip and the chain. It's the last thing I remember too.

"I came out of the womb and there they were waiting for me. They were my mother and my father. The slaveowner snatched me from my real kin the day I was born, which was in the year of 1853 not '59 like Irving has put up there on my stone. The whip and the chain—they were mama and papa to me. But they couldn't break down my spirit. They only built it up.

"Now the funny thing about being born a slave if there was anything funny to it at all was that I was not an Afro-American, a black person or a Negro or any other kind of nigger. Yes, it's true that when I had skin, it was black skin—but I don't know how it got there. The family name they gave me was Gonzalez and I was supposed to be an Indian of some kind. I have nothing against black people—I was called black all my life, Lord knows—but I'm just not black. I can't explain it any more clearly than that.

"I was 11 when Abraham Lincoln gave us our freedom and I came out of one slavery and into another. Mr. Oliver Gathings, a colored gentleman, took me to his home in Waco, Texas and put me in his chicken coop. He chained me up and whipped me raw and used me for his sexual necessities. Captain Albert Parsons, a Confederate soldier, heard about it and set me free and after that, I belonged to him.

"Mr. Parsons was a good man and I dearly loved and served him but in his way he wanted to enslave me too. Mr. Parsons had come to see the error of his ways in fighting on the side of the slavers and now he wanted to help the Negro people. His intentions were honorable. He was then publishing a newspaper for freed men and women and I showed him that I could read and write so he asked me if I wouldn't help him with it, and I was only too happy to oblige. We fell in love and got married in a secret ceremony but it wasn't safe. The Ku Klux Klan was raping and lynching there in Waco—they raped 20 black women right on Main Street in broad daylight one fine day. Being white and black—although I wasn't really—we were violating the miscegenation laws and the Klan burned us out. So now we followed our freedom star up to Chicago.

"When we got to that city, I had a dream which was not really a dream at all but what I really saw. 'And I did see men wander/up and down this cheerless earth/aimless, homeless, without hope. . . .' How does that sound to you, poet? That was the first lines I wrote when I came up to Chicago.

"Chicago was not freedom—at least not the way I imagined freedom to be. The people looked at me like I was a nigger and Mr. Parsons had to come to my defense often to explain that I was not a member of that race. Besides, Chicago was just another kind of slavery, an industrial slavery. The workers were chained to their machines just like slaves and the overseer still cracked the whip, which was called their wages. Mr. Parsons and myself embarked upon a great crusade to free the wage slaves. We embraced Johan Most's 'propaganda of the deed' and decided to take direct action. We were abolitionists every bit as much as Sojourner Truth and John Brown but what we wanted to abolish was the Capitalist system itself.

"I organized tramps and sewing women and Mr. Parsons machinists and printers and other manufacturing workers. We both caught the eight-hour bug and well, you know very well what happened after that. The Capitalists hanged my husband and his comrades until they were dead.

"I'm not going to talk about it anymore. I swore off. I talked all about how they hung my husband for many years, half my long life. I talked from lecterns and soapboxes, from meeting wagons and streetcorners and the Turner Halls, I spoke from church pulpits and down on skid row. I talked from dawn to dusk, told it every night, night after night, year after year, Haymarket was my religion. I was chained to it just like I was a slave.

"Our enemies were the Capitalist bosses but between them and us there stood the police. It was Captain Schact and that crook Schleuter and Black Jack Bonfield who took it upon themselves to frame our husbands. They did it to earn the praises of their masters whose shoes they lapped clean. And it was the police that blew up poor Louis Lingg. It was the police who gunned down the strikers at McCormick's. It was the police who stripped me naked with my children in a cold jail cell at the very hour that the State murdered my husband. I do not know if it was Rudolph or Edward who threw the bomb at the Haymarket but as long as police officers were killed and maimed, I cannot condemn this brave act of class retaliation.

"I had two children with Mr. Parsons and both of them did not work out. The Capitalist system took my Lula Eda from me when she was not yet nine years old. She never had a chance in this horrid world. Right at the start, they put that she was a 'nigger' on her birth certificate—that's just how they wrote it—and they wouldn't listen to me when I demanded a retraction.

"My other child, my eldest, Albert Jr., I don't know what got into him. He just went bad on me and I had to put him away.

"People told a lot of stories behind my back that weren't true. They said I was a pitiful figure in my long skirts and old-fashioned hats, that I lived in the past and was obsessed by my husband's fate. A crazy old black woman, they said—'But I'm not black!' I told them to their face.

"Emma Goldman spread those lies about me and Martin Lacher. He was a cute guy but he wanted to make me into a slave too. And besides, he had a wife who lived just two blocks away. When I told him to get out, he accused me of selling my affections to someone better-equipped to provide for my upkeep and took an ax to my furniture. Sure I hauled him into court just out of spite but I didn't find any justice there.

"I was only 34 when Mr. Parsons was hanged and still had a long life in me. I published many newspaper articles on anarchism and traveled around the country giving lectures against the Capitalist system. It was kind of like being on the stage. We were professional entertainers and we packed our pamphlets around to sell at the engagements. I even sailed over to England and had tea and crumpets with a real-life duchess out there.

"I often crossed paths with that whore Emma Goldman on the lecture circuit. She was not a member of the working class. She sold her book for $7.50, a price no working man could ever hope to accumulate. She wrote her books and articles for bourgeois libertines.

"Emma Goldman was a loose woman with loose lips and loose morals. She was a gossip and a snitch. She wrote obscenities that should never have been published in any respectable anarchist magazine. I wasn't above taking lovers in my lengthy lifespan but Emma Goldman took them all at once. You know, I tried to protect my boy from her variationist smut but he found it in my dresser drawer and he pleasured himself with it. And it drove him mad. Free Love is against the family.

"Haymarket was not the end of my life. I stood with Debs in '92 during the Pullman strike when President Grover Cleveland sent in Indian killers from the Dakotas to break the railroad brotherhoods. I had many high-class acquaintances, like Miss Jane Adams who was jailed with me once. I must have been taken to jail for my free speech more than a hundred times. I joined the Anti-Imperialist League and spoke out against McKinley's war in the Philippines and all the babies burning there. I lost my own son, my first born, to that war.

"After Emma put that poor Czolgocz boy up to assassinating McKinley, I publicly renounced Johan Most's 'Propaganda of the Deed.' To my mind, it only brought greater repression down upon radical labor and the anarchists.

"I was the second woman behind Mother Mary Jones to sign up in the IWW—Big Bill put that red card in my hand himself. I raised money to buy guns for Pancho Villa and I was a suffragette although getting the vote didn't matter much if there was no one to vote for.

"I organized the homeless out there in San Francisco when a thousand men would sleep in the hard rain each night down on

Market Street. From the first day, I took up poor Tom Mooney's defense. They framed him for the Preparedness Day bombing just before Woodrow Wilson put us into the war. It was all a show to hoodwink the workers into signing up to fight for imperialism. I grew old defending Tom Mooney on the streetcorners of America but I did live long enough to see him freed. Poor man died just a month after me.

"I got old enough to march for the Scottsboro men and help the CIO organize the autoworkers into an industrial union. When I died, the Communist Party said that I had been a member but that was a bald-faced lie. Two things I never was: a Communist or a Negro.

"Nina Van Zandt, who is scattered just over there, was crazy and she smelled bad. She married August Spies in prison and then went mad when he was hanged. She never believed that the State would hang him. In his place, she kept a horse in her bedroom and a thousand stray cats. Every year on May 1st and November 11th, the anniversary of our husbands' hangings, we would fight over who got to sit in the seat of honor. So finally I went to Nina and I told her it was unsightly for two old bags to argue like that in public. We made a bargain—who ever died first, the other would be the orator at the funeral. Well, I spoke at hers but she didn't speak at mine.

"I always warned my friends not to trust in the siren dreams of the left. To be practical and put a nest egg aside in case the revolution was detained. I managed to tuck away a little for my old age but never thought I would get that old. I lived nearly a century. I could barely remember Mr. Parsons anymore and often confused him with my George. I started to worry that I was never going to die.

"My last public appearance was February 23rd, 1941. I spoke to the workers at the International Harvester plant, which had once belonged to Cyrus McCormick, where the Haymarket story really did begin. Carolyn Aspaugh has recorded it in my biography but to tell you the truth, I don't remember a thing. My mind is gone.

"I was burned up in a fire on March 7th, 1942 in the cottage George Marksell and I shared for 30 years on Madison. My eyes had gone bad and I bumped into the wood stove and the living room caught on fire. All my precious books were lost.

"George had gone to the store for the newspaper and came running home to rescue me but it was too late and he got burnt up too. Oh my, it was a real mess although it did save on the cremation payments. Irving buried both of our ashpiles down here. He even threw in my son Albert Jr. when he found the urn after the big fire. That makes three of us in this little hole. It really gets cramped down here sometimes."

"Hello, I'm Irving 'Three-for-One' Abrams. You asked me to bury you at the foot of the Monument, remember?—and that's exactly where you are, Lucy Parsons. You shouldn't complain. So it's a little crowded. But you have to remember this is prime real estate right here by the Martyrs."

"That's easy for you to say, Irving. You and Esther have separate plots. But I have to live with two other people, at least one of whom is half crazy, for an eternity."

"Listen Lucy, let me ask you—are you paying rent here? The Pioneer Society has always put out for your upkeep. But did I ever hear a 'thank you' for this generosity?"

"I'm the one who should be thanked. Didn't I leave the society my house and my library in my will?"

"Lucy, I told you long ago we didn't want the house. We're not a rental agency and the title company said it would cause trouble with our tax status. Besides, what house and what library are you talking about anyway? It was all burned to soot and ashes. I had to pay out of my pocket to have the debris hauled away. You have nothing to complain about. You got your front-row seat."

"Great. Thanks. But I had to die to get it. . . ."

"Ingrate!"

"Slumlord!"

"O.K. Sister Lucy—that's it! I'm having the office man move you in with the gypsies."

The Testimony of Irving Abrams

"Hello, my name is Irving Abrams. Did I already introduce myself? I don't know that we ever met before. Lucy tells me you're a writer. I've written a few books myself but my big claim to fame is that I was the last surviving member of the Pioneer Aid & Support Society. To tell you the truth, being the last surviving member caused me nothing but grief.

"I was the one who single-handedly took care of the Monument. I pulled up the weeds and the crabgrass and wiped off the pigeonshit. If there was a scratch or a ding, who do you think took care of it out of my own wallet? Do you have any idea what bronze statue parts cost these days?

"Did anyone even offer me so much as a glass of water to thank me for it? No. But it was my responsibility. All the rest of the members of the society were dead. We couldn't even have meetings anymore.

"Another thing. You see most of these people stretched out here? I collected them all. I myself made sure their contracts were in order. If there was no trust fund, I paid the grave fees. They would be in Potter's Field right now if it wasn't for me. And you heard Lucy Parsons complaining. All they do is kvetch, kvetch, kvetch about the arrangements. What do they expect me to do? It wasn't my business to see who was sleeping with whom. There was a vacancy. So it was next to a communist? That was what was available.

"My family went straight from St. Petersburg to Rochester, New York. Who knows why? When I was 12, I had a job delivering used furniture with my wagon. The boss was Mr. Goldman, a very nice person who often gave me tips. I didn't know then that he was the father of Emma Goldman! This is a true story. Emma Goldman and I both grew up in St. Petersburg, Russia and both of us moved to Rochester when we were kids but we didn't know each other. We didn't meet until much later right here in Chicago when Dr. Ben Reitman, an expert on venereal diseases, was her lover. It must have been fate.

"I don't remember the Haymarket bomb because I wasn't born yet so I can't tell you who I think threw it. But I heard all my life about the men who were hung for it. They were my models and my inspiration although I did not formally meet them until I too was dead and took up residence right here at their feet.

"I came to be a cutter in the garment industry. I tried to organize an IWW local at Hart, Schaftner, and Marx (not Karl) but the workers wouldn't hear of it. The IWW never had much luck with Jewish workers. The Wobblies were mainly a goyish outfit with all those blonde Nordic types like Joe Hill and Big Bill Hayward.

"The garment factories were all owned by Jews who had come here with no money. Now they were rich men and the worst kind of exploiters. I'm not an anti-Semite—how could I be? But I'm not for the bosses, either.

"After the Wobblies were crushed by the government, the so-called Socialist Party tried to organize the garment trades but they were in bed with the bosses. We used to have a song about them: "The Dubinskys and the Debs and the Thomases, they are making by the workers false promises . . ." The Communists weren't any better.

"You ask me who do I remember from those times? I remember Johan Most, the 'Propaganda of the Deed' fellow. He had a twisted jaw and was very angry all the time. He would suddenly fly into a rage up there at the lectern and curse Capitalism so vehemently that the ushers had to restrain him from breaking the chairs. Perhaps it had to do with him being so disfigured, an outcast.

"The book of Most's that impressed me was *The God Pestilence*. It convinced me to call myself an atheist. I didn't have to believe in God just because I was Jewish.

"I remember when Joe Hill came to Chicago. After the copper bosses killed him out there in Utah, they brought his body direct to Chicago There was a big wake—as a matter of fact, my tenant Lucy Parsons spoke there as did Hayward and Gurley Flynn, 'the Rebel Girl,' who fell in love with Joe after she went to visit him in jail. Then the IWWs had him cremated and his ashes sent around to every local in the country except those in Utah. There's a little of him sprinkled out their in the field along with Big Bill. We put Joe in a salt shaker to make sure he was distributed evenly.

"Of course I remember Big Bill, Mister One Big Union. He was a tall, bulky guy who wore a western sombrero to cover the scars on his head that the mine owners' goons had put there. 'Irving,' he told me, 'I hope to be able to repay those bastards for this one day.' Big Bill was a hard, whiskey-drinking man until he got the Wob religion and he never took a drink after that until he ran away to Russia and found out about vodka. It's a crying shame how Big Bill wound up over there, stranded in a dingy Moscow hotel, wasting away from sugar diabetes. When he died, they put half of him in the Kremlin wall with his comrade Jack Reed, and sent us the rest. We sprinkled him out in the field with Joe H.

"I remember Lenin and Trotsky and what happened to the poor fellows at Kronstadt. How could I forget it? We were rooting for the Soviet revolution to win. We were labor anarchists and, of course, we wanted to believe in it. But Lenin and Trotsky betrayed the hopes of Oktober. It was hard for us to trust the Bolsheviks anymore after they massacred the Kronstadt boys in the snow in 1921. It was then that I came to see that the

Dictatorship of the Proletariat was a nightmare for the working class and I never wanted to visit the Soviet Union like so many of my colleagues did. Kronstadt caused a lot of bad feelings here. Anyone who spoke out against the killing of the sailors was branded a Capitalist bootlicker by the Party.

"I remember the 50th anniversary of the Haymarket. I arranged a nice ceremony out here but the Communists wouldn't come. You would have thought they would be the first to show up to honor Haymarket but their stupid dogma kept them at home. And today, so many of them are buried here. Too many, if you ask me.

"I remember the great Negro singer Paul Robeson who is not buried here but who I brought to Waldheim on a rainy night in 1952. It was after a benefit party for the Civil Rights Congress, which was the CP's Negro front group, and Robeson expressed a wish to visit the Monument. Irving here will take you, his comrades suggested. So we caught a cab and sneaked in down by the river because the gates were locked. Robeson stood with his face to the Martyrs and sang 'The International' for them in his grand bass voice. It was like a private concert. I swear I could hear the Martyrs clapping when he was done.

"Do you know that Paul Robeson was the only All-American football player who was stripped of that title by America. Joe McCarthy and his crowd said you couldn't be both an All-American and an un-American at the same time and they removed his name from the record books. The 1928 All-America football team has only ten guys on it.

"Maybe I shouldn't be talking too loud about these things. You've heard that rat McCarthy is buried just across the state line in Wisconsin? Some say he's got Waldheim wired.

"I remember September, 1939 with much sadness. Although I did not trust the Communists, I could not imagine that Stalin would sign a nonaggression pact with that beast Hitler. Frankly, I was shocked. The blood is on both their hands. Shame!

"For a long time after that, all I could think was save the Jews, save the Jews. They were already lining up for the cattle cars to Auschwitz. I became a Zionist and got involved in a harebrained scheme to resettle the Jews in Surinam. I lost $25,000 on the deal, which was a lot of money to lose back in those days.

"Other places we looked into to find a home for the Jews were Uganda and Texas. I support Israel where it is now. After 2,000 years, the wandering Jew finally had a place to hang up his yarmulke. The Palestinians were the pawns of the Ottoman Empire and the British Imperialists. They had no claim to our land which was deeded to us in the Old Testament. But I'm not such a Zionist now after seeing how they've wrecked our dream of Israel.

"I remember Chicago, this big, boiling city, 'hog butcher to the world.' We had our poets, Carl Sandburg, Vachel Lindsey, and the crew over in Bughouse Square. We had our gangsters in nice fedoras and lovely suits. We had an anarchist on every streetcorner. I remember shooting liars' dice and downing shots with Nelson Algren at the Dill Pickle Club—Slim, the bartender, is out here with us too, and I remember Clarence Darrow smoking Havana cigars in the men's room at the courthouse. I remember that kid who called himself "Studs" after James T. Farrell's *Studs Lonigan*—he always carried a tape recorder with him.

"But I guess I remember Emma Goldman best of all. She was the world's most outstanding addict to liberty. No government or ruler was too high and mighty to withstand her scorn. I can't say the same for Sasha Berkman who was a scheming weasel and a real schmuck.

"When Goldman passed away up in Toronto in 1940, I wanted to get her here right away. The Communists tried to blackball her but I told her friends in Canada to just put her on a train and ship her to me. They were short of funds so I said sure, send me Emma C.O.D I always thought that they would pay me back someday but, of course, like everybody else, they never did. I was left holding the bag, as usual. I figure I'm out about a thousand bucks on Emma Goldman."

"So Irving, are you saying that I wasn't worth the freight charges? Me, Emma Goldman, your second-most-popular attraction here in Waldheim? Actually, I've been keeping a headcount and many more visitors come to see me than that tasteless tin monument over there. Instead of griping about the carfare, you ought to thank me for acquiescing to be buried in this industrial suburb. I had offers from Paris as you know and my adopted hometown of Rochester, submitted plans to embalm me and put me on display 24 hours a day in a clean, well-lighted glass case. But no, I had to be stuck down in this worm-eaten ground surrounded on all sides by left-wing losers."

"You see what I mean, folks? Do I have to put up with these insults until the end of time? Did I die and go to Hell? Maybe it's time I sold off the whole kit and caboodle for pet food."

Testimony of Emma Goldman—Her Life and Lovers

"I was hounded and humiliated, persecuted, imprisoned, and eventually deported for love. For my love of liberty. For my love of the right to love freely. I am proud to have been the world's leading advocate of free love and 'variationist smut' as my detractors like the mulatto Mrs. Lucy Parsons over there have dubbed me.

"When I was a young woman and not wise in the ways of the world, I took an apartment on the Lower East Side of Manhattan. I soon noticed that all the other apartments were rented by young women who entertained large men night and day. In my naivetè, I had moved into a brothel! Brutes would break down my door in the middle of the night looking for their whore. I came to see this was unfree love! Capitalist love! This was love for sale! I was a homely Jewish girl who just loved to fuck. My love was given and taken freely without fiduciary considerations. Some like Ben Reitman M.D., that cad smirking over there in the next row, took it a little too freely.

"My first love was little Petrushka, the peasant boy who came every day to see me at our home in St. Petersburg. We would play horsey and I would squeal in ecstasy when he rode me around on his back. I could feel this delightful sensation between my legs. Sometimes Petrushka would touch me there and my little body would grow warm. In the night, I would stroke myself and once my mother caught me so enraptured and chastised me for being 'a dirty girl.' She whipped me until my bare bottom was bright red. And I think this was when I achieved my first orgasm!

"The first man who took me to bed—I do not even know his name! He was a hotel clerk, a nice, presentable boy I thought. I would walk by his hotel, which was up the street from the Hermitage and we stood under the awning and flirted. Then one afternoon, he asked me if I would like to see what the rooms looked like. I was not yet 14 and unschooled in the schemes of males. The rooms were beautifully done, with silk hangings and thick carpets and dazzling chandeliers. He gave me wine and threw me down on the soft bed and jabbed his rod way into me as if it were a lightening bolt. I didn't get home until after dark and I felt sick and violated. I pleaded with my mother not to punish me but she administered a sound whipping and it ached like sex."

"Enough of this filth, you obscene old windbag! This is nothing but variationist smut! Irving, this woman is ruining the neighborhood and lowering the property values! Irving? Irving, are you listening to me?"

"This is the last time I'm going to tell you not to interrupt me, you crazy witch. Besides, Irving's either dead or in the bathroom. Variationest smut? Don't you wish! You're just jealous because I had a good time. Besides, this is a free-speech cemetery and there's nothing you can do to shut me up.

• • •

"Jacob Kirshner was my first husband. We worked together in the corset factory when I came to Rochester. He was a handsome fellow but not too bright. He asked me to a dance and I had never been dancing before. When we danced close, his flesh was hot to my touch and my heart beat like a tom-tom drum. I was so dumb I thought it was the dancing.

"On our wedding night after we had been to see the Rabbi, Jacob lay down by my side. We were both naked but he would not touch me so I reached over and took his penis in my hand and stroked it gently but he could not get hard. I put it in my mouth and licked at it strenuously but still Jacob was flaccid. And then I realized that it was my bad luck to have married an impotent man.

"I stayed with Jacob for three years. We married and divorced twice. I stopped sleeping with him after the Haymarket Martyrs were hanged. After Jacob, I never married for love or visited a rabbi again. I did not really need a rabbi to tell me which men I could sleep with—or which woman either. Am I right, Voltairine?"

Testimony of Voltairine de Clyves

"We were free anarchist women! No man could rule us! My name is Voltairine de Clyves and this is my testimony—"

"Not now, dear, this man has come to talk to me about my life and my long list of lovers."

• • •

Testimony of Emma Goldman (post-interruptus)

"I was obsessed with the Haymarket Martyrs. They say that when a man is hanged, his member fills with blood and gets stiff and hard. I fantasized that I was making love to Parsons and Spies, Fischer and Engels, all of them at once. What that would have been like!

"Johan Most was my first lover when I came to Chicago. He was a brooding man. His jaw had become infected when he was a child and he was misshapen and misanthropic. He tried to hide his deformity beneath a wild and tangled beard but even unseen it weighed upon him like a curse. But Most's darknesses only made him more fascinating to me. I went to see him at a lecture in Chicago at the *Arbiter Zeitung*. 'Destruction is the only salvation!' he thundered and my whole body trembled. When I visited him at his hotel later, he sat me down on the sofa and warned me that anarchism was a steep and painful path. Then he suddenly collapsed at my feet and claimed he had fallen in love with me when he first saw me in the lecture hall and what was my name? He began to weep for fear that I would reject him because of his disfigured face and I was crying too and our tears mingled and I told him he was beautiful to me and before I could say 'Peter Kropotkin,' he had my bloomers off and his trouser snake was coming for me.

"I was 19 and loved to flirt with the anarchist boys. It was only natural. Johan Most grew insanely jealous at these harmless flirtations. He came to my door and accused me of being unfaithful. He made such a ruckus that I was asked to leave the boarding house. It was an impossible situation and I tried to break it off many times but he took to stalking me. Later, when I was with Sasha Berkman, he threatened our lives and once tried to throw acid on my clothes. After Sasha shot the millionaire Frick during the Homestead Strike, Johan Most lied that it was a put-up job and that Sasha was a government spy and had just done it to arouse sympathy for the bosses.

"I knew well how Sasha had suffered when he saw that Frick had survived and I resolved to teach Johan Most a most painful and humiliating lesson. I bought a horsewhip and at his next lecture, I rose and asked if it was true that he had called Sasha a tool of the ruling class? He began to shout that I had joined with his enemies to murder his life work, whereupon I leapt up on the stage and pulled down his pants and horsewhipped the great anarchist orator until he begged for mercy. It felt so good. I even wet my panties. Then I broke the horsewhip in half and threw it on him and stomped out of the lecture hall. That was the last time I ever spoke to Johan Most.

"Sasha Berkman and I were together for 30 years and we never once made love. You could not love his body nor could he love the woman that yearned for fulfillment inside my inverted womb. Sasha did not like to be touched which was a big problem when the authorities tortured him. You could love his brilliant, searing mind but forget about it below the neck.

"It was even worse when he came home from prison. I put a red rose in his hand and crushed him to my ample bosom but he wiggled free. 'I cannot be touched!' he shrieked.

"Whenever Sasha would come home weak and bruised from waging the revolution, I would take care of him and build him up with Jewish food—he particularly loved blintzes and stuffed dermas. I would bring him back to health and he gratefully called me 'his Big Nurse.' But he would never let me practice my talents as an erotic masseuse on his poor, scrawny body.

"Then Sasha was sent to prison and my fingers were forced to go to work. I loved to feel the flesh of men bend and become supple under my hands. And besides, frankly, I was broke and needed the money. I rented a rooftop apartment on 17th Street near Union Square and printed up handbills: 'Have a red-hot time with Red Emma!' I had many younger men as regular clients and I loved up them all, especially Dan, my golden-haired Princeton fraternity boy.

"How many lovers did I take in my time? 10,000? Less than Wilt Chamberlin but more than an old maid like that prune-faced Lucy Parsons Gonzalez ever did.

"I can't deny that I liked the young ones. Beautiful Leon Czolgocz with his dreamy blue eyes and apple cheeks and tiny girlish mouth. Blonde Lars, my Swedish Delight, who I took up with after Sasha and I escaped from Moscow. I could not get enough of his sleek, tan body. But alas, he was 29 and I was 53 and one night in Berlin, he went out for a pack of cigarettes and, well, you can read about it in my autobiography.

"Ed Brady was a millionaire who kept me in expensive new clothes from Saks Fifth Avenue. He was trying to buy me and I went along with the game and spent many intoxicating nights with him in the lap of luxury—but like all the rest, he just wanted me to be his maid and his mommy. Marriage is nothing less than indentured servitude—I was married three times, twice to Kirshner, and once to the Welsh coal miner, Mr. James Colton, but that was only so that I could continue to stay in England. Many men proposed to me—good men like Harry Kelly right over there but I didn't want to be chained down. As Harry used to say, I just liked that free-love stuff.

"I had affairs with so many writers it's a wonder I wasn't mentioned for the Nobel Prize. I knew Henry Miller carnally in Paris and Jack London in San Francisco. Jack and I met during the Great Earthquake—or at least they said it was an earthquake—and we went up to the Berkeley hills with a bottle of wine and watched the city burning across the bay and when Jack mounted my naked body, the earth trembled beneath me.

"I had sex in London with Dr. Havelock Ellis. It was clinical but he taught me a few tricks he picked up from the *Kama Sutra*.

I never slept with James Joyce but I read *Portrait Of An Artist As a Young Man* in the New York Tombs and bedded down with the book between my legs.

"Frank Harris and I were off-again on-again lovers for ages. He taught me how to drink French cognac and smoke fine cigars. I finally read his book *The Bomb,* which blames Rudolph Schnaubelt for the Haymarket, when I was living in St. Tropez working on my best-selling volume *I Was Disillusioned With The Russian Revolution.* I don't believe *The Bomb* was supposed to be true. I never had occasion to know either Rudolph or Edward Schnaubelt but from what I understand, it was Edward, not Rudolph, who was the real Haymarket bomber. Whichever brother is guilty, it was an irresponsible act.

"Jack Reed was another gay young blade who I always lusted to take as a lover but the opportunity never presented itself and that Louise Bryant was always hanging around. Louise was a shallow and ordinary woman who looked like she was sucking on a lemon all the time. She did not at all resemble Dianne Keaton in *Reds* and I often wondered what Jack saw in her.

"Then one day Jack burst into my hotel room at the National in Moscow. He was burning up with fever and I put him to bed and nursed him back to health in record time. In fact, by the third day, he felt so frisky that he pulled me under the quilts with him. He had a very unusual penis, with a red star tattooed on the tip.

"I'm convinced that Jack Reed was duped into mouthing the Communist line. By the time he died, he had grown disillusioned with Lenin. 'I'm caught in a trap, I'm caught in a trap'—those were his last words as he lay dying of typhoid fever in frigid Estonia. He kept on saying them over and over again long after he was dead and the commissars had to brick him up in the Kremlin Wall just to keep him quiet.

"I fell in love with young Elizabeth Gurley Flynn the moment

I spotted her speaking at a streetcorner meeting in Union Square. She was just a slip of a thing and she had the loveliest complexion. I took her back to my hotel room and showed her my dildo. She was horrified. I'm proud to say that I carried my dildo from one end of the revolution to the other. I never went off to the class war without it.

"I fought the revolution for love. All of those lovers who used me and abused me, threw me away, called me a traitor and a trollop, I forgive and absolve them today. All except that son of a bitch, Dr. Ben Reitman, M.D.

"Reitman was everything that I abhorred in a man. He was alien to all my ideals of what a human being should be. I hated his American swagger on sight. The first time he came to see me, he was wearing a huge black hat like a cowboy, which he certainly was not, a flowing, dandified tie, and a great gold-headed cane. 'I've come to see the little lady,' he bellowed at my secretary, half frightening the poor thing to death. The little lady! I mean, if you please! Emma Goldman! The little lady!

"And yet for all his bluster and misogyny, I was drawn to Ben Reitman M.D. as if he were my preordained destiny. He was tall and dark, a handsome brute. When he fastened me in his dark, leering eyes, the physical magnetism was like an irresistible force of nature. But what fascinated me most about Ben Reitman M.D. were his hands. Large working man's hands with the dirt encrusted up under the fingernails. I just wanted to take him home and scrub them clean.

"Reitman had come to make me an offer he said I couldn't refuse. The Chicago police would not let me speak anywhere in the city in those days. Every hall I rented would be raided by Captain Schleuter and the Red Squad—Schleuter had hounded the Haymarket Martyrs and jailed poor, gaunt Eugene Debs many times. Now Ben Reitman had a storefront down on west Madison where the hobos and the vagrants could get out of the cold, and he offered it to me free of charge to hold my meetings there. But he was in cahoots with the cops even then.

"Reitman called himself the 'King of the Hobos' but I doubt that he ever even rode on a railroad train. Ben Reitman M.D. was a pathological liar.

"But I could not escape my fate. I was impelled into his powerful arms by the hurricanes raging inside me. I craved his manly physique—you have to understand that he was exceptionally well-hung. I was so obsessed with him that whenever we were apart, even for just a few hours, I would grow agitated and depressed.

"My friends universally considered Ben Reitman M.D. untrustworthy and constantly warned me to break off our relationship. But I would not listen to reason and plunged recklessly ahead and trusted him with my life.

"Reitman had grown up in an unsavory demimonde of hobos and tramps, prostitutes and petty thieves and yet, despite his low ways, I took him hungrily to my bed and served him my heart on a porcelain platter. Foolishly, I made him my manager and granted him exclusive rights to book my lecture tours. He accompanied me all across the United States and carried my books and pamphlets, arranged for lodging, and the best of meals, regardless of expense. I kept a sharp eye out on things and soon began to notice that the literature sales were coming up short every night. I confronted Ben about this but he vigorously denied any wrongdoing and cried that I no longer loved him. Torn by my addiction to his sexual prowess, I would retreat into silence for fear of driving him away. I had become his love slave.

"But that was not all there was to my nightmare. Ben Reitman M.D. began disappearing after the lectures with the women he would meet there. He did not even learn their names before bedding them, he confessed. Sometimes, he would be away for days, and then come crawling back to me on his big hands and knees and declare that he loved only me. All he had to say was 'Yoo-hoo mommy doll' and I would melt like sweet butter.

"I will tell you another thing about Ben Reitman M.D. He was fixated on his mother, a grotesquely obese woman who consumed large amounts of chocolate. It wasn't healthy. Every day, Reitman would bring her a heart-shaped box of bon-bons—if he was out of town he would have them delivered—and sit there and watch her devour the contents. Sometimes, he would feed them to her and she would lick his fingers. It was so disgustingly Oedipal that I had to laugh.

"Sasha cautioned me about my strange infatuation and urged me to dump the man but I was hopelessly hooked on his enormous member. It was like morphine and I could not bring myself to kick the habit.

"Then one day, I walked into a restaurant in the Loop and saw Reitman there eating and joking with Captain Schleuter from the Red Squad like they were old pals. I almost died with shame to think that I had given my body to a . . . a . . . a . . . police agent! That I had even serviced this fink with oral sex!

"Later, he came to me with his 'yoo-hoo mommy doll' routine but this time it wouldn't work. I was through! It turned out that Reitman had been tipping off the cops to where I would be speaking and they came and broke up the meetings. He did it for the publicity, he whined, so that you would get more sympathy from the masses, and like an idiot, I almost believed him.

"This creep wormed his way into my life over and over again until I was finally deported from the United States of America. 'At last,' I said to Sasha as we sailed out of New York Harbor, 'I'm rid of Ben Reitman M.D. for good.' No more! Kaput! And now I'm buried in the same section of this dreary cemetery with the lout. I've often complained to Irving that this is tantamount to sexual harassment—Reitman has been stalking me for years! Do you happen to know a good lawyer?"

Testimony of Dr. Ben Reitman, M. D.

"My name is Dr. Ben Reitman M.D. and my reputation is being spit on here. I was a medical doctor and an expert on venereal diseases. I am the inventor of the world-famous 606 ointment, a sure cure for syphilis, a couple of tubes of which I have right here with me for sale today.

"I was also known as the King of the Hoboes. I rode the rails from sea to shining sea. I jumped freight trains with Boxcar Bertha and cooked my stews in the hobo jungles with T-Bone Slim. I heard the lonesome whistle and I dodged the railroad bulls. I knew all the Wobbly songs by heart and counted Joe Hill as a personal pal. For Emma Goldman, perhaps the most pathological liar of all time, to question my authenticity, is a literary hoax.

"Goldman's allegations are actionable and it is a good thing that I am not a litigious man by nature. Good anarchists do not recognize the bourgeois courts.

"For the record, let it be known that I played a pivotal role in Emma Goldman's political and literary career. I was instrumental in crowning her the Queen of the Anarchists. I promoted her tours and lugged around her voluminous books, was her faithful bodyguard and part-time lover. Her petty jealousies pushed me away and drove her to desperation. To label me a police agent is both scurrilous and libelous, not to mention frivolous and ridiculous. I would ask damages but one can get no blood from a stone, even as ostentatious a stone as hers.

"My political credentials are an open book. You can read all about them in *My Life As An Outcast,* published, of course, by the Charles Kerr people. I just happen to have a few copies on discount with me.

"I was only seven when they hung the Haymarket Heroes and it changed my life. Ever since, I have worked ceaselessly for the liberation of the working class. The bomb? From the rumors I picked up around police headquarters, it seems like both those Schnaubelt brothers were mixed up in it.

"I organized the grifters and the drifters into the Migratory Workers & Hoboes Union. I opened up the Hobo College down on 10th and Madison, which wasn't exactly an institution of higher learning. The opera diva Mary Garden, a deliciously buxom wench, donated large quantities of food and we had the finest soup line in the Windy City.

"I joined the Wobblies and rambled all over the land. I was tarred and feathered in San Diego during the free-speech fight there. That alone should prove that I'm not a police fink. Joe Hill will tell you all about it.

"I am anything but a misogynist, as Goldman has libeled me. I took up the cause of a woman's right to own her own body and went to work for birth control. I was arrested time and time again for passing out Margaret Sanger's pamphlet "What Every Woman Should Know." I was jailed in Cleveland for two months and you know what? That Sanger woman never said a word in my defense.

"As I grew in age and stature, I became a much-requested orator at Left-leaning funerals. I spoke at the spreading of Joe Hill's ashes and those of Nina Van Zandt. I was asked to officiate at Lucy Parsons' interment and I even said a few words over Emma Goldman herself. I don't remember that she complained about it back then.

"Finally, you best leave my mother out of this, thank you."

"Ben Reitman M.D., you deserted and humiliated me in my hour of greatest need. After Sasha and I were threatened with prison in 1917 for counseling young men not to fight in Wilson's imperialist war, you led the police right to our doorstep.

"You came to us and lied that you had to take an emergency

trip to Chicago because you had gotten a young woman in a family way. But it was all a sham to cover up the fact that you, Ben Reitman M.D., had ratted Sasha and I off to the Department of Justice. You gave us up to them and then fled into the night! You're nothing but an unscrupulous stool pigeon!

"Attention! Attention! This is a warning! My fellow dead comrades, there is an informer loose among us. Take heed!"

"You'd better watch your tongue, bitch, or I'll have your bones carted off to the dog pound.

"In my defense, I call as my first and only witness Joseph Hillstrum, also known as Joe Hill."

Testimony of Joe Hill

"Joe Hill is my name
and songwriting gained me fame,
the copper bosses gunned me down
in 1915 in a Mormon town
but my only real crime
was dreaming up rhymes
for the working class of people.
'It's doggerel' the bosses critiqued,
we're going to have put this dog to sleep
but what they forget to exorcise
went on to organize,
went on to organize.

"Or something like that.
I'm working on a draft.
Songs sometimes come to you right away
and sometimes you can't put a final line

to 'em any old day.
I wrote hundreds of tunes when I was young
but I must have 10,000 ditties
swimming around my brain
that never got sung.
I wasn't exactly a Tin Pin Alley kind of guy.
Soapboxes and souplines were more my style.

"I sang for my supper and I sang for my bread
but singing for the cops, I be better off dead,
I'm a radical rapper and I'm not going to chill,
until the working class has eaten its fill.

"When I was still a greenhorn
and wet behind the ears,
I sailed the seven seas
from Swedish fjords to Chinese shores.
I came to California
and organized the stevedores
all the way to Vancouver port.
I learned to hop a freight train
and fool the railroad bulls.
I hunkered in the boxcars
where the bindlestiffs did gather.
I preached to them about sabotage
and how if each of us would just practice it
ten minutes every single day,
we'd have more jobs and better pay.

"I marched into Mexico—not me alone
I went with the brothers Flores Magon,
We got as far as the town of Tecate
when there appeared the *Federales*

so we retreated back across the line
to fight the revolution another time.

"I knew Ben Reitman in Dago town.
The year was 1912 and
they was shutting our free speech down.
Ben jumped up and took a stand.
1,500 men had already gone to the can
for crooning my tunes about revolution.
So he got on the box
to read them the Constitution.
For being an ornery Wob,
the deputies fed him to the mob
and he was feathered and tarred on the spot.
So far as I can tell
fellow worker Reitman was no police fink.
I can't figure out why
Emma's making such a stink.
Sounds like a love/hate thing to me.

"Well, I filled up the *Little Red Songbook*
and was starting to write another
when the call came in from Utah
that the miners were in a lather.
So I rode the rails to that desert place
and took me a slave in the Tucker mine.
The Wobblies came from every part
and those that wasn't soon signed their cards,
we called ourselves One Big Union
and fought the bosses for One Big Solution.
We called a strike and shut it down
but when we walked out the scabs walked in
and that was where the class war begins.
We sang them songs and threw some stones

and the owners sent in the Pinkertons.
'Just defendin' private property' they said.
Hell you are, you're stealin' our bread.
It was a damn good struggle
and we gave them mucho trouble
but in the end, we lost the battle
and had to skedaddle, some to Seattle
and some to Salt Lake City just down the road.

"It was a dark January night in that gritty city
and I was bedded down with my secret sweetie
Then her pop walks in
and pulls out a pistol.
I ducked and dived as the bullets whistled
but I caught a slug and that made me holler.
So I skipped out to the sawbones' parlor.
Old Doc McHugh fixed me right—
gave me morphine and called the po-lice.

"Now on this same night, two tough cookies—
Turk Christian was one of those bums—
heisted up a grocery store
and killed the owner and his son.
But when the cops heard I'd been shot,
the Chief snarled go get that Wob.
That rascalous red has sung his last song.
Go get that radical pill they call Joe Hill.
Right then, I knew I was a goner.

"They took me down to the city jail
and told me wasn't going to be no bail,
you shot those men and they shot you back,
it's open and shut and those are the facts
You're nothing but a trouble-making troubadour

but you're not going to be making trouble
here anymore.

Joe Hill, you've sung your final song,
Joe Hill, you've sung your very last song,
but they were mighty, mighty wrong,
I kept on singing on and on.

"They put me on trial and I looked sunk.
The judge was a skunk
and my lawyers were drunk.
I fired them both and defended myself.
You got the wrong man I decided to fight.
I wasn't out grocery shopping that dark night.
My alibi was a woman friend
but I can't reveal her good name
because I'm a gallant kind of gent.
As you might expect,
the jury didn't buy my story.

"Tell us her name and we'll give you a break
but that was a deal I just couldn't make.
Today we're all dust so it doesn't much matter
if her name is revealed to the rest of you rabble.
She was a beautiful lass from the upper class
by the name of Virginia Stephen Snow—
her daddy was the big boss dog
in the Mormon show.

"Three times they gave me a date to die,
'Enough's enough!' I wanted to cry.
The King of the Swedes pled for my life
but the law wouldn't listen and I was denied.

Wilson the president whom I always despised
he even gave it a halfhearted try.

"Big Bill said we had to mobilize
to save Joe Hill's tough old hide,
so the Wobs came to town
and soapboxed up and down
said they was going to blow up
the Angel Maroni
if the State didn't stop all this baloney.
But the judges denied the appeal
and my fate was sealed.
I wrote Big Bill and philosophized
don't mourn for me—organize!
And them words themselves
went on to organize,
went on to organize.

"Now, Big Bill knew the turmoil I was in
so he sent me an angel named Gurley Flynn.
She was a Rebel Gal, a real Rebel Gal.
Came into my cell, kissed me on the cheek,
said 'We'll have you out of here in a week,'
but the weeks became months
and the months a whole year.
I said to Gurley, I'm already dead
and we dead men
have nothing to fear.

"Now, I don't think that its a sin if I tell you,
I fell in love with Elizabeth Gurley Flynn.
I told her go away, I'm already fried chicken.
I'm just a drop in the bucket

and there's an ocean to win.
'I'm sticking with you Joe,'
cried my sweet Gurley Flynn.
She was a Rebel Girl. A real Rebel Girl.

"So my time ran out and I told my friends
so long, good-bye, how swell it's been.
All this *au revoir* stuff
was getting really monotonous.
I'm heading out to Mars
to organize the canal workers up there.
And we're going to sing
the old songs so loud and clear
that the learned stargazers
are going to have to concur
there is intelligent life out in the universe.

"The Warden came to my cell
and asked me how I wanted to depart.
'We can hang you by the neck
or shoot you right through the heart,
What's your pleasure, you red thug you?'
How do you want us to snuff you?
It didn't much matter
but I chose the latter—
I figured one bullet in the biff
was one bullet less
for the next working stiff.

"On the 19th of November
Nineteen centuries down the pike
after they whacked fellow worker Christ,
they came for me with a gun in their hand

but I figured I still had a fighting chance.
I grabbed a sharp stick and made my stand
they beat me with clubs and tied me to a chair,
told me I had better start saying my prayers.

"They stuck a bullseye to my heart,
and put a black hood on my head,
said I was about to be deader than dead,
Ready, Aim! the captain commanded.
You better fire away, I demanded,
and my executioners forthwith obliged.
That was my final and favorite breath
and I couldn't have asked for a finer death.
Next day in the *New York Times*,
they said I was more dangerous
dead than alive.

"Now I made one last request
and of course it was in rhyme.
Haul my old bones across the state line.
'Won't be caught dead in Utah,' I advised.
They paraded me through that city of shame.
Six lady pallbearers carried me to the train.
Bought me a first-class ticket all the way
to sweet home Chicago.

"10,000 workers met me at Union Station
and Big Bill spoke at my consummation.
The ovens reduced me to a pile of ash
and Bill Haywood divided up the stash.
Sent little packets to every state—
only Utah didn't get no flakes.
Didn't want to be caught dead in that place.

They sprinkled me here at Forest Home,
scattered me east and out in the West,
what was left they tossed up in the desk,
and here comes the part I like to tell best:
Comes 1920 and the Palmer raid roundup,
Feds bust down the door and grab the comrades
took away the Wobs for being dirty reds,
took away me too, although I was dead.
Said I was evidence.

"Now there's one more thing.
It's about that song they wrote,—
the one that says I never croaked.
Being mushed up like that gets my goat.
They say they see me in their dreams,
a-standing by their beds.
Is this supposed to be some kind of joke?
Earl Robinson and Lee Hayes wrote the music and the words,
Robeson sang it everywhere in the world,
and Joan Baez brought it to the suburbs.
Takes more than guns to kill a man.
Says Joe, 'I didn't die.'
That's what I'm supposed to have replied.
But I'm here to tell you, now, today,
I caught that lead.
I'm not like Elvis.
I'm really dead.

"Finally, before I pull the pin,
I need to sing you one more hymn.
It's for the still-beautiful Elizabeth Gurley Flynn
who I'd like to take out for a spin.
Not just because she's a girl
but because she's the Rebel Girl:

"There are women of many descriptions,
in this queer world, as everyone knows,
some live in beautiful mansions
and wear the finest of clothes,
there are blueblood queens and princesses
who have rings made of diamonds and pearls
but the only real thoroughbred lady
is the Rebel Girl.
The Rebel Girl,
to the working class,
'she's our most precious pearl!'
And here she comes now.
She's the real-deal Rebel Girl."

Testimony of Elizabeth Gurley Flynn, aka "The Rebel Girl"

"Thank you, Joe. I appreciate your kind words and its always a thrill to be regaled by that silver tongue of yours.

"First off, I should like to say that I am not a character witness for Ben Reitman M.D. He was and remains an insufferable buffoon. But if Emma Goldman despises him with a purple passion, he can't be all bad.

"Emma Goldman was a personal heroine of mine, a role model for my generation. But she flaunted our trust and sold out the Russian Revolution to the *New York World* 'for a pot of porridge,' as my old dad would say. She betrayed the Great Lenin and the Great Stalin, and the Bolsheviks were entirely justified in booting her out of Moscow for attacking Socialism when the reactionary bandits were besieging the city.

"From my first gasp of life to the last breath I drew, I was a mortal enemy of Capitalism. I don't care anymore if that swine McCarthy up there in Wisconsin is tapping the root phone. Capitalism is an evil criminal enterprise and I dedicated my life to its destruction.

"Oh, I certainly paid the price for acting 'the Rebel Girl.' I saw the insides of a lot of hoosegows, state pens, and federal reformatories from Paterson, New Jersey to Alderson, West Virginia to Butte, Montana. When I was over 60 years old, the so-called government charged me with failing to register as a foreign agent in violation of an unconstitutional law called the Smith Act because I was a frontline leader of the Communist Party USA. They took a dozen of us to trial and we were convicted of teaching and advocating the violent overthrow of the government.

"The evidence entered into the transcript was *The Communist Manifesto,* which I had first read in 1904 to my freshman classmates at Morris High School in the Bronx. When I burst out laughing in the courtroom, Judge Harold Medina held me in contempt, which pretty much describes what I had for him. Years after we were sentenced and served our terms, the courts threw out the convictions. It was a witch hunt, pure and simple.

"I was sentenced to two years in a proper women's penitentiary in Alderson, West Virginia, where the great Negro singer Billie Holiday was incarcerated on a dope charge. We often walked the yard together and she would sing for me—I particularly enjoyed the song "Strange Fruit," which was written by my old friend Abel Meerpol (who took in the Rosenberg children after Eisenhower fried poor Julius and Ethel). 'Strange fruit hanging from the poplar trees'—the song is all about the lynching of the Negro people in the South. The way she sang it would break your heart.

"On my birthday, Billie came into my dorm and dedicated 'Red Sails in the Sunset' because I was a Communist. Billie Holiday's singing made the time fly by.

• • •

"My mother and father were from the old sod by way of the granite state of New Hampshire. Mary, my mom, was a green-eyed colleen and my father stole her away when she was only 15. She went to work early in the sewing factories and all her blessed life, supported Tom Flynn, a rarely employed layabout, in his screwball schemes.

"While Mary toiled 12 hours a day, my father lounged around the house, reading books and spouting wild ideas. He loved the political meetings and took me with him—he would put me up on his strong shoulders so that I could see the speakers and I thrilled to watch how they could keep a crowd spellbound. At bedtime, Tom Flynn tucked me in with tales of the San Patricios, Irishers who had fought the *Americanos* during the invasion of Mexico and who were hung from the lampposts of Mexico City for it, and the Molly McGuires, the 19 brave lads who went to war against the anthracite barons in Pennsylvania and slaughtered their share before they too were rewarded with the noose.

"The great Irish working-class speaker James Connelly often slept on our couch on 133rd Street in Harlem and the Gaelic poet Sheamus O'Sheele was a frequent houseguest. Money was collected in our living room for the Irish Dynamite Fund to purchase explosives so the boys could blow up Parliament.

"Every November 11th, Tom Flynn would bundle up Mary and my sisters and we would go down to Union Square for the annual mourning of the Haymarket Martyrs. Afterwards, Mr. Flynn would splurge and take us over to Luchow's for early dinner. As long as I lived in New York, it was a special treat for me to eat at Luchow's.

"I kept the portraits of the Martyrs of Chicago over my bed, along with Jesus and the Virgin Mary, and I learned their faces in my heart. Wasn't it Louis Lingg who threw the bomb at the Haymarket?

"I learned from the street meetings and was considered a child prodigy as an orator. I spoke on Harlem streetcorners at 15 years of age. I was a member of the Harlem Socialist Club and we traveled all over the city to speak at union meetings and spread the working-class gospel. I loved particularly the workingmen's saloons on the Lower East Side where I would address the German pianomakers and the Jewish garment cutters about the benefits of socialism. I was just a young slip of a thing but I had a voice like a jackhammer and when they pushed me out on stage, I could really pump up a crowd.

"When I was 16, and with my parents' blessing, I traveled to Chicago and joined the IWW and that is when I first met the gentle giant Big Bill Hayward. 'I'm a two-gun man from the West—want to see a card trick?' he winked and tried to coax me into sitting on his knee.

"Big Bill was the big man in the Western Miners' Federation and the mine owners cursed his name mightily morning, noon, and night. One afternoon in 1903, the ex-governor of the state of Idaho, Frank Steunenberg, who got William McKinley to put army troops on Hayward's boys after they blew up the Bunker Hill mine, went to open his mailbox and a dynamite bomb flew him into the next county. Big Bill was in Colorado and had an alibi but they picked him and the other mine union leaders up in the middle of the night and sent them on a train in chains all the way to Coeur d'Alene. Clarence Darrow came out from Chicago and mounted an eloquent defense that showed Big Bill couldn't have done it. In the end, Haywood went free and became the most popular working-class hero in the country, and was elected general secretary of the Wobblies.

"Big Bill drew me up a list of all his comrades out in the West and sent me there to agitate. 'Gurley, with that gravel voice of yours, you'll scare the pants off the bosses and their scabs,' he joked with a twinkle in his one good eye. So I traveled west and watched the big country go by. I had no idea America was so big! I visited all the hot spots like Cripple Creek and Leadville and Ludlow, where John D. Rockefeller turned the machine guns on the miners' wives and children, and I heard their terrible stories.

"I went to Butte, Montana, which was like the city of the dead. The Anaconda smelter gassed the babies with cyanide and the miners called the place Poisonville but they weren't going to take it anymore. I loved those rough miners and cowboys and broncobusters.

"The IWW locals provided me with an escort from town to town and said I'd be as safe with them as if I were in god's pocket—and I was too. One long, lean drink of water was assigned to accompany me on the train to Spokane and he wasn't real comfortable about riding on the cushions. 'You have some beautiful scenery out here,' I remarked, just to make small talk. 'Don't know about that sister,' he drawled back. 'No time to look at the scenery until we destroy the Capitalist class.' That made me laugh.

"I went up into the Mesabi range and talked to the iron miners and their families. They were all tough Finnish people. That's where I knew my first husband, Jack Jones, an IWW organizer known to everyone as plain old Jonesy. I was not yet 18 when we got hitched by a justice of the peace up in Hibbing and Jonesy was arrested on our honeymoon for planting a bomb in the post office, but it was a put-up job.

"Now, one problem with the Industrial Workers of the World was that it was a man's world and the sisters always felt like they were the ladies' auxiliary of the One Big Union. Hayward and his cronies smoked these evil-smelling cigars. They were meat-and-potato men and they laughed at me because I was a vegetarian—I could never look another piece of meat in the eye after William Z. Foster gave me a guided tour through the Chicago packinghouses. Another thing I told Big Bill was that I didn't much care for all that dynamiting and sabotage his boys were carrying out. 'What's the matter Gurley? You going soft on us now?'

"I joined the Women's Party because I wanted to vote. It outraged me that women didn't yet have suffrage. We followed Woodrow Wilson around with a roving picket line for nearly two years every time he poked his face out in public and there was a terrible persecution for it. The sisters were beaten and thrown in prison and when they went on a hunger strike to protest, they were put in straitjackets and carted off to the mental hospital. But we persevered.

"I met many heroic women during these struggles. Mrs. Lucy Parsons over there was one. She traveled the country knocking on union-hall doors to clear her husband's good name. She was a warm, dark person who always had a word of encouragement for us younger rebels. It shocked me to hear how she had locked her son in an insane asylum because he disobeyed her and enlisted in the military.

"Another woman I knew and loved was Mother Mary Jones. She lived a hundred years and always wore her sunbonnet when she went out to march. Old Mother and her wild women would take after the scabs with their brooms and their pails. When she died, she went straight up to Coal Miner's Heaven and became a star in the firmament and later, in a magazine.

"The Triangle Shirtwaist Fire changed my life. Hundreds of women were trapped inside a sweatshop on the top floor of a building just east of Washington Square—the NYU lunchroom is there now. The doors had been locked to keep the girls from wasting the boss's precious time going to the bathroom, and to keep the union organizers out. One-hundred and forty-eight young women were burned to death or threw themselves through the windows into the street. The Triangle Shirtwaist Fire took place on March 25th, 1911 and that night, I swore that I would dedicate my life to organizing women workers for decent conditions.

"I told Big Bill that I was going up to Lawrence, Massachusetts to help organize the textile mills. Joe Ettor and Mr. Gianitti were already there. When we tried to speak in the street, the cops would call us 'agitators' and beat and arrest us. Our demands were bread and roses. You heard me right. There were a lot of women workers and they wanted roses. They deserved them.

During the first winter of the strike, there was no coal and the mothers could not feed their children or keep them warm. So we organized the Children's Crusade and the kids were sent off to New York City, where well-endowed society matrons bought them woolen clothing and saw that they ate three times a day.

"When they came back in the spring, the kids were fat and the women had won the strike and the roses and the bread. The sisters and brothers came to Lawrence from everywhere—there were Slavs and Italians, Portuguese, and even Syrians and Cape Verdians, but somehow they all spoke the same language.

"It was in Paterson, the silk city, where I received the title of 'The Rebel Girl,' I guess for going to jail so often. Joe Hill heard about me on the grapevine and wrote the song and pretty soon, whenever I got up to speak, the strikers would all join in for a rousing chorus or two. It was kind of embarrassing.

"Hayward came and stood with us and young Jack Reed organized a workers' pageant at Madison Square Garden to build up a strike fund. But the silk kings had a bigger bankroll and, in the end, the strike was lost. Well, in my case, not entirely. It was in Paterson that I met the love of my life, Carlo Tresca, the Italian anarchist. We lived together for 14 tempestuous years and I became an honorary Italian.

"As a child, whenever Tom Flynn would get a little rowdy at his political meetings and the cops carried him off to the precinct, Mary would send me down to collect him. It seems like all my life, men have been after me to get them out of prison. Big Bill said I had a knack for it. By now, he had taken over the IWW General Defense Fund and he sent me back out west to visit class-war prisoners. That was how I came to know and love Joe Hill here.

"Joe was a handsome blue-eyed boy and a heck of an accordion player, too. When they put him before the firing squad he was only thirty-one, the same age as Jesus when they crucified him on the cross. Actually, Joe looked a lot like Jesus if only Jesus had been blonde and Scandinavian. The first time I saw Joe Hill I looked into those baby blue eyes and I said to myself, 'This fellow has to be innocent.'

"For years after that, I saw Joe each night standing by my bed and smiling with his eyes. Says I but Joe, you're ten years dead. 'I never died,' said he.

"You know, I never knew the name of his alibi woman until this afternoon when Joe told us that his secret sweetie was the daughter of the man who ran the Mormon Church. Isn't that something?

"I went out to San Francisco to set up the defense committee for Mooney and Warren Billings and worked with Lucy Parsons there. They had been framed by the owners of the municipal railroad for the Preparedness Day bombing. Both were fine union organizers and they were trying to sign up the streetcar workers—their pictures hung in every car barn. The persecution of Mooney and Billings was the first sign of how the government was going to use war hysteria to bust radical labor.

"Now, there was no question that the IWW was against going into Wilson's bloody imperialist war. But there was a group of fellow workers who argued we shouldn't be risking our neck getting involved with the antiwar crowd. Emma Goldman and others were against America, they said. There was a big debate about it and Big Bill put it out there that we were fighting a bigger war, the class war, and we shouldn't be losing sight of that. So, in the end, we left signing up to the individual members. But that didn't stop the government from using the war to break up the One Big Union.

"By 1917, the IWW was at the height of its organizing powers. We had 50,000 lumberjacks on the bricks out in the woods of the Pacific Northwest and another 20,000 Mexican copper miners lined up to strike in Arizona. The Wilson government saw that we had all these workers in vital industries organized to resist Capitalist exploitation and branded us as unpatriotic and subversive because we wouldn't order our members to run right out and register to fight the Germans. The Ku Klux Klan and the American Legion led lynch mobs against our local halls.

"They dragged Frank Little out of the Butte office in August of that year and made him kiss the flag and when he refused, they tied a rope around his neck and threw him from the nearest railroad trestle. Three times they flung him down and hauled him up and then they left him there dangling and dead in the Montana wind with the numbers 7-3-77 written on his undershorts, the dimensions of a grave in the state of Montana. 7-3-77. It became the mine owners' motto.

"Now, Frank Little was more American than his lynchers. He was an American Indian. Nearly 200 boys had been burned up in a mine fire that year and Frank's Indian blood was boiling. He declared that we would defeat the Capitalist class by any means necessary and the copper bosses heard that and put a price on his head.

"Barely two months after Frank was lynched, with the nation at war, the attorney general issued warrants for the arrest of 168 fellow workers who allegedly had conspired with one Frank Little (now deceased) to 'hinder and delay execution of certain United States laws.' In other words, they were rousted for conspiring with a dead man.

"The Radical Division of the Department of Justice, where J. Edgar Hoover was a rookie agent, broke down the doors of our Chicago headquarters and dragged Big Bill off to jail. This was the beginning of the great repression. Over the objections of the rank and file, Hayward had concentrated the membership lists and the finances in the Chicago office and the government walked off with everything, even poor Joe's ashes.

"If convicted, Big Bill faced 20 years in Fort Leavenworth, Kansas on sedition charges. He was no longer a young man and it was probably with this in mind that he issued a general call from Cook County Jail for all of the 168 fellow workers listed in the indictment to surrender to the government. It was the biggest mistake Bill Haywood ever made—if it was a mistake. We just couldn't understand why he would want to make it so easy for the Justice Department like that, and it got around that Big Bill had gone over to the other side.

"I joined the Wobblies at the tender age of 16 and I was a tough old bird of 30 when Attorney General Mitchell Palmer put us out of business. I saw a lot of bad stuff happen during that time and it didn't all come from the bosses and the government. To tell you the truth, the IWW was an unruly bunch. The Wobblies couldn't agree on anything and they were always acting out, as if they had some sort of infantile disorder. The IWW needed a Lenin or a Stalin to keep the rank and file in line.

"I had heard the word 'Bolshevik.' I didn't really know what it meant but I wanted to be one anyway. In September, 1919, the Communist Party—actually two communist parties—was officially formed. I went to the convention of the Communist Labor Party with Jack Reed and William Z. Foster, who were delegates—Bill Foster had just organized the most significant steel strike in the nation's history. I didn't join right away. I was a fellow traveler for many years but never actually had a party card until the 1930s, after my breakdown.

"Big Bill got sprung from Leavenworth on a $20,000 appeal bond posted by Miss Mary Marcy, who ran the office at Charles Kerr, the radical publishers. I suppose he was worried sick about being sent back to Kansas if his appeal turned out badly so he jumped bail and ran off to Russia with Foster and Mother Ella Bloor on a labor delegation, and he never came back. Sure, Big Bill was sick with ulcers and diabetes and didn't want to die in jail, but Mary Marcy lost her home and she later committed suicide.

"Big Bill was a gentle giant but he had feet of clay and they broke his will on the wheel of Capitalism.

"It was Carlo who got me mixed up with the Italian anarchists and so I came to know Nicola Sacco and Bartolome Vanzetti like my own brothers. They were part of a group in the Boston area and Carlo helped them with their newspaper. They had both fled to Mexico in 1917 so that they wouldn't be conscripted into an imperialist war. When they returned to Boston, Mitchell Palmer was deporting foreign radicals by the boatload and they were often harassed by the red squad.

"Then, in 1920, an anarchist named Andrea Salsadeo either jumped or was pushed from the fifth floor of an office building at 15 Park Row in Manhattan where he was being 'questioned' by Hoover's boys. Bartolome's comrades sent him to New York to find out the true facts of Salsadeo's death—I know the date because I cooked dinner for him and Carlo that night—linguini and pesto and clams. I had become a regular Italian housewife by then.

"The next day, Bartolome left for Boston and I had a bad feeling that something wasn't right. Then he and Nicola were arrested on a streetcar and accused of a payroll robbery at the White Shoe Company, where Sacco had once worked. A guard had been killed in the commission of this robbery so it was a death-penalty crime. The only description of the holdup men was that they were 'foreigners with mustaches.' One eye-witness testified that she knew they were foreigners because their faces 'looked blue, the way foreigners do after they shave.'

"On this kind of testimony, they convicted Nicola Sacco and Bartolome Vanzetti of murder. My brothers were tried twice—the real gunman, a tough Portuguee from the Moreli gang down in Providence came forward and said he was the guilty party and that he had shot the guard at the White Shoe Company. But it made no difference. Justice was deaf.

"I worked to save the lives of Sacco and Vanzetti night and day for seven years. When the State of Massachusetts executed them before dawn on November 3rd, 1927, something snapped and I went bats. Bats! Do you hear me? Bats!"

• • •

The Testimony of Nicola Sacco and Bartolome Vanzetti

"Buen giorno, my name is Nicola Sacco and this is my accomplice Bartolome Vanzetti. We are not really bats. We just look like that. These are our souls flapping around. We don't really live here. We're buried back east but we fly out here to Waldheim at least twice a year to visit with Elizabetta and fill up on the memory of her pesto and clams. Although she was raised on Irish potatoes, Elizabetta is a secret Italiana.

"I was just an honest shoemaker but I had this Big Idea. The Big Idea was that man could be free. No police, no government, no boss, no god, no authority. Just free. I was ready to die for my Big Idea but not to kill for it. The Big Idea meant that you could do no violence. I taught my children this. I taught them that no matter how cruelly they hit you, you must not hit them back because it only made you just like them.

"I was a shoemaker and I learned that life is a little like a good shoe. If it fits, keep it and wear it in good health but it may need a little mending from time to time."

"I'm Vanzetti. I was a lonely man who went my own way. A poor fish peddler who never married. I lived in Plymouth, Massachusetts where the Pilgrims settled America but I never felt to be a part of this country. In Plymouth, every family knew me for my fish wagon.

"On the day of the robbery at the White Shoe Company, I was selling eels in the streets of Plymouth. Here is the receipt that shows how much I paid for the eels. See, it says 'one barrel of live eels delivered to Bartolome Vanzetti.' Now, eels are a delicacy for us Italians. Would I be out robbing a shoe company if I had eels to sell? For an Italian, this is a crazy idea.

"I showed this receipt to the court—it was my Exhibit A—and they would not believe me. I was executed merely because I was a foreigner with a taste for eels and an anarchist. For no other reason. Where there is no justice, there is no peace. Only a hunger for revenge."

The Testimony of Big Bill Hayward

Howdy, my fellow workers. My name is Bill Hayward, 'Big Bill Hayward' they liked to call me, the Gentle Giant With Feet of Clay, and I just want to say that from the bottom of my big heart, I apologize. I'm speaking out today because I want to make amends for the pain and suffering my weaknesses have caused the working class. I'm truly sorry.

"Well, if it helps I'm not so much Big Bill nowadays. 'Barely Bill' would be closer to the mark. I'm just a shadow of my formerly paunchy self, crunched down to a single shabby cell a-blowin' in the wind.

"I was a western man. Ma and Pa came out there in a Conastoga wagon to strike it rich and live free. They died young and dirt-poor and left me to find my way as an orphan.

"I growed up around mines and railroad towns out there on the alkaline flats of Utah and Nevada. When I was just a lad, I learned about being a powder monkey. I'd go down in the hole and load up the charges, and hightail it out of there as fast I could. I loved the thrill of the explosions.

"I was just breaking in as a hard-rock miner up in Colorado when the Haymarket came along. I cheered for Lingg and those Schnaubelt boys and all their comrades in the dynamite business.

I wanted to be like them. But after I blew out my left eye on a sabotage job up in Leadville, I began to have second thoughts about it. I apologize for those second thoughts. The only way the ruling class ever sits up and takes notice is when the workers use force and violence.

"Wherever the dynamite went off, they went looking for Big Bill Hayward. They tried to hang me in Coere d'Alene for blasting Governor Steunenberg to kingdom come—lord knows he deserved it. They brought in that Pinkerton scum McParland who had hung the Molly McGuires back east in Pennsylvania but they couldn't get a conviction. A stoolie name of Harry Orchid finally took the fall. Clarence Darrow came out from Chicago and dazzled the courtroom in my defense and they had to set me free. Can't say the same for my co-defendants George Rathbone and Charles Meyer, who did 20 years of hard time. I'm really sorry about that, boys.

"There were details in the Idaho case that never could be known. Many years after I was acquitted, a young feller came from New York and tried to get to the bottom of all of it. He wrote a pretty good book, *Big Trouble*—I recommend it. But there were things about this case he couldn't find out for sure. The court records won't tell you the whole story. There is a lot of fiction in history. I guess that young feller thought he got it wrong and he upped and killed himself over it. I'm awfully sorry about that too. For making it all so complicated.

"I made plenty of mistakes when I ran the IWW. I trusted the wrong people and then I didn't trust anyone at all. The rank and file were right to question my decisions. I feared the organization was too dispersed and tried to run it all from Chicago but there was just too much to attend to. We just didn't have the muscle to be fighting the class war in Bisbee, Arizona and Spokane, Washington at the same time. We could never organize Jewish workers and we had precious few colored people in the One Big Union. Women thought we were roughnecks. We smoked too many cigars and got to be more like a men's club. I apologize for making a mess of the revolution. I should have listened more and run my mouth less.

"I was personally against Wilson's 'war to end all wars.' That was just bad gas. The 'war to make the world safe for democracy' was a war to make the world safe for the bosses—it was a war against the working class. But I didn't want the Wobblies to be slammed for being unpatriotic. We were Americans, after all.

"They came after us anyway—right on the very day Wilson declared war on the Krauts. They said we had violated the Sedition Act for knocking the government. We were criminal syndicalists. We took money from the Kaiser.

"So now they had me in Cook County Jail and Judge Kennesaw Mountain Landis, the same gent who became commissar of baseball, the American pastime, said he was going to send me to Leavenworth for 20 years if I didn't tell my boys to give themselves up. Yup, I can't deny I issued a call for the comrades who weren't already in jail to come on in. The federal men promised me they'd go easy on them. The war was nearly over by then—it was just a matter of months— and the G men told me everyone would be released when it was. I figured that we would still have the IWW to go home to. That was the biggest mistake I ever made, trusting the government boys. Some of my feller prisoners were still doing time long after I was dead and gone.

"I apologize for my poor judgment. I bear the burden of blame for destroying the lives of many fellow workers. But I know it won't make up for what they went through in prison.

"I got sent to Fort Leavenworth out there in Kansas. There were a lot of anarchists and anti-conscription protesters there. I got to know Ricardo Flores Magon who was thrown in prison for violating the Neutrality Act when he tried to take back his own country during the revolution there. The jailhouse dirt was that the guards strangled him in 1924 for having a Mexican flag in his cell.

"In April of '18, I finally raised bail pending a new appeal. Sister Mary Marcy from the Charles Kerr publishing house put up her home. I went back to Chicago and tried to get the General Defense Fund back on its legs. I figured that with Armistice Day just up ahead, pretty soon we'd be back in business. But, as usual, I was wrong.

"On Armistice Day, November 11th, out there in Centralia, Washington where the Wobblies had just won a big strike in the woods, a mob pulled our organizer Wesley Everett out of the hall. Wesley was a decorated war hero but it mattered not to those so-called 'patriots' and they castrated him and stuffed Wesley's sex organs into his mouth. After that, I saw there was no salvation and that it would be my fate to lose my appeal and die in prison. I apologize for losing my nerve and falling victim to despair.

"The attorney general sent Hoover and the Radical Division to close us down for good just after midnight on the first day of 1920. There was a federal dragnet out and 8,000 Wobblies and reds were caught up in it. They culled out all the foreigners and deported them back to where they came from. The bigshots like Goldman and Berkman departed for Red Russia first class but most of the comrades were sent steerage.

"I was convinced that the IWW was a sinking ship and I started to get chummy with the Communists. I went to the party's founding convention and liked what I heard. They invited me to see the Russian Revolution for myself and so I went over there and never returned. I know it looked bad after I had gotten all the boys to surrender, what with them still being in jail and here I was running away to Russia. I left poor Mary Marcy holding the bag and she took her own life. I didn't know she was in that bad a way. I really didn't. I apologize. But that's not going to bring her back.

"I went to Russia and became their 'yes man.' We arrived in Red Square on May 1st and they put us right up there on the big grandstand with the Great Lenin. Phalanxes of workers marched beneath us, an endless sea of proletarians, and I asked the Great Lenin if it was true that the workers really did control the means of production, and he responded, 'Comrade Big Bill, that is Communism.'

"Well, I thought I'd died and gone up to workers' paradise but I hadn't and I wasn't. Some of the workers had it good, or at least better than the rest, and others didn't even have a crust of bread. It all depended on where you were situated within the Party. I couldn't say these things out loud of course—there were spies everywhere. I saw what Trotsky had done to the Kronstadt boys and I have to say now, it was as bad as anything Rockefeller did to the miners and their families at Ludlow. But I kept my lip buttoned and I'm sorry for not speaking up. I really mean it.

"They put me up in a big hotel room in Moscow and made me a Peoples' Hero. I got a medal and a bust of the Great Lenin. Emma Goldman said I was a debutante and that really stung. I was given a stipend by the Soviet Communist Party, which I gladly joined. I planned to organize the masses back in the United States but I was too far away, and besides, no one trusted me anymore after Mary Marcy cashed it in.

"The American newspapers printed that I was despondent and disillusioned and tried to escape over the steppes into Turkey. That was pure horseshit. Truth was I didn't ever leave my hotel room anymore. I had found out about Russian vodka. I had been a rye whiskey man until I gave up the sauce for the revolution. But Moscow was freezing and the vodka kept a fire burning in my big belly. Besides I had terminal sugar diabetes and figured two quarts a day of that poison would finish me off a lot quicker. The most important part was that I died in bed, a nice feather bed. I apologize about that feather bed. It was too soft for a worker.

"They put half my ashes in the Kremlin Wall with John Reed and the other Peoples' Heroes. Reed wouldn't stop yapping about being 'caught in a trap.' We were all sort of caught in a trap.

"The rest of me they sent back here to Forest Home where I belonged in the first place. I'm sorry for taking so long to get here."

Testimony of Emma Goldman—Her Disillusionment with Red Russia

"The country was mad with war fever and our every waking breath was spent trying to stop Wilson from taking us into the conflagration overseas. After Ben Reitman M.D. betrayed us, the Justice Department charged Sasha and I with conspiring to keep young men from going to war and we were handed two-year sentences each, the maximum penalty at the time. That was June 27th, 1917, my 48th birthday. My friends brought a cake, a chocolate fudge cake, my favorite, but it didn't have a file baked into it.

"I was sent to the Jefferson City, Missouri Women's Reformatory, far from civilization as I knew it, and Sasha went to the federal penitentiary in Atlanta with Debs.

"Unlike native-born antiwar activists, we were ordered to be deported upon the completion of our sentences. Sasha had never become a U.S. citizen—he didn't see any use in it. Although I was now an American, I was resolved to accompany him into exile. Our lives in America had been busy and exciting but we were disappointed that so few Americans had the spunk to stand up to the tyranny of Capitalism. That was the sad truth.

"Now we were embarking on a new adventure! The Russian Revolution blazed in the East and we were on our way to join up.

'Is this the end of the line for Emma Goldman?' an impertinent New York reporter asked me as I mounted the gangplank. 'No, sonny,' I replied quite firmly, 'this is only the beginning!'

"They held us for deportation at Ellis Island, a cruel joke. Our fathers and mothers had first landed at this pestilent immigration station in New York Harbor to escape the Tzars and their Cossacks, the pogroms and the famine, and now America was booting us out through this same door. We had come to build up America and now we were ordered to vacate the premises. I felt bitter and joyous at the same time to be sailing off to a new life.

"The date of our departure was December 21st, 1919, and it was so cold that the few tears I could manage froze to my face. We went up on deck and I discreetly raised my middle finger to the two-faced Miss Liberty as we slid by.

"The *Buford* had been leased by the Justice Department to take the hated Reds away from America. There were 249 hard-core radicals aboard and troops had been posted to keep us in line—but we were too seasick to revolt. The crewmen came to us and complained of low pay and lousy working conditions. They said they wanted to mutiny and would we join them. I was so sick I just spit up all over the young man's shoes. . . .

"Yes? What's all the fuss over there?"

The Testimony of Voltairine de Clyves (aborted)

"My name is Voltairine de Clyves. I was a free anarchist woman. No man ruled me. My life was destroyed by two bullets. . . ."

"Not yet, dear Voltairine. I'm about to tell this young man of my disillusionment with the Russian Revolution. . . ."

"But you said later and it's nearly my bedtime."

"Oh, let her speak, you old filthmonger! You've already told your story a thousand times and everyone here is sick to death of hearing it yet again."

"Don't you start in now, you crazy mulatto. Mind you, I've got nothing against colored people—if you really are a colored woman. But I hate hypocrites and you're a hypocrite, Lucy Parsons. You locked up your son in an insane asylum because, you told the judge, he was your 'personal property.' We anarchists don't believe in private property in case you haven't heard."

"My name is Voltairine de Clyves. I was a free anarchist woman. No man ruled me. My life was destroyed by two bullets. . . ."

"Girls! Girls! This is Irving Abrams, your host and your friend, and, as the last member of the Pioneer Aid & Support Society, your sponsor here, I've asked myself to chair this session. Emma, you have the floor, and Voltairine, you're on deck. Fellow worker Goldman, take it away!"

Testimony of Emma Goldman—Her Disillusionment with Red Russia (cont.)

"Much obliged, Irving. You're the last gentleman left in Waldheim.

"The *Buford* dumped us ashore in Finland and we had to trek the frozen tundra without galoshes. The moment that we crossed over onto Russian soil, I threw myself upon the snowy ground and kissed it passionately. At last I had returned to the bosom of Mother Russia! My *matushka!* My sacred land and magic people! Now I had come to serve her and her radiant dream of equality for all men and women, in which the workers would partake of the fruits of their labors and a thousand flavors of intellectual freedom would flourish and ferment. I was so overjoyed, I had an orgasm right there in the snow!

"We wanted to go at once to see our dear friend Peter Kropotkin who lived near Moscow, but we were taken to St. Petersburg instead with the other deportees, a dreary lot really, from whom we soon detached ourselves.

"Sasha and I went immediately to the Cheka for permission to travel but we were denied the necessary papers on the pretext that our safety would be endangered. Did we not know that Russia was at war? There was no time now to accommodate revolutionary tourists! We went back many times to renew our applications. We applied to visit the factories in the region to see if it was true that the workers controlled the means of production but this too was not permitted.

"The weeks passed into months and still our travel plans were in limbo. Mostly, we stayed in our shabby rooms at the hotel and huddled around the samovar for warmth. The food in the restaurant was an insult to responsible nutrition—cabbage after cabbage and maggots crawled from every potato. We discovered that there were 34 classes of rations in the Soviet Union—Party officials received monthly allotments of caviar but the workers had to boil their belts to survive. I made friends with a local aparatchik and gave him cigarettes. He promised to bring me lamb chops. I am such a fool for lamb chops! But of course, the lamb chops never appeared.

"When we met with our fellow anarchists, it was always in secret places, and they spoke in hushed tones because the walls reported back to the Cheka. Every day, they whispered, their numbers were fewer. Their comrades were being sucked up into the dungeons of the State and they themselves soon vanished into the underground. We received a note from their valiant general, Makhno. He had declared war against Lenin and Trotsky and invited us to join forces with him. But we did not yet understand the anarchists' desperation.

"Yet we knew that something was terribly wrong. That the revolution was being poisoned from within. I was determined to warn Comrade Lenin before it was too late. I was still naive enough to believe he did not know what went on outside the Kremlin walls.

"My petition for an interview with the Great Lenin went unanswered for many months. Then, one morning, a limousine was sent to my hotel—Sasha was still in St. Petersburg. I was driven deep inside the walled city of the Kremlin. I followed my silent guides through many winding corridors and was finally seated in a dim alcove and told to wait. The clock ticked and chimed many times. It crossed my mind that I had foolishly flung myself into the jaws of the Cheka and would soon join my anarchist comrades in the dungeons. But at last my guides returned and escorted me to a set of imposing brass doors at the deepest point of the labyrinth, and when the doors swung open, there he was, the Great Lenin, a small, intense man in a deep blue tunic, his goatee bristling, beckoning me to enter.

"Upon first impression, he seemed to be dwarfed by his great desk but as I drew closer, I could feel his brilliance radiating upon my naked skin. A map of the world lined one entire wall of the room, and Comrade Lenin seemed to be seated at its control panels. I took my place in a small chair at his feet, trembling all over. I felt as if I had never been so close to such sheer power before. I tried to speak. 'Comrade Lenin,' I tried to say, 'the anarchists are rotting in your prisons'—but the words froze in my throat.

"Nonetheless, Lenin, whose telepathic genius was legendary, read my mind right away. 'Tovarisch Goldman,' he said, 'the anarchists suffer from an infantile disorder and we have no time for their counter-revolutionary flapdoodle now with the White Wolves at the gates of Moscow.'

"'Do not allow yourself to become a sentimental *burhooy*,' he warned me, 'revolutions are forged in steel and we do not flinch at our task, Yes, we will sometimes seem harsh and unrelenting. But you must trust that our ends are glorious and they always justify our means. Da, you hear me correctly, Comrade Goldman! Our ends always justify our means! Do you believe?"

My head nodded yes but my heart did not agree and Lenin had read the doubt there.

"'You may go now.' And I was dismissed.

"From that exact moment, I knew that I was a marked woman and my days in the Soviet Union were numbered.

"We were finally permitted to visit Kropotkin. He lived in Dmitrov, about a half day's journey from Moscow. We found him frolicking naked in his garden. He was still a stallion of a man. Lenin had tried to make him into a museum piece but Peter had resisted. Yet he had no doubt that when he died, the government would have him taxidermied and set out in front of his charming cottage, for the tourists to admire.

"'The State is inherently evil,' Peter Kropotkin posited, 'it commits unspeakable crimes to justify its existence and crushes all dissent.' We ate fresh dandelion greens from his garden and the old man gleefully disparaged the size of Lenin and Trotsky's penises for hours on end.

"Of course, Peter was not allowed to make such jokes much longer. Within months, he was dead of a 'ruptured spleen.' Sasha was asked to organize the funeral and all the arrangements had to be done in secret. After the ceremony, Kropotkin's cadaver was hijacked from the cemetery by the Cheka and never reappeared again.

"There was no way to escape the Party apparatus. It controlled every nuance of our lives, from every sheet of toilet paper to our freedom to write what was on our minds. Its dogma encrusted every surface and felt slimy and cold. You could see its rheum in every eyeball and every tongue repeated its venom. I dreamed that I was drowning in dogma and I cried out in my sleep to Sasha to save me. But he was still a believer.

"Kronstadt was the final blow to Sasha's faith. The beautiful boys of the Baltic fleet, the heroes of Red Oktober, could no longer abide the betrayal of their revolution. When Trotsky crushed the workers during the general strike for bread and coal in St. Petersburg, the sailors rose and Lev Davidovich condemned them as 'tzarist terrorists' and signed their extermination orders. The Great Trotsky had grown fat and arrogant and in no way resembled the humble intellectual I had once sipped tea with in the Bronx so many years before. For Trotsky, like Lenin, the ends justified the means and he had become a cold-blooded butcher of his own people. I can say that here without fear of rebuttal. There are no Trotskyists buried in our cemetery.

"The destruction of Kronstadt lit up the sky for leagues around. You could see the fires burning red as blood in the night. The beautiful blonde sailor boys were paraded through St. Petersburg in chains and shipped off to Siberia to die. After Kronstadt, I could no longer remain silent. Silence had become an act of criminal complicity. Now 'The International' was a funeral dirge to me, and the Hammer & Sickle the revolution's shroud. Escape became my burning obsession and at last Sasha agreed. We would leave at once for Europe and write our books denouncing what we had endured in Russia.

"By 1921, Moscow had become a sort of Lourdes for sycophant socialists. We saw Hayward there and found out that poor Mary Marcy had taken her life when he jumped bail. 'It was a yellow trick!' Sasha shouted at him. 'You sold out the IWW and now you've been promoted to do your dirty business for the Kremlin!' Big Bill turned his back on us and just shambled off. He was already a broken man and we never saw him again.

"We ran into William Z. Foster there. He was traveling with Mother Ella Bloor and Earl Browder—they were still great pals back then. They were all blinded by the Great Lenin's magic act and ignored us as if we were lepers when they heard that we were on the outs with the Party. Many people here in this cemetery have treated me similarly.

"Being thrown out of the Soviet Union was less dramatic than our deportations from America. We were actually allowed to leave to attend an anarchist congress in Berlin but ordered never to return.

"It was December again, two years since we had first set sail for the Soviet Union with such extravagant hopes, and the snow covered the ground again. But now I knew what hideous sores lay underneath. Our dreams had been crushed flat by the machine of the State and our hearts sat like stones in our breasts. Nonetheless, *My Disillusionment with Russia* would soon be a runaway bestseller in America and Sasha's book, which was a bit more theoretical, would receive excellent critical reviews.

"Who would you like to see play me in the movie? Too bad Winona Ryder got pinched. What do you think about Courtney Love as the young Emma and Streisand as the more mature version?"

"What do you say to Bela Lugosi, you fraudulent two-bit vampire of the American Left! You drained the lifeblood of the glorious Russian Revolution and sold it by the column inch to the New York tabloids! You blasphemed the Great Lenin and the Great Stalin! You went around Russia bribing workers with Pall Malls to tell you malicious lies about Communism. You became a reactionary tool, a Capitalist running-dog lackey, and a low-down stool pigeon. I have conclusive evidence that you were on the U.S. Secret Service payroll!

"Who am I to make such accusations? I am William Z. Foster, one of the great American Communists of all time, and I demand a show trial for this traitor to the working men and women of the world. Can I get a second on this motion?"

"Fellow worker Ben Reitman M.D. right here and I'm with you on this one, Brother Foster."

"Now Irving?"

"Break a leg, sister. . . ."

Testimony of Voltairine de Clyves (finally)

"My name is Voltairine de Clyves. I was a free anarchist woman. No man ruled me. My life was destroyed by two bullets. But that came later.

"I marched with Albert and Lucy Parsons for the eight-hour day. But I had to break with them after the bomb blew up at the Haymarket. I could not accept violence. The Schnaubelts were police spies.

"During the riots following McKinley's assassination, I was beaten severely around the head and was never quite the same after that.

"I offered myself up to be shot by any bigot who wanted to kill an anarchist—but on the condition that I would get to explain anarchism first.

"Emma Goldman says I was her friend and lover but she really only wanted to list my name in the index of her two-volume autobiography. Emma is a conniving name-dropper and I was opposed to having her brought here in the first place. I voted against it at the time.

"I suffered from paralyzing headaches all my life. They were particularly excruciating after meetings. I would have to take morphine and retire to my bed for days. I really hated those meetings.

"Then one of my students, a Jewish boy, shot me twice in the head. He was in love with me and only wanted to ease my suffering.

"Although I was a lifelong pacifist, I believed in the Mexican revolution and supported the Flores Magon brothers with my time and my money. I always dreamed of traveling to Mexico to shake hands with the famous Zapata but my headaches kept getting worse and worse. I believe I finally died of an abscess of the brain but I've lost all the paperwork. I have to take a nap now. Thank you and goodnight."

Testimony of William Z. Foster

"My name is William Z. Foster and I'm a recovering Communist. I admit that I had no power over Communist dogma and followed it slavishly into addiction and abjection.

"My tragic flaw was that I had no sense of humor. As a boy, no one in my family ever laughed so I grew up without hearing laughter and did not even know what kind of sound to make for it. When I found myself in a social situation where I was called upon to laugh, I invented a horrible chortle that made my comrades nervous. I soon learned that it was best not to have a sense of humor for the good of the revolution.

"I was an original member of the Communist Party USA. The date of our founding convention was August 31st, 1919, and the place was Blue Island Avenue, the Pilsen District of industrial Chicago. I had been an IWW organizer but that was unraveling fast and I needed a new dogma desperately to hang on to. I was addicted to dogma.

"I came to the Communists from Big Steel, the red-hot heart of the U.S. working class. In 1919, we shut the steel mills down and the furnaces went cold for six long months. Two-hundred-thousand workers hit the bricks to win union recognition. We didn't succeed that time but a couple of years later, we had a collective bargaining agreement for the industry, the first in the land.

"Steel was a real American strike—bohunks and polacks, micks, squareheads, limeys, dutchmen, poor white trash and blacks. Fanny Mooney Sellins was a Hillbilly lady from Natroma,

Pennsylvania. She went up against Alleghany Steel and the deputies shot her down in the street. In her dying breath, she gasped in my ear the immortal words of Solidarity Forever: 'When the union's inspiration through the workers' blood shall run, there can be no greater power anywhere beneath the sun. . . .'

"As Fanny lay dying, her killer picked up her hat and put it on his head, dancing around and squealing to mock her, 'I am Fanny Mooney Sellins.' Fanny's neighbors got agitated about that and tore the hat from his head and his head from his body and nailed up the bloody torso by the roadside. That was how I came to know and fear the terrible fury that stews in the heart of the American working class.

"I saw the great power in steel and saw that we needed a party that was as unflinching as steel, a party steeled to resist the class enemy, a vanguard party that would channel the revolutionary fury of the people and establish the Dictatorship of the Proletariat once and for all. I felt called upon to personally lead such a party.

"Our party had many names—the Communist Party, the Communist Labor Party—the two fused underground in 1921 and sometimes emerged in part or as a whole in the Workers Party, the Proletarian Party, the Women's Party, the Farmers Party, the Labor Party, the Farmer-Labor Party, the Progressives. We absorbed the left wing of the Socialist and the Socialist Labor parties. Our splits were the stuff of legend and winnowed the wheat from the chaff. The government simplified our task by deporting all the foreign-born reds. 8,000 comrades were rounded up during the Palmer raids and we were reduced to a hard core. We became a fist.

"We drew our logic and our fire from the example of the Soviet Union. I made many trips there myself in the 1920s, which is where I had the misfortune to bump into Goldman and Berkman. The two of them suffered from an infantile disorder. Emma Goldman always treated the revolution as if it were a sort of vaudeville.

"I was an important Communist and a delegate to the Comintern. I met the Great Lenin on many occasions and shared privileged information with him that I am still not at liberty to disclose. I attended his funeral in the troubled winter of 1924 and visited with his embalmed remains in his Kremlin crypt for many years thereafter.

"Upon the Great Lenin's death, I accepted the Great Stalin into my heart. Stalin! His name of steel rang out all across Mother Russia! Stalin! The most brilliant brain of Marxism-Leninism-Stalinism!

"Our most pressing mission was the defense of Communism, at least in that one country where it first took flight—the Glorious Soviet Union! Leon Trotsky was a scab and a rank opportunist. His call for world revolution would have sacrificed the Soviet Revolution upon the altar of the International Capitalist Conspiracy. We here in the CP-USA diligently weeded out the Trotskyist pollutants. The Cannonites were sent packing and the Schachmanites expelled. I personally purged that professional intriguist Lovestone, a notorious Thermadorian Bakuninist.

"I sometimes wonder where it is that Trotskyists go to die. Perhaps to Mexico City where we Stalinists finally nailed their idol. As you can see, no Trots are buried here and none ever will be. At least none that admit to that affliction.

"The 1920s were a saturnalia of Capitalist excess. Wall Street gorged at the banquet table the workers set for it and power was concentrated in fewer and fewer hands. The presidents who administered this orgy of greed were hopelessly corrupt. Warren Harding committed suicide as soon as the slime of Teapot Dome slithered out. Calvin Coolidge was a Yanqui skinflint and colonialist bozo whose gunboat diplomacy kept our Latin brothers under the Imperialist thumb. Meanwhile, Mooney and Billings, Sacco and Vanzetti, lived and died in a

Capitalist hell. While the flappers were frivolously flailing their fannies in gay speakeasies, our Negro comrades were swinging from every other tree in the Jim Crow South and the hunger marchers were being bayoneted by the fascist generals McArthur and Eisenhower on the Capitol mall.

"And then the bubble burst. On Black Tuesday, October 29th, 1929, Hoover's chicken-in-every-pot came home to roost and the facade of Capitalist America crumbled into dung. Almost six thousand banks shut their doors in a single day, taking with them the life savings of millions of hard-working citizens. Seventeen million unemployed workers trudged the dark streets of our cities and battled with clubs and broken bottles over scraps from the garbage heap. The banks foreclosed on the farmers and the land dried up and blew away. Capitalism had failed!

"The comrades broke out the champagne to celebrate its demise. The breadlines and apple stands stoked our thirst to overthrow the ruling class with Scientific Socialism. Worse was better! The Great Depression presented the CP-USA with a once-in-a-lifetime opportunity to prove that our theories had been right all along.

"First, we needed to have followers, many followers, so we created front groups, many front groups, so many front groups that there were not enough combinations of letters in the alphabet to name them all. The masses joined by the carload, some as card-carrying Communists and others as fellow travelers. We took over the Works Progress Administration and brought Socialist Realism to the walls of American post offices, insidiously spreading the message of Communism in the subtle backgrounds of our murals.

"We infiltrated every significant social institution in the nation, from the National Association for the Advancement of Colored People to the American Federation of Labor, and fought for our program: the greatest good for the greatest number! The Congress of Industrial Organizations, founded in defiance of the labor aristocracy, sprung from our loins and grew by 4,000,000 members from 1936 to 1940.

"We organized sitdown strikes in the cotton fields of California's Imperial Valley, built the Alabama Steelworkers and Sharecroppers Union, rallied the Workers and Peasants of Flatbush in Brooklyn. Nick Bordois, a Communist, was gunned down in the streets of San Francisco and his killing sparked a general strike that shut that port city down tighter than a drum in the summer of '34. Harry Bridges, the firebrand Aussie seaman who led the strike, joined the Party and brought the rugged longshoremen along with him.

"Communists Wyndam Mortimer and Walter Moore were on the firing line at the Fisher Body plant in Flint, Michigan 1936. To the dismay of Roosevelt and the rest of the tycoon class, the workers seized the means of production and camped out inside the factory for 72 days, shutting down the the most powerful industry in the land from coast to coast. The National Guard was called out and kept the women with the lunch buckets from feeding their men. Grub was running short when General Motors finally caved in to the workers' demands. Communists helped win the first contracts in Big Auto and Big Steel, the engines of the economy. And Communists were gunned down on Memorial Day 1937, the little steel massacre in Youngstown, Ohio. We never miss a massacre.

"We were against the bosses and the fascists, the phony politicians and the labor fakers. We were the first to defend our Negro comrades on the shop floor. We were there for them.

"Our chief nemesis had three names—Franklin Delano Roosevelt. Roosevelt and his New Deal ilk were sucking labor back into the Democratic Party with their "Happy Days Are Here Again" horseflop. We had to stop the hemorrhaging before they all drifted off.

"You could not avoid electoral politics. The workers needed to have a voice and the Communists would be that voice. I took it upon myself to run for president on various occasions. In 1932, at the bottom of the Depression, with revolution just around the corner and Roosevelt blubbering to the National Association of Manufacturers that they either got him or the Communists, I volunteered to run for the presidency and received a grand total of 102,000 votes—never again would a Communist candidate garner such a large percentage of the presidential turnout.

"In the midst of this arduous campaign to put a Red in the White House, I suffered my first heart attack and could no longer continue the crusade. But my running mate, James Ford, the communistic vice-presidential candidate, valiantly carried on in my stead.

"I am proud to say that James Ford, a Negro male and credit to his race, was a great friend of mine, and Esther and I had him often in our house for dinner. The day that the Communist Party nominated the Negro James Ford as my vice president is a day that will live as long as the Emancipation in the history of the Negro people.

"Thereafter, the Communist Party became the Party of the Negro. They even called us the Nigger Party in the South and we were proud to be so designated. Many prominent Negro clergymen supported our cause, among them Father Divine, a charlatan who ministered to the downtrodden, and the Very Reverend Adam Clayton Powell, who held Harlem in the palm of his hand from the pulpit of the Abyssinian Baptist Church.

"Our program was that the Negroes were an oppressed race and needed to have their own nation in the black belt of the South, as outlined in Harry Hayward's *Negro Nation* plan. I agreed with Harry Hayward in principle but the plan troubled me. I never really liked using that word 'black.' I was brought up to say 'Negro' or 'Colored.' It's more respectful.

"Now, we Communists studied the National Question and we were guided by the world's leading experts on the Negro race, the Great Lenin and the Great Stalin.

"The Communist Party USA had great sympathy for the Negro struggle and we stood with the Negro Fig & Date

Workers and the Colored Motion Picture Operators Association when they were oppressed. We demanded the death penalty for all lynch mobs and defended Angelo Herndon, a civil-rights worker, in an Atlanta courtroom in 1936. The Communist Party was the friend of all Negroes female and male. We went to bat for the Scottsboro Boys. . . ."

"One second William Z, but who you calling *boy*?"

The Testimonies of (in order of appearance) William Patterson, Claude Lightfoot, Henry Winston, and Pettis Perry (with a cameo by Mrs. Lucy Parsons)

"Put it there—William Patterson, Mr. Civil Rights, that's what the Party called me. I was the Scottsboro defendants' lawyer for many years and when I knew them they were grown men. The last victim of that racist frameup did not get out of jail until 1950 when he was nearly a senior citizen but the Communist Party always insisted upon calling him a 'Scottsboro boy.'

"I was a civil-rights advocate. Apart from the Scottsboro 9, I defended the Trenton 6, and the Martinsville 7, and did my damnedest to save poor Willie Magee from the Mississippi electric chair. As a young man, I was outraged by the injustice meted out to Sacco and Vanzetti and so I enrolled in law school. I became a crusading civil-rights attorney traveling the south trying to save black men from the hangman's noose. I became obsessed with the lynchings.

"The Communists were campaigning to make lynching a

federal crime subject to the death penalty and that was enough to convince me to take out a Party card. They sent me to classes so that I could find out just what this Marxism-Leninism-Stalinism-Fosterism-Browderism stuff was all about. Mr. Browder assigned me to do Negro work seeing as I was a Negro. That's what they called us back then.

"I was a founder of the National Negro Congress but when the Loyalty Board declared that the Negro people were themselves a Communist front, I had to change the name to the Civil Rights Congress. We demanded equal employment in Harlem stores and an end to segregation and lynching in the Jim Crow South. Paul Robeson did many benefit concerts for us and Canada Lee and Rex Ingram put in special appearances. But the whites just kept on lynching.

"Us Negro Communists invented many front groups—the Harlem Unemployment Council and the United Negro Veterans of America were two of them. Even our front groups had front groups. We needed the front groups to win the Negro people to Communism. The Negro people are brainwashed. They believe a Communist is someone who doesn't go to church on Sunday.

"The Scottsboro case kept me gainfully employed for many years. I toured the U.S.A. with the Scottsboro Moms, holding rallies and raising money for legal fees. We had a weekly quota that we had to meet. I even accompanied the Scottsboro Moms to the Soviet Union, where they had the pleasure of shaking hands with the Great Stalin himself. Sometimes, we didn't have a Mom with us and I found that just about any old colored woman would do. We all looked alike to the ofays anyway. Besides, like I told you, we had a quota to raise—Mr. Browder kept on us about that."

CL: "Lightfoot here. There were Choctaw Indians on my grandfather's side—that's how I came by that name. But we considered ourselves Afro-Americans. My aunt and uncle raised me and they were Garveyites. Black Zionists. They were going to ride the

Black Star Line back to Mother Africa. They could never understand why a black man might want to be a Red.

"The Soviet Union was rumored to be selling oil to Mussolini on the spot market to fuel up his invasion of Ethiopia. To the Garveyites and the African Blood Brotherhood, Ethiopia was the black holy land and Haile Selasie, the black Moses. Black nationalists kept their distance from the Communists. 'Marx was a redneck,' my uncle Arthur would thunder. 'You crazy hanging out with those white folks, boy.'

"But what I saw in the Party was certain white people trying to be the friend of the Negro. That was O.K. with me—we needed a lot of friends. They were nice to us and saved their hand-me-downs for Geraldine and the kids.

"My notion was that I was black first and then red next but the white comrades convinced me it was the other way around. At that time, Harry Hayward put forth the proposal for a Negro Nation in the Black Belt of the South but William Z. Foster vetoed it and argued that, although we black people were especially oppressed, we were still part of the proletariat and couldn't have a separate country. I suppose he was right at least theoretically but Harry Hayward became depressed and left the Party.

"The whites had the idea that we Communist blacks should form a United Front with the so-called black leadership. But black leaders red-baited and shunned us just as the Nationalists had. Roy Wilkins accused Robeson of starting the race riot at Peekskill when it was the other way around and A. Philip Randolph told the sleeping-car porters to kick us off the train. Jesse Owens was a rock-ribbed Republican Red-hater and Jackie Robinson said he didn't need the Communists to break the color bar, even if the Russians had invented baseball.

"Walter White purged all the black Communists from the NAACP—even Dr. Dubois, who claimed to be a Marxist. Dr. Dubois, detested the CP-USA because of the way we had sported around the Scottsboro boys, I mean, men. Dubois was 83 years old when the N-double-A kicked him out the door. The Subversive Activities Control Board ordered him to register as a foreign agent but never specified of what country. We came to his defense and named our youth clubs for him but Dr. Dubois always rejected our solidarity. 'The commies are making a monkey out of you, boy' he would tell me.

"Despite the rejection of our own colored brothers, I refused to give up the dream of a Socialist America. Even when McCarthy singled out the black Communists to witch-hunt and Hoover labeled us 'the hateful spawn of Moscow,' and I was indicted under the Smith Act for advocating the violent overthrow of the government even though I was a mild-mannered man, I remained faithful to the Communist Party USA."

HW: "I too was imprisoned for being a black man and a Communist. I went blind in Lewisburg Federal Penitentiary because of a tumor in my head. Henry Winston they tell me it says on my tombstone. Glad to meet you.

"I was a frontline Smith Act defendant before young Claude here. My co-defendants were Gus Hall and William Z. Foster. But Foster suffered one of his convenient heart attacks and his case was separated from the rest.

"I came to the CP-USA because I believed in Communism and thought it was the only way to save the black race. American blacks just couldn't do it alone. We needed to be part of the working class. I read Marx and Engels and understood the economics of how Capitalism worked. I became the first Negro president of the Young Communists League. I saw the Soviet Union as a model of racial justice. I flew the Hammer & Sickle from my heart.

"After 1936, the Party began to hide its true colors. They took down all the red flags and hoisted up the Stars and Stripes. I protested long and loud but comrades Browder and Foster argued that we were in a United Front Against Fascism now and we had to at least pretend to be Americans.

"I gave my eyes to the Party but the Party never could see me. The real me. The Communist me. The white comrades saw me only as a black man. That was fine with them, the blacker the better. They wouldn't have minded if I were to sweat ink, like Ellison wrote. So long as I didn't say what I was really thinking. To them, the Communist me was an invisible man.

"But then I went blind and the white comrades became invisible to me. Although they made me Party chairman, I never saw them again."

WP: "Between 1885 and 1930, 3256 black men were lynched in America, an average of 73 a year. More than once a week, a black man was hung from a tree or burned alive by white folks. Eighteen more brothers would be lynched during World War II while we were over there fighting for U.S. freedom.

"Wars were bad for lynchings—13 black soldiers were lynched by a white mob in Houston, Texas on September 17th, 1917, a few months after the U.S. entered World War I. The years directly following that war were fat times for the lynchers. The Klan had swollen to 5,000,000 members but the government looked the other way and cracked down on the IWW and the reds instead. From 1919 to 1921, more than 200 black men a year were hung, burned, shot, stabbed, or stomped to death by their white brothers and sisters in America.

"Lynching was the American pastime. A mob would hang up a black man and maybe cut his balls off or set his corpse on fire and then go play baseball and picnic on their front lawns as if it were just natural to brutalize a Negro. Postage stamps were canceled to commemorate memorable lynchings. A lot of this information is in a book I wrote, *We Call It Genocide* by William Patterson.

"We call it genocide! I told that to a congressional witch-hunting committee once and they cited me for contempt. 'What did you say?' this Ku Kluxer from Georgia named Lovelace yapped. 'Genocide' I told him, 'you know, like when you just wipe a whole race of people off the face of the earth. I know it must be a big word for you.'

"'Why, you black son of a bitch!' Lovelace yelled, and tried to punch me in the nose. Of course, I was the one that got hauled out of there for contempt."

CL: "I have a question for Brother Foster that has always troubled me. Why did our black brother Paul Robeson have to sing spirituals at the Party fund-raisers? Spirituals are nothing but bourgeois Christian slave songs. Couldn't he have been of equal use to the Party if he sang opera or scat?

"Paul Robeson was a tragic victim of Left-wing chauvinism. The CP-USA tried to make him into the Noble Negro, rolling his eyes and smacking his big lips while he sang slave songs like 'Ol' Man River' in a voice as deep and muddy as the Mississippi. The Party used Robeson like a red Stepen Fetchett, a Kneegrow jeffing for the white Red folks. It was breaking poor Paul's heart.

"We went to the central committee to protest the stereotyping of Comrade Robeson. We told the commissars that we were sick and tired of being used as bait, that the Party was full of racists who lived in all-white neighbors and belonged to all-white clubs. Party bosses like Mr. Foster here got real defensive and after that, the CP-USA abolished the color black to avoid problems. It wasn't in the Party's color scheme anymore. We were all supposed to be some neutral color now as if there was no such thing as hue and pigment. Meanwhile, outside the Party, the world kept getting darker all the time. Africa rose and the Arabs became oil niggers. 'Even the Chinese Reds were black,' Malcolm said that. But inside the Party, no one seemed to notice."

PP: "Hey, I'm sorry I'm late, boys. My baptism name is Pettis Perry but y'all can call me Pete. I'm older than most of these young men here. I chopped cotton out in California and hoboed around and met all types of people. I was never a prejudiced person. I didn't see black and white. Then one day I was lolling around on a park bench in Pershing Square, downtown L.A., and I received a leaflet about the Scottsboro boys from a nice young white lady. She invited me to a Labor Day picnic and I went and felt right at home.

"My new comrades taught me how to read and write. They were always correcting my diction. They said I could be a true leader of the Negroes but I had to talk correctly. By correctly, they meant that I had to talk like a white person.

"Well, pretty soon I got the picture. It seemed like we blacks were being invited to the meetings so that there would be a proper number of dark faces there. We were sort of like interior decoration. But we weren't supposed to interrupt. After the meeting was done, then we'd be asked to entertain. You know, dance around like we were all Bojangles or something. I refused to go along with the game and the white comrades criticized me for being resentful. I was acting like a black man they said. Communists only have one color—red.

"They held a show trial and I was forced to rectify. By then, I'd been around so long that the Communists were my only friends so I went along with the program and mastered Marxism-Leninism-Stalinism-Fosterism-Browderism and went to prison for two-and-a-half years to show them how well I'd learned my lesson."

LP: "Excuse me, gentlemen. I apologize for interrupting your conversation. It's all very edifying. My name is Mrs. Lucy Parsons and I just want to say that the Communists used me too and I wasn't even a black woman. They got me up on their stage and I spoke out in defense of the Scottsboro case. I was only too happy to do it—I wanted to help out. But I never did know where the money was going. I always felt like the Communists were using me and, as I explained, I'm not even a member of the Negro race."

WP: "While the lynching was underway, vendors would work the crowds, selling hushpuppies and soda pop. When it was all done, the mob would take home an ear or a knuckle or a tooth or maybe a shoe if it was in good condition, as a souvenir. Black men got lynched for not taking off their hat to Mr. Charlie or not stepping off the sidewalk for Mrs. Murphy. Black men got lynched for telling the boss what for and they got lynched for not being out of town by sunset. But mostly they got lynched because of white women.

"The sexual powers of black men drove the whites crazy and diminished their manhood. So they hung and castrated us by the thousands. A 14-year-old white-trash girl named Ruby Bates accused the Scottsboro men of raping her in a boxcar while traveling through Alabama and no one ever questioned her story until I started poking around.

"After going overseas to save the world from Hitler, Issac Woodward came home to South Carolina and a lynch mob gouged out his eyes for looking at a white woman. Young Emmet Till got shot in the head, trussed up with barbed wire, and thrown in the Tallahatchee River. All that for supposed to have wolf-whistled a white lady in a grocery store. Emmet Till was a stutterer and to stop stuttering he sometimes whistled. That was why they murdered him. Emmet Till was but 14 years old when they lynched him. We call that genocide.

"I wrote that book and Robeson read it and told me that when he visited Dachau, all he could see were the bones of black people. Together we took the book to the United Nations and Mrs. Eleanor Roosevelt accused us Communists of 'ignoring the progress black people were making under Capitalism,' and she walked out of the meeting room. Foster, who strived to stay on Mrs. Roosevelt's good side, tried to smooth it over and suggested that we stop calling the slaughter of black people in America, 'genocide.'"

The Testimony of William Z. Foster (rebuttal)

"The Party really had a lot more important business to attend to than the whining of a disgruntled minority. The future of Man- and Womankind was at stake. Humanity faced the most stupendous threat of butchery and enslavement in the recorded history of civilization. The Fascist Ogre was on the march and headed straight for the throat of the Soviet Union. Only the Great Stalin stood in the way of Hitler's mad schemes for world domination. The Bolshevik Revolution had to be defended at all cost.

"The Nazi putsch forced us to retool our strategies for an American revolution. On the eve of Roosevelt's inauguration in 1933, Hitler torched the Reichstag. The jackboots were already marching in the streets of America. Father Coughlin and Gerald L. K. Smith spouted their racist poison from the radio tubes. Charles Lindbergh, Henry Ford, and the American Bund were encouraging their Führer to launch a preventive strike on Moscow. At the seventh congress of the Comintern—I was a delegate—Comrade Georgi Dimitrov laid down the line. Our task now was to build the United Front Against Fascism. Negro and Trade Union work would have to wait.

"Spain was the first test for the United Front Against Fascism. Franco and his black legions rose out of Africa in July, 1936, against the democratically elected loyalist government, with the backing of Hitler and Mussolini, and later, the Luftwaffe bombed Guernica, the first aerial bombing ever perpetrated against a civilian population. But Roosevelt and the

Capitalist class sat on their hands, impervious to the agony of the Spanish people. Then Dolores "La Passionaria" Ibirruri issued her blood-curdling cry for the workers of the world to save the Republic from the fascist barbarians and the International Brigades were organized. *No Pasaran!*

"We joined with the Canadian Mac-Paps, the Italian Garibaldis, the Polish Dumbrowskys, the Bulgarian Dmitrovs, and the ill-armed, ill-trained proletariat of 51 other nations, to rescue Spain. The CP-USA sent our best and bravest as members of the Abraham Lincoln and the George Washington brigades. We held the fascists at Teruel and the Rio Elba. We stood with the masses in Madrid while Franco's hordes flung themselves on the city in waves. *No Pasaran!* Milton Herndon, Oliver Law, and Alonso Watson were Negro comrades who gave their lives so that the world could be free from fascism. *Freiheit!* The blood of these brave comrades mingled with that dusty soil and they each grew into a strong olive tree.

"In the face of indifference from the rulers of the Capitalist world, Communists alone stood in the path of the Hitlerian onslaught."

Testimony of Eddie Balchowsky

"Yo, Eddie Balchowsky here somewhere. Although I'm listed in Mark's graveyard guidebook, I have never ever been able to find my own bones.

"I was crowned the King of the Alleys. I knew every rathole and lowdown dive in this windbag city. I was a poet and a painter and a barrelhouse piano player although I could play the classics too. I was a fixture in Bughouse Square where I knew Ben Reitman M.D., who was even crazier than I was.

"It must have been the autumn of '36 and I was out of work as usual. What else is new? Down at the unemployment hall, I spotted this poster with four hot-looking Spanish broads on it. I didn't speak the lingo but close as I could figure, they were inviting horny young studs like myself to come and fight in the war over there. Gee, I had never fought in a war before but those girls looked like they might be worth it so I signed right up and set sail to battle the fascists.

"We learned all the songs right away—'Los Cuatro Insurgentes Generales.' 'Rumbala, rumbala, rumba-la!' We could sing all the verses by heart but we were an ill-trained and ill-armed lot and when we got up to the frontlines, my comrades started falling left and right.

"I joined a demolition team and me and this Italian boy were trying to blow a bridge over the Elba when the dynamite went off in my hand. I lost my whole arm and part of my shoulder. Ouch, that hurt! I'll never tickle the ivories again, I mourned. My bum luck. But later I learned how to play with one hand, all bass notes, your basic boogie-woogie. I could really rumble down there.

"The comrades evacuated me up to Barcelona and I lay in a hospital most of '38. I met the usual beautiful nurse and hung around pitching woo in my lousy Spanglish. When the Soviets pulled the plug on the Loyalists and carried their gold off to Moscow, I knew it was time to get into the wind. I was never much of a Communist anyway. I crossed the Pyrenees in the spring of '39 and there were fascists in back of me and Vichy France was just up ahead.

"They kept us in the internment camp all summer. Food was scarce and the heroes of the International Brigades got to fighting among themselves over the crumbs. Finally, we shipped back to the States and I was arrested right there on the pierhead by the FBI for violating something called 'the Neutrality Act.' 'You're full of shit,' I told them, 'I've never been neutral in my whole life.'

"I was in a federal jail in New York when I heard that Stalin had made a pact with the Nazis. It hurt worse than losing my arm to see Joe Stalin shake hands with that bastard Adolph."

The Increasingly Dubious Testimony of William Z. Foster

"Thanks for your comments, comrade. Your analysis is ridiculous and your conclusions misguided. But thanks just the same.

"Moving right along now, the paralysis of the Capitalist class allowed the fascists carte blanche to attack the Soviet Union. Chamberlin tried to use Stalin as a cats' paw to pull his chestnuts from the fire in Munich—whatever that means (I wrote it in a book once). Anyway, the Soviet Union stood naked and vulnerable, surrounded on all sides by ravenous Capitalist beasts. Alone among world leaders, Joseph Stalin, the greatest Stalinist on earth, sought to safeguard the peace. The people of the world applauded him when he forged a nonaggression pact with the German National Socialists. This brilliant maneuver purchased precious time for the glorious Red Army, the world's most valiant fighting machine (now that it had been purged and purified by Joseph Stalin, the world's greatest military genius) to prepare for the coming battle in defense of Man- and Womankind.

"It is a vile canard spread by bourgeois maggots that we sold out to the Nazis. Our sole goal was the salvation of Communism, the only hope for the Human Race.

"As for the Jewish question, the scent of roasting flesh had not yet risen to our nostrils. Our enemies only reveal their own anti-Semitism when they accuse us of ignoring the crematoriums. Besides, the Communists always had many Jewish friends and members. In fact, according to *The Protocols of Zion,* we were charter members of the International Jewish Communist Conspiracy.

"While the war raged in the Soviet heartland, the Party was under attack from without and from within on the homefront. Browder, with whom I had had a principled falling out, was spreading the spores of 'American Exceptionalism.' According to this crackpot thesis, the class war was kaput and we had to join forces with J.P. Morgan to enslave ourselves. I called upon myself to exterminate this venomous snake while it was still in the egg, before it devoured the CP-USA. Browder was nothing less than a revisionist opportunist and Roosevelt bootlicker who preached Munichism and class collaboration—he received far fewer votes when he ran for president than I did back in 1932. But the Party foisted him on the U.S. working class after I suffered my fifth heart attack in 1940.

"In 1943, the Great Stalin, the world's greatest strategic thinker, ordered the Comintern to liquidate itself in order to unite all peace-loving people and eliminate sectarian divisionism. Browder was an enthusiastic liquidationist and utilized the pretext of my sixth heart attack in 1945 to dissolve the Communist Party USA completely. While the glorious Red Army was trampling the Nazi rats into the snow at Stalingrad in the most decisive battle in the history of the modern cosmos, Earl Browder was selling off the furniture and embracing Henry Ford. The doctors kept the news of Browder's deceit from me for fear it would be the fatal blow to my declining health.

"So the Browderites took down the portraits of the Great Lenin and the Great Stalin and in just two minutes time his clique in the central committee voted the CP-USA out of business. A quarter of a century of social struggle went down the tubes. Now we were The Communist Education Association—Browder even campaigned to take the word 'Communist' out all together.

• • •

"Our Soviet comrades had suffered 23,000,000 casualties in the War against Fascism, four times the number of Jews and Gypsies incinerated by the Nazis, but they had stopped fascism in its tracks. And yet the moment peace was declared, Red Russia became Public Enemy Number One. Patton offered to march straight through Berlin on Moscow. Truman dropped the atom bomb and vaporized hundreds of thousands of Japanese just to show the Soviet people what would happen to them next if they didn't throw off the yoke of godless Communism. We had to get Stalin the bomb before Washington launched a pre-emptive strike.

"In March of 1947, Harry Truman declared the Cold War against Communism. Capitalism cannot survive without a war to keep the furnaces of the munitions plants belching.

"The Cold War, like the First and Second World Wars, was a war against the American proletariat and its vanguard party. The Smith Act had been passed in 1940 to round up native-born Nazis. Now it was turned against the CP-USA. Since we were supposed to be taking orders from Moscow, we had to sign up as foreign agents or go to jail. It became a crime to be a Communist without signing up, and when you did, you were automatically adjudged guilty of advocating the violent overthrow of the government. It was a devious Catch-22.

"My health revived in 1946 and I got out of my sickbed and took the Party back. I took the portraits of the Great Lenin and the Great Stalin out of the closet and hung them back up again, and I kicked Browder and his whole family out of the CP-USA for good. But you could tell it wasn't the same. The times they were a-changin'."

• • •

A Brief Colloquy on Life, Death, Damnation & Eternal Hope Between William Z. Foster and Senator Joseph McCarthy (Rep. WISC.)

"You bet your sweet bippy, Willie Boy. The times they were a-changing—in the favor of us red, white, and blue-blooded Americans at last. Senator Joe McCarthy here on a conference call from the All-American city of Appleton, Wisconsin across the state line up by Oshkosh and Green Bay. We're real hot cheeseheads up here. Have you ever noticed how cheese is like death? At first, it smells real bad and then the odor dies down and only the good stuff is left.

"Appleton has always been my hometown. Only real Americans have hometowns anymore. I grew up and learned to hate here. Now I reside in well-kept grounds, St. Mary's cemetery, the same church where I was an altar boy. Another native son, Harry Houdini, an active member of the International Jewish Communist Conspiracy, is buried across town with the other sheenies. He's a tricky type and I keep a sharp eye on his movements. Don't mind me. I'm retired now and investigating dead subversives is my only entertainment.

"The Cold War was my heyday. I found a Red under every bed and a dozen fellow travelers in the closet. I cleaned the commies out of the pumpkin patch, the union halls, the nigger churches, the State Department, the U.S. Army, and, of course, the White House. The Red Menace had taken over stage, screen, and radio. I was like the fumigator. They brought me in to get rid of that vermin. Red Channels blacklisted the subversives and locked them out of the television industry but there were some who sneaked in through the keyhole. Sid Caesar and Imogine Coca were dangerous pinkos.

"The commies had infiltrated Hollywood, too, inserting their perverse anti-red-blooded-American messages up on the silver screen. I hounded the Hollywood Ten into prison—Alvah Bessie, Herbert Biberman, Lester Cole, Edward Demitrich, Albert Maltz, Samuel Ornitz, Dalton Trumbo, Adrian Scott, and Ring Lardner Jr. I never forget a name.

"At the height of my meteoric rise to power, I had princes of the Roman Catholic Church—Fulton Sheen, Cardinal 'Porky Pig' Spellman—eating out of the sweaty palm of my hand. So what if I fudged my military record and destroyed hundreds of lives with my lies? By 1950, the presidency was in reach!"

WZF: "Joe McCarthy was a two-bit chistler, a bottom-feeding political con man, a disingenuous demagogue, and a mean drunk. He and his gang of stoolies—Whittaker Chambers, Looie Budenz, and Herbert 'I Led Three Lives' Filbrick—gave anticommunism a bad name. Among professional red-hunters, Joe was a bad joke. Yet McCarthy lent his name to a decade of political persecution.

"The deans of the witch-hunting industry were fascists like J. Parnell Thomas and the Subversive Activities Control Board, Pat McCarren's Senate Internal Security Subcommittee, HUAC, Walter Winchell and Westbrook Pegler. The moneybags was H. L. Hunt, the tomato king. Tom Clark, Ramsey's father, was attorney general and by 1948, he had compiled a list of 160 subversive organizations.

"The blacklist snowballed out of control. A few years later, HUAC claimed to have 608 groups on the list. Everything from the Joint Anti-Fascist War Relief Committee to the Ethical Culture Society. There was no end to their calumnies.

"Besides the organizations, the government kept 43,000

Americans under permanent surveillance. Everyone was a suspect. If you signed the Stockholm Peace Petition. If you subscribed to *The Nation.* If you voted for Henry Wallace and Cowboy Glenn Taylor.

"We were red-baited out of the CIO, an organization we had built with our sweat and our blood—a million workers, longshoremen, electricians, mine, mill, and smelter workers, Marine cooks and stewards, Ben Gold's furriers—all given the bum's rush.

"The FBI tapped our phones and read our mail. Their agents hid behind potted palms in hotel lobbies and parked in front of our homes all night long. They sent our entire leadership to jail under the Smith Act, ultimately proven to be an unconstitutional law. Gus Hall, who would succeed me as the Party's obligatory presidential candidate, swam the Rio Grande and escaped to Mexico but the F.B.I. nailed him in a motel room down there with a hooker named Guadalupe and dragged him back in chains.

"Our apartments were broken into and our meetings were infiltrated and bugged. Pronouncing the words 'Dictatorship of the Proletariat' was forbidden for security reasons—if you got an urge to talk about it, you had to write the letters DOP on the blackboard.

"Many Americans said they would rather be dead than red and built bomb shelters to prove it. Our members grew depressed and drank themselves to death or blew their brains out with small-caliber pistols. Do you know how depressing it is to always be on the losing side? Always. In spite of what the Great Lenin and the Great Stalin had to say about the victory of socialism being inevitable?

"By 1950, the stress was getting to me and I suffered my seventh heart attack. My case was separated from the rest of the Smith Act defendants and my doctors urged me to go to Florida and forget about Communism.

• • •

SJM (Rep. Wisc.): "J. Edgar Hoover, a well-known transvestite, was my handmaiden and those two fag jewboys, Cohn and Schine, did my dirty business. *Confidential Magazine* spread the muck around. I blackened the names of many Reds, near-Reds, parlor pinkos, and liberal Jews, but I guess I bit off more than I could chew when I went after the commies in the Army. Oh, they were there all right, just like sleeper cells. Russky lovers, agents of the Red Chinese in Korea. My investigators found a Red under nearly every bunk. But I underestimated the power of the military-industrial complex and their Red Jew flunkies.

"The public is fickle. I began to lose influence and even Winchell wouldn't take my calls anymore. No one would believe me when I warned that the Red Chinese were massing in Baja California. I became a national caricature. Walt Kelly drew me as a weasel with five o'clock shadow. I drank hard and my liver died of cirrhosis at 48. It was all a commie plot.

"But I'm coming back. There are still some old-time diehards out there and a whole new generation of anti-Communist, anti-nigger, anti-faggot skinheads is coming up. Every year now we have a patriotic hot-dog feed right here in Appleton on my birthday. An accordionist plays 'God Bless America' at my graveside and I am decorated with American flowers and flags. The John Birch Society and the National White Peoples' Party are lobbying to make my birthday a national holiday, and they're petitioning the post office to put my mug on a postage stamp. Yup, I'm coming back strong all across America. Like it says on our bumper stickers: 'Joe McCarthy was right!'

WZF: "The Red Scare spiked like a raging epidemic and slowly began to subside. Communists poked their heads out of the foxholes. The democratic forces in Eastern Europe rose up against the reactionary oligarchs to establish comradely peoples' republics, and the darker nations of the third world threw off the colonial yoke.

"Most importantly, the Soviet Union got hold of the atom bomb and even built some jet planes to deliver it. That balanced out world power a lot more than when the bomb belonged exclusively to the Capitalists. Say what you will about Ethel and Julius but they were true proletarian heroes. They should have been nominated for the Nobel Peace Prize.

"Then the Great Stalin died, poisoned in a Kremlin imbroglio no doubt sponsored by the C.I.A. His alleged crimes against the Trots and other divisionist slime became public knowledge and we held criticism and self-criticism orgies to purify ourselves and our Party.

"By the middle of the 1950s, we could see the light at the end of the tunnel. The Korean War was winding down and Smith Act convictions were overturned. Our comrades came out of jail and the closet. Negro brothers and sisters in the Jim Crow South would no longer sit in the back of the bus. Young people became impatient with Capitalism and began to wiggle their pelvis. The HUAC tried to hold a witch hunt in San Francisco and there were so many protesters on hand to defend longshoreman leader Archie Brown that the cops washed them down the city hall steps with firehoses.

"The CP-USA and its many front groups are bouncing back. With the Great Marx, Lenin, Stalin and Foster as our guides, our dogma rings more true than ever. We are a strong and resilient party resolved to squash the late Earl Browder and other class collaborationists, weaklings, confusionists, turncoats, renegades, and stool pigeons. As the immortal Molotov of cocktail fame once proclaimed: 'All roads lead to Communism and our victory is assured.'

"What was that you mentioned about a wall? Which wall? A wall that came down? Our Wall? You mean, our victory was not assured? You mean we didn't win?"

The Declaration of the Haymarket Martyrs

"Might I have your attention, comrades? I know it's late and you've been dead a long time and you're tired—but the eight Haymarket Martyrs have prepared a short statement in respect to our continuing participation in the class war. It was drawn up collectively and I, Albert Parsons, have been delegated to present it to the plenary buried here in the shadow of the Haymarket Monument, heretofore to be known as 'the Monument.'

"First of all, I would like to remind the police spies out there that regardless of your pathological intolerance of our many dogmas and anti-dogmas, we have a constitutional right to assemble here around the Monument. Besides, in most cases, our cemetery fees are current.

"The eight Haymarket Martyrs would like to express our eternal gratitude to all of you for following in our footsteps, one way or another. You have been an inspiringly lawless rabble. Yes, some of you led while others lagged, some of you zigged while others zagged, some believed in dynamite and others in doing no violence at all, most furled the flag of one -ism or another, embraced fallacious dogmas and anti-dogmas, trusted false leaders, followed parking meters, and did not have a weathervane to know which way the wind blew. But all of you soldiered in the class war to change the balance of the world in favor of the many over the few and we applaud you for keeping on keeping on. You form a profoundly American continuum of rejection and resistance to Capitalist tyranny and you can take comfort that without you, the rulers would have been more secure.

"All of you are Americans by virtue of being buried in American soil and having been eaten by American worms. Although some of you spoke other tongues and arrived from lands other than this one, you participated in an American revolution. You have fought the Masters of the Universe from inside the Belly of the Beast. There is no more noble struggle than to take on the Imperialist Monster on its own turf. Our future depends on those who dare to struggle for justice in this most Unjust State on earth. And although you battled to set America free, you are also citizens of the world, intractably linked to the international working class and sworn to break the chains of this most pernicious of enslavements—Capitalism!

"History is a conspiracy and all of you are under indictment for having stuck your nose into it. You huddled over pitchers of beer in the workingmens' saloons and steaming cappucinos in cosmopolitan coffee houses, to plot the next march or rally or strike or prank or bombing or film or uprising or revolution. You carried that flame of hope in your own private heart but fathomed that it took every private heart to overthrow the State and you organized those hearts into a bonfire that will one day consume the rulers and their rules. Of that, I have no doubt. Congratulations! You have been sentenced to hang until you are just as dead as the next working stiff but at least you had the satisfaction of fighting back. It is an honor to have been hung with you, our dear fellow workers.

"Did we win? We fought for the eight-hour day and today, too many Americans are working 10 and 12 hours just to make ends meet. We fought to destroy the Capitalist system and today, Capitalism continues to snuff out the lives of the working poor of the world. Did we lose? They said it was the end of history and that proved to be one more Big Lie. They said the Wall came down but the Wall between rich and poor is taller than it has ever been and demon Globalization has made it more impenetrable. Did we win or did we lose?

"Just as at Haymarket, what counts is that we fought back. Our resistance is as permanent as our deaths. And just as at Haymarket, our silence is still more powerful than all the voices Capitalism throttles every day.

"I've talked too long and the hour grows late. Thank you, comrades for your time and attention. To close this chapter, I'd like all of you to join hands under the earth and raise your voices in silent song:

Arise ye prisoners of starvation,
Arise ye wretched of the earth.
For justice thunders condemnation,
a better world's in birth.
'Tis the final conflict,
let each stand in their place.
The International Union
shall be the Human Race.
The International Union,
Shall be the Human Race."

Parsons was right. It had grown late. Twilight was falling fast and the gates of Forest Home were about to clank shut. It was time to go.

But first I had to bid a fond adieu to Mrs. Lucy Parsons and when I did, she expressed one last request.

"Hey, big boy" she cooed, "bend down here quick but don't let my husband catch you." I dropped to my knees and suddenly Lucy's cold, old stone levitated to my lips and planted there a gelid but juicy kiss.

"Take that back to California with you for that cute Rudy Schnaubelt" Lucy giggled, and it was then that I remembered why I had visited Waldheim in the first place.

The Cemetery

The Midnight Dog was crammed with the usual low-rent rabble ceaselessly shuttling between the cities of the Pacific Northwest. The bus air was stale with snores and farts and it was kind of cosmic relief to step into a driving predawn North Coast November rainstorm. After parking my pack at the digs of Sidney Twenty Bucks, a long-time co-conspirator, I slogged off down Stagecoach Road towards the local boneyard with Lucy's kiss still imprinted on my lips.

The Trinidad town cemetery in November is often a desolate and water-logged sanctuary, the dead in their season curled up in fetal repose beneath the mud, the rain slanting from the cheerless heavens, pelting the plastic flowers and crumbling markers without remorse. Up by Saunders' surveillance fence, a still-comatose Eddie Schnaubelt drank deeply from the porous heavens.

I doubled over and planted Lucy Parsons' long-distance kiss upon the mottled stone, and settled back to await a sign.

The metabolisms of the dead are hopelessly occluded by decay and darkness. Although my calibrations were not amiss, re-establishing contact with E. B. Schnaubelt (if that indeed was his true name), was not instantaneous. The hours limped by, the rain drizzled and squalled. Retreating to Sidney's, I purloined a tarp and strung it up around Schnaubelt's plot as if it were a live-in construction area, or one of those strange tents Thomas Pynchon had noted up in the telephone wires in *The Crying of Lot 49*.

Finally, on the third morning of my vigil, movement was measurable around the base of the anchor-decorated cenotaph. Now I could detect an esoteric creaking, fibers unspooling, the stifled gurgle of a dead man desperately trying to clear the dirt from where his mouth used to be situated. By mid-afternoon, the moist soil packed around the tomb was visibly palpitating. Something very old was waking up.

I was jostled from numbing, dreamless slumber by a piercing scream. It was after midnight and Eddie Schnaubelt had at last emerged from his self-induced coma. "Arise Ye Prisoners of Starvation!" he caterwauled over and over again, a cracked, crazed chant that channeled right through me. Indeed, I was not to blame. I

had only been the vector of his revival, having transported the imprint of Lucy's lips halfway across the continent on my own.

In his understandably muddled state, Schnaubelt became convinced that his long-ago lover had at last acknowledged his undying passion and was now perched at his graveside. Obscene smooching sounds reverberated from the love-starved tombstone for days.

But as the hours dripped by, the old man's dementia began to subside. His maniacal renditions of "The International" tailed off and he became curious about just where exactly his bones were buried. So it is when the dead wake up—and they are still dead.

By now, it was evident that what remained of Schnaubelt's mind was short-circuiting dangerously, flickering on and off as if he were in the throes of a posthumous power blackout, the rats chomping on the whorls of his DNA, biting off little cheese wedges of his personal history. There was not much left to nibble on.

Schnaubelt was deeply disappointed to learn that I was not Lucy and sobbed quietly to himself. He only dimly recalled who I was. "Oh, it's you. When did you get back to town? Where have you been, anyway?" he faked, grappling to remember my name and my story, cautiously listening for any clue I might drop about my identity. As I march into my own sunset years, I know the syndrome well.

To ease Schnaubelt's troubled mind, I reintroduced myself and reminded him of how we had been collaborating on our memoirs when he suddenly went blank. After that, I explained, I had gone to Chicago and Waldheim to seek Lucy's counsel about summonsing him from his extended narcolepsy. It had been her idea to send the kiss. I gently chided him for his temper tantrum and obstinate clam-up, and assured Eddie that he would get first billing on the title page. A publisher had shown interest, I feigned. The ancient anarchist seemed so very frail, as if he might slip from me and memory at the slightest tremble of the earth.

As the weeks drifted into December, the rain slashing viciously into my back, and old "Glen Saunders" getting more suspicious each day about what exactly was shaking under the mystery tarp, Schnaubelt's interest in resuming our project waxed hot and cold. Some days, he seemed eager to forge ahead, and even encouraged me to continue the 5,000-word-plus autobiographical sketch that had driven him into silence in the first place. I demurred, not wanting to provoke him back into disconnect. No, no, he would insist, his short-term-memory bank was now so severely damaged that all that he was told, he forgot immediately. I should feel free to proceed with my story. No one would be listening to it anyway.

But on other days, the rain dampened the transmission lines and Schnaubelt would grow dour and withdrawn, emitting only erratically spaced grunts and wheezes in response to my incessant chattering.

One matter I urgently needed to clarify related to Lucy's confusion. Had her long-ago lover been Edward or Rudolph Schnaubelt? Both had been tall, handsome men with ginger beards. Moreover, many of the denizens of Waldheim had expressed conflicting opinions in response to my questions about the brothers' involvement in the Haymarket bombing. Eddie—if that is who I was in touch with—had himself told me about switching identity papers with Rudolph at the train station, and even confessed that there were moments when he thought himself to be his brother. But who it was that was buried here and who it was that had actually tossed the bomb that had ignited the class struggle in the U.S.A., was a secret that could only be wheedled inch by inch from beyond the tomb.

My strategy, then, was to take up Eddie Schnaubelt's invitation to pick up where I had broken off my narrative and hope that sooner or later he might tip his hand. I would speak to him of recent struggles and how the radical history of this country did not disappear with the end of the war upon Vietnam—although the saga has sure veered into uncharted waters with the Fall of the Wall and the death of dogma.

Hallelujah. I think.

The Life of Ross (restored)

Just like you Schnaubelt boys, I was drawn to the coastal forests after years running the mean, littered streets of American cities. The light filtering through the last redwood stands seemed to me the most radiant and mystical of all light, the distillation of poetry into a living physical presence.

And beyond the spiring, primeval forests, the land embraced the shoaled, salmon-thick sea, sweeping from the rocks close upon the shore where the spirits of dead Indians flew into the souls of migratory sea birds, all the way to the horizon at the edge of the earth. At sunset, you could feel the planet tilting into the heavens from the Trinidad bluffs.

Or maybe it was the Acid.

Revolutionary politics as usual did not make much sense out here. There was no Vanguard Party in the forest and everyone took their proper position in the food chain. But like you Schnaubelt boys, because this here was a place with forests to be leveled and oceans to be trashed, it was under permanent sentence of being Murdered by Capitalism. That, I suspect, became the nugget of the dogma that came next, after dogma was dead.

The Humboldt Bay Nuclear Power Generating Facility had been one of the first commercial applications of the technology that reduced hundreds of thousands of unsuspecting Japanese civilians to ashes on

August 6th and 9th, 1945. Inaugurated during John F. Kennedy's unhappy tenure at the helm of the nation, to guinea-pig the effects of nuclear-power generation upon a civilian population, the Humboldt Bay Nuke was a calamity from startup. Radioactive garbage flew out of its stacks and landed on the playground of the grade school across U.S. 101. Geiger counters clicked frenetically the closer you came to the site, which was just south of the pulp-mill city of Eureka, California on the shores of a once-flourishing wetlands. The Nuke's managers fed the rabbits who lodged here store-bought pellets rather than allow them to forage on the native vegetation, for fear that when tested by inspectors, the bunnies would glow in the dark. Fishermen reported one-eyed mutants feeding around the outflow. The gaseous discharges from the stacks, when combined with the toxic effluvia from the pulp mills, made it difficult to distinguish Eureka from Mordor.

We rattled a lot of mojo to rid our place of this Great Satan. We marched and sued and shouted our poetry at its gates. Pacific Gas & Electric, which operated the leaking utility, insisted there was NO DANGER TO THE PUBLIC. Then geologists discovered that the Humboldt Bay Nuclear Power Generating Facility had been sited on a confluence of three earthquake faults. In 1977, PG&E suspended operations hours before the Nuclear Regulatory Commission was to have ordered the utility to cease and desist.

To celebrate our victory, we formed affinity groups with amusing names like No Nukes of the North and caravaned around trying to shut down killer nukes from Seabrook, New Hampshire to the Canyon of the Diablo on the sunny Southern California coast, penetrating the perimeters and driving the operators nuts.

After the Humboldt plant had been off-line for several years, the Redwood Alliance had the temerity to demand that it be removed from the (our) landscape and that the wetlands upon which the plant had been erected be restored to their original contours and fecundity as the NRC's guidelines required. I wrote an optimistic piece for *Mother Jones* magazine titled "How To Take Apart Your Neighborhood

Nuke" but of course, no technology existed to disassemble a nuclear power plant once its operating life was spent. No one had ever seriously considered the back end of the nuclear cycle, Ralph Nader told us sadly. The industry thought itself to be immortal.

In the end, the regulators decommissioned the Humboldt plant, the first commercial generating facility ever to be taken off line for good. The offending nuke was placed in "safe storage" where it will remain for the next millennium or so, a grim skeletal monolith out there at the end of the land. Did we win or did we lose? the Haymarket Martyrs had to ask.

Back in the saddle of the '70s, with the dream of Redwood National Park in reach, a protected enclave that would provide sanctuary for the tallest trees, the most ancient and sacred groves, which had stood before America was fixed in Christopher Columbus's spy glass, the timber beasts went on an unparalleled chainsaw rampage. First they massacred the tallest tree in the proposed park and then the next tallest. They murdered a 300-year-old redwood and chainsawed it into the shape of a peanut which they then drove across country on a flag-bedecked flatbed truck and deposited on Jimmy Carter's doorstep. Environmentalists were hanged in effigy on the North Coast and spat upon at public meetings by the pawns of the timber companies. They treated us just as badly as they did you old-time anarchists.

At this point in my story, each time I spoke of the trees, my co-author emitted a heart-rending shriek of Alzheimic terror—or perhaps he was merely imitating the rip of the saw blade that still resonated deep in his bones. There seemed to be no way to quiet him.

Up river, old Indians like Charlie Tom hunkered down in their house trailers, shaking eagle feathers, and prophesying doom. The Forest Service was determined to carve out a logging road from Gasquet on the Smith, California's last wild river, over the Siskiyu ridges past Doctor Rock from where the Yuroks looked at the world. We raced up there to head the Smokies off, together with a handful of visionary Indians, at least one of whom believed he had been taken up in a flying saucer. At the Indians' behest, no menstruating women were allowed in the encampment.

The G-O Road battle marked Earth First!'s first escapade in the bioregion but even back then tree-hugging was a popular pastime around here. My pal Aura Denise Sullivan bedded down for three days and nights in an old pine tree down in Arcata while the bulldozers hungrily circled below. And that was nearly two decades before Julia Butterfly inhabited the high branches of the old growth redwood she named Luna. Much like Aura's pine and the ancient giant reduced to a peanut by cro-magnon loggers, Luna too got chainsawed and nearly died in a windstorm days after Julia had descended to the forest floor after a year in its arms. The loggers murdered Gypsy Chain by felling the tree in which he was sitting during the great battle to save the old growth of Headwaters Forest from the bean-counters of Charles Hurwitz's junk-bond empire.

It was Capitalism that killed the forests and those who defended them and it was Capitalism that bombed Judi Bari and sent her to an early grave. When Judi lay upon her death bed, propped up on pillows and looking hard at the other side, she splayed a spidery hand on Dennis Cunningham's wrist and whispered legal instructions. "Never settle," she told her lawyer. "Never Settle!" Now a new generation is up there in the trees and they heed St. Judi's doctrine: Never Settle In Defense Of Place.

Saving the last redwoods or the last whales, the wild salmon, the spotted owl, the marbled murrelet, or even unlovable critters such as the crocodile and the scorpion, was to some like doing God's work. Tree-spikers and monkey-wrenchers, eco-terrorists and unabombers, became the Hezbollah of the environment, calling down jihad on the despoilers of Place. I don't know, Eddie, maybe these kids seem a little extreme but Capitalism is destroying our home and the urgency of defending it requires martyrs. To me, this place, Trinidad and the North Coast, is to die for.

Hey, wasn't that what happened to you?

• • •

Defending the republic of the trees and tides necessitated secession from the United States of North America. Whether you called it Ecotopia or Jefferson State, the Emerald Triangle or Shasta, or defined the bioregion by its watersheds, we were in revolt against the way things were done in the rest of this TV nation. As in hundreds of pockets of resistance stretching from the left coast to the right one in the post-Vietnam rollout—back country communes, hamlets of new-age homesteaders, university towns radicalized by the war, urban enclaves where squatters grouped around bowls of brown rice—we were obliged to invent alternative institutions to serve the needs of the communities we were creating.

Piecing together political options was paramount in a county like Humboldt where city councils and boards of supervisors were dominated by timber-corporation puppets. Down in Arcata, the state university drove the economy, and a mid-'70s liberal coup d'etat wrested power from an entrenched handful of fogies who had controlled local politics since Brizzard and Zehndner called the shots. Now, nominally new-wave politicos converted city government into one of the most progressive bodies in California. A quarter of a century later, the Arcata City Council would become the first elected body in the nation with a Green majority.

The Open Door Clinic threw open its portals to colorful travelers in 1971, first as a hippie crash pad and then, an alternative to commercial health care. The octagon-shaped Equinox Free School was raised up by volunteers to provide an option to the intractable flypaper of public education. The Arcata Coop fed the hungry, advocated organic produce, baked its own bread, and tempered the temptations of mindless consumerism. The North Coast Environmental Center championed recycling and provided an ideological nexus for the multiple defenders of places and species.

Most of these counterinstitutions have survived into the new millennium, albeit in sometimes unrecognizable shapes. One popular bumper sticker reads "The Coop—We Used To Own It!," and the Open Door is now a for-profit medical complex. City Council liberals tend to represent small-business constituencies and have little sympathy for transients. The Environmental Center has been under the management of a single director longer than Rafael Trujillo ruled the Dominican Republic. Equinox is now an annex of an upscale charter school.

Back in the old days, alternative venues popped up like psychedelic mushrooms to accommodate the thriving cultural beat that had come to the near north woods. A whiskey-brown loggers' bar was rechristened the Jambalaya Club and hosted an ebullient stew of boogie bands, bebopists, bluegrass pickers, and bipolar poets for nearly two decades until the yuppie set ripped out its guts and started serving blackened fishes to branch-office managers and tenured professors. A series of irregularly issued underground weeklies and monthlies flourished and fizzled. I scribbled my soul out for them all.

We invented our own calendar and decreed new holidays—most pertinently, the North Country Fair which 30 autumn equinoxes later still celebrates the bounties of the season.

We first envisioned the fair as a sort of peoples' takeover of the physical center of Arcata—its McKinley-dominated plaza—after losing a bruising battle to stop a state-sponsored freeway from tearing the town in two. Nonetheless, the city fathers and mothers, packed as the council was with liberals we had personally elected, were at first reluctant to grant permits for the party because a 1973 Rotary Club salmon dinner had gotten out of hand and a mob tried to burn down the Bank of America, which corners the square, *a la* Isla Vista. Nonetheless, more than a generation down the pike, the Earth flag still flies over the packed plaza on Fair days and the belly dancers wiggle long past the Pacific sunset.

The economic base of Ecotopia was not all Tofu, tie-dyes, and curative-crystal sales. Agricultural pursuits—only marginally organic tomatoes—underwrote and leveraged the alternative universe we were constructing.

The first sinsemilla was harvested in 1970 in the southern Humboldt hills by Berkeley dropouts with educated green thumbs. The next year, underground agronomists traveled to the Hindu Kush and brought home seeds and samples of the fabled Purple Indica. The lovingly cross-pollinated product was soon in commercial circulation, both a blessing and a curse upon the land.

Each November, under the autumn rains, the trimmers gathered in country kitchens and backwater bunkers clipping and bagging the huge dripping colas, the fragrant residues accumulating between their sticky fingers. Fortunes accrued like the finger hash and the boom did not escape the attentions of those who lived out there in the other America. The greedy flocked to Humboldt County and Capitalism threatened murder.

The State declared war and invaded in 1979. The Campaign Against Marijuana Planting (CAMP) changed the nature of the industry, driving growers indoors and the price into the $5,000-a-pound range. One afternoon up on the New River near Denny in Trinity County, I escorted two *Das Spiegal* reporters whose heads we had trussed up in Safeway shopping bags so they could not see how they got there, into a 200-plant patch while CAMP helicopters droned in the distance. 'Hear that?' my compadre, a onetime Columbia University–trained anthropologist turned mountain man, inquired. 'That's my price support-system.'

The risk factor generated undreamed-of surplus value and some growers felt a little guilty about it. My buddy, the mountain man, an outlaw with a fondness for bear-heart breakfasts, still forks over a sizable chunk of the profits to the eco-warriors who put their bodies on the line to defend this place.

So here we were in our own self-contained paradise, a bubble of our own blowing. Only problem is that it never stopped raining and the precipitation bred galloping depression. The chemical pall emanating from the pulp mills had neural implications too. The colossal consumption of alcohol at Jambalaya and the six other bars and two booze barns around the Arcata Plaza must be figured into the mix.

Love was mostly free in that hothouse pre-AIDS ambience and

bed-hopping de rigor. On any given night, any given patron at Jambalaya had probably slept with half the other patrons. The incestuous pairings-off spawned high drama between the sexes and within them, and the community—or whatever it had morphed into—constricted and turned upon itself.

New dope money washed through county commerce—we're talking millions a year. With the moolah came the cocaine and everybody who was anybody choogled around town in a sort of me-first daze. Me? I was mostly out of the loop, subsisting solely on the sale of my food stamps or bulb-farm minimum-wage stoop labor, moonlighting so to speak as town clown and poet in residence. I often spent my days cadging drinks and my nights sleeping out in the rain, pining for some lost love. 'When a man loves a woman. . . .'

After repeated appeals, the government of Uncle Sam finally conceded me five hundred bucks in crazy money each month, most of which was consumed in one excess or another by the tenth calendar day. When summoned by the government offices to explain my psychosis, I would sometimes pull out my pecker and piss on the nearest portrait of the president.

Although distance and weather held the North Coast incommunicado for whole seasons, news of what went on in *USA Today*–land, occasionally filtered through the Redwood Curtain. A poet now deceased of bad whiskey once wrote a poem about me writing a poem about watching the Symbionese Liberation Army burn to a crisp in their Watts safehouse.

I remember that the war finally ended on the Jambalaya TV screen with hysterical Vietnamese collaborators scrambling aboard helicopters on the roof of the U.S. Embassy in Saigon.

Watergate, which I covered for the local university station from a pay phone in a downtown Arcata shopping mall, certainly made an impression. On the night of Nixon's abdication, I harangued the masses from the Jambalaya pool table calling for "power to the persons." Later that evening, the town gendarmes would pin me to the pavement and lead me off in handcuffs for making criminal whoopie.

I costumed myself as Zippy the Pinhead and tried to vote for that noble idiot savant in the 1976 election but was turned away from the polling precinct for electioneering within a hundred feet of the polls, and I sought to register for the draft at the Arcata post office in a gorilla suit when Jimmy Carter threatened to wage World War III in Afghanistan.

Three Mile Island kind of caught my eye. But mostly I lived in an Ecotopic state of mind, thinking locally but not acting very globally, lolling on the nude beaches of Trinidad or swimming in the whiskey-brown miasma of Jambalaya, lost in the trees or up here with you snoozing in the boneyard. The outside world was a distant planet orbiting my insular head space. Ross to Earth. Earth to Ross.

By 1977, Francisco Franco was presumed to be defunct and Mom was running a jazz club "Dot's Place" on the southern coast of Andalucia. I temporarily shifted operations to the Straits of Gibraltar.

You don't remember when I left? I came up here to say good-bye and we shared a final dram. I even sent postal cards from Morocco.

You could see all the way to Africa from Mom's roof garden and I spent a lot of time over there meandering through the Maghreb. In the late afternoons, Paul Bowles conducted a salon in his tiny Tangier apartment behind the British Embassy and I once met the hallucinatory Moroccan writer Muhammad M'rabat "M'hashish" there, complaining loudly about a bogus traffic ticket. One night we gathered around the kif pipe and Paul and M'rabat begged me to tell them the saga of Patty Hearst.

In Xouen on the border of Katama Province where the best hash is grown and pressed, we consumed all-night bowlfuls up at the abandoned mosque above the fragrant valley and rose before dawn with the ghost songs of the muezzins.

I journeyed to meet the blue people at the great camel market down in Goulemine on the edge of the Sahara and took the suicide bus ride to the end of the line at Tan Tan, not all that far as the vulture flies from Timbuktu where the late beat poet Ted Jones was then encamped.

In Marrakesh, I squatted in the dust at the feet of the storytellers in the bazaar of the Djema al Fnaa and learned their miraculous legends in a language I could not understand.

I stayed by the Blue Gate up in Fez and Arbi Mimguni, the middleweight champion of Morocco, took me to his gym in the palace walls with the full-length portrait of Battling Siki leading a leopard through the streets of London, posted up on the pink plaster.

One afternoon, deep inside the Medina of Fez, Hassan Saber entrusted me to watch his leather-goods stall while he attended to a family emergency. It sometimes took days for white people to find their way out of the Medina. I felt as if I had reconnected with the world.

Back on the European edge of the Straits, I availed myself of ne'er-do-well poet Ralph Nelson's hospitality in Pamplona where he and his family occupied a small apartment in the Casco Viejo.

Although administratively the province of Navarre, Pamplona is a hotbed of Basque nationalism and Euskara Ta Askatasuna (ETA), "Basque Homeland and Liberty," considers it part of Pais Vasco. I fought in the streets shoulder to shoulder with the Abertzalez' all the summer of '78 after the *Ikirena* (Basque flag) had been raised in the bullring during the San Fermin fiesta and the *Grises* (Gray Police) stormed into the *corrida,* spraying tear gas and rubber bullets everywhere to extinguish this insidious display of independence.

We marched in San Sebastian and at the Limonez nuke site near Bilbao before ETA would bomb the containment building. That winter, I lived in a 400-year-old farmhouse up on the snowy flanks of the Pyrenees and wrote a book I've never had the nerve to offer for publication.

During the long icy nights, I became a convert to magic realism and traveled down to Barcelona to interview Gabriel Garcia Marquez's doorman, and a gypsy deputy in the Spanish parliament. I traveled to London for the great Carnival riot along Portobello Road that August. At Carnsore Point in Ireland, I spoke at the first all-out anti-nuke rally in the Emerald Isle's rebellious history.

When I returned to California, Ronald Reagan was being elected president. Rosalie Sorels, the kick-ass cowboy soul singer and I perched on stools at the Jambalaya Club watching the returns come in. And when the votes were all counted, there wasn't any place to hide anymore. Now it was time to return to the cities and build up the barricades once again.

Each Saturday, the Nicaraguan *compas* would gather at the 24th Street BART station in San Francisco's Mission District to curse the Somoza assassins and holler *Vivas* for the Frente Sandanista. The Mission is a poly-American barrio, a point of refuge for political and economic exiles from everywhere in Central America as well as Mexico, and the Nica community, in particular, had a half-century history of smoldering anti-Somoza hatred bottled up inside. My fellow poet Roberto Vargas, born in Managua but raised on Bernal Hill above the Mission, quit his day gig as San Francisco Neighborhood Arts director and flew off to fight on the southern front.

Then, on July 19th, 1979, the *muchachos,* like Fidel's *barbudos* so many years before, rode triumphantly into Managua, toppling statues of the dictator as they advanced on the abandoned presidential palace. The victory was sweet payback for decades of Yanqui occupation of Nicaragua, for the assassination of Cesar Augusto Sandino in 1928, the overthrow of Gaitan in Colombia ('48) and Arbenz in Guatemala ('54) and Salvador Allende in Chile ('73), for all the coups against all the peoples of the south forever being hatched in the inner sanctums of the Central Intelligence Agency. In San Francisco, we renamed the esplanade around the BART station Plaza Sandino and many exiles followed Vargas home to join the revolution.

Meanwhile, next door, El Salvador, the little flea of the Americas, had sunk into Grand Guignol nightmare. By now Ronald Reagan had checked into the White House and in his first pronouncement as his secretary of state, Alexander Haig drew the line against Communist guerrillas just two-days-drive from Harlengen, Texas, and gave the military and the death squads the green light to annihilate the "subversives." 800 were massacred at Mozote up in Morazon. The corpses piled up each morning at the El Playon garbage pits in the capital, and frightened refugees were soon streaming north to the Mission.

The assassination of Monsignor Romero on March 24th, 1981 uncorked a torrent of blood that prayer alone could not stanch. I marched from Dolores Park carrying a cross that bore the name of Father Rutilio Grande, the story of whose death I came to know. Until Salvador, I had never felt comfortable with believing Catholics. Now I would sit in the back pew at St. James' Church on Guerrero Street, drinking in the Mass.

Just as in 'Nam, the horror of Central American had to be brought home. In Guatemala, General Efrain Rios Montt, a leader of the Church of the Word, an evangelical cult founded by Jesus Freaks from Eureka, had taken power and was roasting Mayan Indians alive in Quiche province. Each Sunday, during their services, we threw blood-spattered dummies on the Church of the Word's front lawn and our solidarity group invited Rigoberta Menchu, whose father and brother had just been incinerated by Rios Montt's *Kaibiles*, to Eureka to debate the Jesus Freak elders about Christian responsibility.

We hauled those bloody dummies around everywhere. Once we threw them out on the Arcata Plaza in a stunt designed to disrupt the annual good-time kinetic-sculpture races and Japanese tourists snapped photos wildly. And once I ripped the expensive suitcoat of Adolfo Calero, the head of Coca Cola Nicaragua and the most bloodthirsty of the Contras, right up the back and San Francisco's Finest whacked me hard in my bad eye, tearing the retina, a trauma for which I continue to pay dearly. But my lesions were minor compared to Brian Willson's loss of both his legs, cruelly torn from his torso by a loaded freight train at Port Chicago, California where arms were being shipped from the local naval weapons station to Calero's hired killers in Nicaragua. The next week we marched on Port Chicago and tore the train tracks from their moorings.

Although I have never earned sufficient U.S. currency to be tithed by the Pentagon, I stood in the doorway of the I.R.S. one morning at the Federal Building with that Grande Dame of West Coast letters Jessica

Mitford to protest the forced U.S. taxpayer financing of the Contras—or at least until Decca got bored and went out to lunch.

Street protest surged in the early '80s. Going to jail to protest South African apartheid became such a popular social phenomenon that I volunteered for arrest one afternoon just to do the inside story from a San Francisco tank cell for a progressive news service.

The power of the word always startles me. Just as I had been rescued by poetry from the dumps of political despair a decade earlier, journalism now allowed me to step back from the barricades and take a larger look. As the '80s caught fire all around me, I gave up strong drink and attended 93 AA meetings in 90 days.

For years, I had been covering drug warfare in the Emerald Triangle for commercial media like San Fran's glorious KSAN free radio and the weekly *Bay Guardian,* and even had suffered the not-so-unique indignity of being ripped off by Rolling Stones' lead thug, Joe Esterhaz, after I wrote a cover story that exposed killer narcs in southern Humboldt, which he published under his own notorious byline.

Early in the 1980s, I went to work for Sandy Close (with whom I had once formed the Ruchel Magee Defense Committee) at Pacific News Service, an enterprise that lived on the cutting edge of American journalism. Sandy raised up a generation of starving freelancers dedicated to getting the story from the ground up rather than feathering the nests of their own careers, and though down the decades, most of us have had our differences with this difficult diva of alternative journalism, I have never been able to shake the PNS commitment to starting the story at the bottom.

I covered a lot of California looking for that story. I trudged through the Stringfellow Acid Pits, tracked rivers of PCBs under the San Francisco streets, delved into how the California Adult Authority manipulated black and brown prison gangs to kill each other, uncovered Contra infiltration of Native-American Vietnam vets groups, exposed liberal lawyers who defended killer cops for extravagant stipends (a story for which *Bay Guardian* publisher Bruce Brugman stripped me from the mast-head, apparently because his pals were implicated in the scheme). I wrote on the futility of the drug war, the lies of the generals, the globalization of murder by Capitalism. It got depressing.

Jesse Jackson and the Rainbow Coalition were a fleeting antidote to despair. Then at the 1984 Democratic National Convention in S.F., as I watched a great American flag descend from the rafters of the Moscone Convention Center and a stand-in step to the microphone to accept the nomination, I suddenly had what James Joyce used to call an epiphany: Although it was only a sound check, I knew now in my

photo by Richard Gibson

heart of hearts that the fix was in. The U.S. had moved so far to the right that there was no turning back and both parties were in cahoots up to their necks. The so-called Democrats proffered mealy-mouthed lip-service while stabbing Good Samaritans like Jesse between the shoulder blades. There was no way out but to get out.

As at the finale of the '50s, I began to drift south, first to Baja, the San Quentin Valley below Ensenada where Mixtec Indian tomato pickers from Oaxaca were being kept in indentured servitude by big growers with McDonald's contracts, and then to the scarred, eroded Mixteca sierra itself. PNS ace Mary Jo McConahy was then driving around Central America from one harrowing newsfront to the next, but Sandy engineered a grant that got me further south to Lima from where I would cover guerrilla action in the Andes for the next year. Eventually, I came to interview mid-level Sendero Luminoso management and earnest young members of Tupac Amaro. In Colombia, I hung out with the M-19 cadre and spoke with Carlos Pizarro, leader of the internationalist Batalion America in a mountain camp above the Cauca Valley.

Near Molongo in the Cauca, a disgruntled guide escorting me up the mountain to an encampment of the all-Indian guerrilla Quintin Lame, pulled out a .357 Magnum and fired in my direction. "I was only joking," he chuckled but I decided to call it a day. And in Santiago, a sergeant in Pinochet's armed forces jammed the muzzle of an automatic weapon up my nose and threatened to blow me all the way to Easter Island during raging street demonstrations there.

I traveled to the Chapare in Bolivia and became the only gringo ever to attend the coca growers annual congress there. Although assailed as a Yanqui spy on the opening day of the conclave, by the closing bell, I was playing three-on-three basketball and chewing coca leaves with the *compas*. Foreign correspondence was full of such surprises.

At 7:19 on the morning of September 19th, 1985, Mexico City was ripped apart by a killer 8.2 earthquake. Between 4,000 and 30,000 mostly poor lives were crushed out beneath the rubble of the toppled buildings, many of which had been fraudulently constructed by thieving contractors. Sandy sent me back in to cover the aftermath and I took up residence in the shattered Old Quarter, the Centro Historico. Two decades later, I am rooted there yet, reeling off these words in a threadbare downtown hotel suite which has been my official address ever since.

The earth was still trembling when I first touched down but the *damnificados* (victims) were already on the march, demanding replacement housing right where their old buildings had fallen. The government, which had been run by one party—the Institutional Revolutionary or PRI—for nearly seven decades, was paralyzed and afraid of its own people. Lalo Miranda, my comrade and barber, headed a brigade that expropriated buildings landlords would never repair. The *damnificados* marched 100,000 strong on Los Pinos, the Mexican White House, and Lalo was asked to accompany the commission that presented the demands of the victims to President Miguel de la Madrid, a moment he never forgets. Indeed, it was that shared experience of momentary empowerment that eventually changed Mexico and got Cardenas elected president in 1988.

A couple of decades of covering this inscrutable republic from the inside out has sent me down a lot of lonely roads with not much more than a Pentel Rolling Writer for self-defense. I've unmasked military death squads, hunted for scorpions in Durango, saved sea turtles in Oaxaca, and fought for the forests of Michoacan. I've tracked genetically modified corn and electoral fraud and ski-masked Mayan Indian rebels from one border to the next.

Mostly, I have written of the resistance of the Mexican people to being *asasinado por Capitalismo,* Murdered by Capitalism, invariably with a U.S. brand-name attached to it. I thought, foolishly perhaps, that these stories of massive defiance to the dictates of the International Monetary Fund, Wall Street, and the White House, a Mexican ruling class that long ago ceded national sovereignty to NAFTA and neoliberalism, could stimulate my countrymen and women into emulating their neighbors just one country south. Did I win or did I lose?

Two stories changed my life forever. The Cardenas victory in 1988 and the subsequent theft of the election by the PRI taught me what Mexico was really all about. I accompanied the Engineer, as Cuauhtemoc Cardenas was universally known, through 20 states in the months prior to the election and saw how he struck a nerve when he spoke of the past and of his father Lazaro, who had once handed out millions of acres of land to the landless. Mexico is a civilization in which the past weighs as heavily as the present and the campaign, driven as it was by history, snowballed from plaza to plaza and polling place to polling place.

And when on election night, the PRI burned the ballots and crashed the computers, a half-million citizens converged on the Zocalo, the great Tiananmen-like plaza a few blocks from my rooms that is at the heart of Mexico's political life. Although the throng thirsted to bust down the doors of the National Palace, which fronts the square, and drag the scoundrels out, Cardenas, fearful of a military bloodbath, pulled his supporters back. For years after that, the PRI assaulted and assassinated members of Cardenas's social democratic party with impunity—more than 500 have died. I covered too many of those funerals.

The other story was, of course, the 1994 Zapatista rebellion in Chiapas, word of which I actually broke in October '93 in that eccentric and exasperating North Coast weekly, *The Anderson Valley Advertiser.*

A week after the Zapatista Army of National Liberation arose on New Year's eve in the first hour of the North American Free Trade Agreement, I accompanied former U.S. attorney general Ramsey Clark into the Chiapas backcountry. While hard-eyed army troops patrolled the broken town square of Chanal and a helpful mechanic repaired the oil pan of the vehicle that had conveyed us to this distant, war-torn corner of the forest, I reminded Ramsey that it had been his Justice Department which sent me to jail 30 years before for refusing to participate in the genocide of the Vietnamese people. That was a long time ago, he sighed. I had to agree.

The Zapatistas caught me in at the tail-end of my middle years, my outer vision fading and my inner one turning jaded. The Zaps restored my political sightlines. I have written three books about how their revolution came about and what it has meant, both to Mexico and to the country whose passport I still carry. Young people buzz around me now at anti-globalization galas and university presentations, telling me of their belief in the Zapatistas' vision of dogmaless revolution. I tell them that the U.S.A. is not a democratic country and the place to put that vision to work is right here in the maw of the monster. Be a Zapatista where you are, Subcomandante Marcos once advised.

I could never have gotten to Chiapas without having first stopped off in Santa Cruz Tanaco. The Nanas and the Tatas taught me more about place and struggle than a thousand Lenins and Marxes and Maos ever did. Indians and trees remain at the heart of my belief system.

Today, a graybeard with senior-citizen discounts, I consider myself more than an expatriate and less than a political exile. I do indeed migrate north whenever Capitalism threatens new murder, sneaking in under the radar to conduct three-week hunger strikes in front of the World Bank, or do battle with a NAFTA that has laid the table for the MacDonaldization of the planet or to march against both Bushes and their evil axis.

In January of '91, in fact, when Daddy Bush first went after Iraq, I flew into Baghdad by the Bay and sat on the Bridge with 10,000 comrades to express my displeasure at this malfeasance. Later, I went to Kuwait to try and rescue Palestinians who were being brutally rounded up and summarily kicked out of that illusory sheikdom under orders from the Yanqui embassy, then followed them into the refugee camps just outside Amman, and back into the West Bank. It was still the first Intifada and I watched horrified as Israeli army troops pummeled old women with rifle butts in Ramallah. 'Jews are not supposed to behave like this,' I shouted at the soldiers, and they laughed viciously.

The Arab world amazes me and I toyed with the temptation of resettling in East Jerusalem, ground zero in the coming clash between the civilizations, but giving up Mexico, an evil with which I am at least familiar (as an old Mexican proverb instructs), soon dispelled the urge. The more deeply a correspondent drinks of the country that he or she covers, the more it costs to move on.

I suppose my estrangement from the land of my birth is an expression of opposition to Gringo Imperialism, but others might consider that my reluctance to return home and fight for the long haul is the act of a cowardly lion or paper tiger. True, my country of residence does put me just out of reach of the Patriot Act but it is really not all that simple. The pain of displacement is palpable when the Giants win the pennant and I'm not there to egg the team on, or when hundreds of thousands of protesters storm through the San Francisco streets and my shoes are not in the line of march.

You know, Eddie, through all of these travels and travails, Trinidad has never been more than a few miles away, a place to which I always come home. No matter to which end of the world I wobble, sooner or later I come teetering back to take my place at your side and confide the secrets of the road and the incurable nostalgia that lards my heart. Now as I shop around for a place to die, the Trinidad town cemetery seems to me an inviting option. Just sprinkle me atop your noble tombstone and we'll piggyback together into left-wing eternity!

For much of this monologue, E. B. Schnaubelt had been screaming remorselessly, a jagged sawblade-like whine that would not be stilled. Now suddenly, he addressed me with abrupt lucidity, inviting me to join him in his loamy lair as if he were selling cemetery plots to trainee corpses.

"C'mon down brother—it's all organic. No chemicals or preservatives. Even the worms are vegan. And they tickle."

Book Four

Kaboom!!!

Bombing the Heartland

I was already perusing my morning *Jornada* and taking in the downtown killer Mexico City rays when the phone trilled. "Turn on your TV," a voice instructed from two time zones away, "you are not going to believe this. . . ."

I did and I didn't.

All morning, I sat there in the great broken brocade chair staring at the jumbo jets plowing into the Twin Towers, the skyscrapers melting and collapsing, the business suits gracefully swandiving into the abyss. Lunchtime came and passed and by mid-afternoon, my belly was growling like an irate bulldog.

At the Madrid *panaderia* (bread store), I spotted Alejandro bent over the *bolillo* bin. I know Alejandro from the marches in the Zocalo, where he invariably stands with the ultras of the left. Alejandro hates North Americans but he likes me. Now he turned from the bin with the bread tray balanced between his fingers and a gleam in his eye bright as a 600 watt bulb.

"Companero!" he shouted, "Did you see it? *Que pilotos!* (What pilots!), *Que Chingones!* " (What great fuckers they were!), *Que guevos tenian!* (What balls they had!)"

"But Alejandro," I pointed out, "thousands of people have been killed. . . ."

"*Que bueno!*" he grinned.

As distasteful as it must seem to my fellow gringos, Alejandro's joy was not uncommon here in what used to be known as the Third World. Nineteen Islamic brothers had seized four commercial jetliners, brandished boxcutters like Holy Swords, and transformed the planes into the most powerful bombs ever tossed at U.S. Capitalism or Imperialism or Globalization or whatever you wanted to call what was inside "the towers built strong and high." The twisted, smoldering wreckage of the World Trade Center and the Pentagon were stark testimony to their unprecedented success. Taking down the Twin Towers was a metaphor the poor could understand all over the planet. The U.S. military-corporate structure had never before been dealt such a cruel blow. *Que bueno!*

> *The black ball arced out of the alley as if it had been spit straight up from the night, a loaded fist, a deadly comet, its rouged tail glowing in the suddenly disintegrating darkness.*

A few weeks after 9/11, I traveled to Chiapas to see if I could find out what the Zapatistas thought about current events. Tzotzil Maya men in short skirts that make them look like extras from *The Iliad,* were still lined up on the narrow sidewalk outside the Elektra store, stoically staring at the banks of television screens, eyeing the reruns of the jumbo jets plunging into the Twin Towers over and over again, with mistrust.

"They think it is just a movie," the white owner told me but that wasn't true. The Zapatista villages had been bombed in 1994 by U.S.-supplied helicopters in the first days of their war. They did not think that was a movie, either.

A friend who often visits the villages in the highlands later told me the *compas* all wanted the 9/11 video. "They see that America is not invincible and it makes them wonder. . . ." I have a feeling that's just how a lot of poorer, darker people in the world south of the United States border looked at 9/11.

• • •

In mid-October, I rode a Greyhound bus through the anguished heartland of a U.S. still reeling from the apprehension that the whole world hates us. The bombings had not yet settled into memory and many citizens correctly feared that only some of the chickens had come home to roost. The country seemed to be curled into a fetal ball awaiting the next assault.

Old Glory was in full furl from every porch, a tri-colored talisman to ward off the evil that lurked among us. Men with turbans were being pummeled by lunchtime lynch mobs or disappearing into dungeons from which few would emerge. Anthrax was in the mail and everyone was finking out everyone else on Baby Bush's TIPS ("Terrorist Information Prevention") hotline.

The left had retreated to its upholstered salons, a traditional posture whenever the shitstorm blows, and my presentations were poorly attended and ill-paid. As I traveled from one Midwest tank town to the next, I kind of related to Red Emma or Lucy Parsons hauling their pamphlets around America for years, hounded by the dogs of patriotism whenever a bomb went off at Haymarket or McKinley caught a slug in the gut or when any deadly blow against the ruling class went terribly awry.

The 9/11 hurt made America a dangerous place to visit. Disguised as an elderly traveling salesman (the Willie Loman of the Zapatista Army of National Liberation), I managed to evade Homeland Security scrutiny and reached the isle of Manhattan in one piece, where I made an immediate beeline for Ground Zero.

The police had just allowed non-residents to re-enter the area but the pall of disaster still laced the air. You could smell it, a whiff like when bad wiring burns up, but with a slight overtaste of corrupted cheese. The somber throng of mourners, patriots, thrillseekers, and firehouse buffs thickened considerably just west of City Hall. Many were out-of-towners, white people, tourists who might ordinarily have been climbing the spiral staircase inside Miss Liberty out there in the harbor, now padlocked because of the terrorist threat.

The tragedy was still a new scar across the chest of America and many were weeping. I watched a well-dressed matron's mascara melt in sobs, her agitated little cinnamon poodle yapping viciously at any who came near to offer comfort. Outside St. Paul's Chapel, National Guard chaplains with soft Georgia accents acted as official huggers.

The route around the Piles transcribed a canyon of kitsch: West African streetvendors hawking Osama bin Laden toilet paper and tons of I Love NY trinkets. Firefighter paraphernalia was everywhere to honor the brave working men ground down to zero by the ragheads with their Allah bombs. Plaques spelling out G-O-D B-L-E-S-S A-M-E-R-I-C-A in copper pennies and what looked like human hair were hung on the wrought-iron fence outside the chapel. Peace cranes, plastic flowers, and Teddy Bears littered the sidewalk. The peeling faces of the missing were pasted to the lampposts, those who had gone to work and never come home. They seemed to be happy, smiling in the favorite photo that relatives had chosen to advertise their disappearance.

The remains of the Towers were still being dismantled. Frightening clanks and groans, the grate of metal girders being torn apart, shrieked from the gargantuan tomb. You could not get close to Ground Zero or maybe you were already at Ground Zero and just didn't know it, the damaged heart of U.S. Capitalism—Wall Street lay just three short blocks to the east, behind the next bank of abandoned skyscrapers.

Body parts of the infidels were being dug out of the rubble every day. I thought about the 16 Mexican workers, most of them Mixtec Indians from rural Puebla and Oaxaca states, who had been bus-boys and whalloped pots up there in Windows On the World on the 108th floor. They must have gotten a truly grand look at the dance of death beneath them, the sleek jets coupling with the gleaming skyscrapers in an aerodynamic ballet of colossal dimensions, the tiny stockbrokers spreading their wings and freefalling into oblivion. "*Pero por que nosotros?* But why us? The men cried out for their cornfields and families as the lights dimmed and died. "We have come here only for the *chamba,* for the work. We are not your enemy, we are not the Capitalists. . . ." But, of course, they would be Murdered by Capitalism just the same.

"Wherever you are, Death will find you, even in the towers built strong and high." *So the Prophet has written.*

As I climbed through the boneyard on the rebound from Ground Zero to tell E. B. Schnaubelt all about how the assassins had stopped the heart of Capitalism with their flying bombs, it struck me that the date was the second of November, and back home in Mexico my neighbors would be celebrating the Days of the Dead, when the families decorate the graves of those who have gone on before with altars fashioned from spun sugar skulls and *cempachutl* flowers, bread of the dead, good tequila, mole of turkey, the *difunto's* favorite cigarettes, the music they loved best so that their old bones can get up and dance. . . .

Writing this book with Ed Schnaubelt has presented me with many new martyrs whose lives demand celebration, and I resolved to build a Day of the Dead altar for the American Left before night fell.

Up on the grassy knoll at the top of the graveyard my co-author was in deep repose but I soon ahemed him from his siesta. "Where ya been, this time ol' buddy?" he asked, sounding just as cool and lucid as when he had tried to sell me a cemetery plot the previous autumn. So I sat up there and told him all about the flags and the Osama bin Laden toilet paper and the jumbo jets plowing into the skyscrapers over and over again on the television. "They bombed the Temple of Capitalism! Thousands have died!"

"Bombs?" Eddie asked placidly. "Bombs?" he repeated not so placidly. "Bombs? Bombs? Bombs? Bombs? Bombs?"

Bombing for the Revolution

The bombs of yesteryear were flying high and hard now deep inside E. B.'s plasma, the chemical collisions unleashing hard-core anarcho-syndicalist DNA.

"'Dynamite! Of all the good stuff, this is the stuff—stuff several pounds of this sublime stuff into an inch or so of gas or water pipe, plug up both ends, insert a cap with a fuse attached, place this in the vicinity of a lot of rich loafers who live by the sweat of other peoples' brows, and light the fuse. Zowie! A most cheerful and gratifying result will follow.' Heeheehee."

The words had a familiar chime to them. Of course! The text was Albert Parson's, a notorious article from *The Alarm*. The prosecution had read it to the jury at the Haymarket trial and Judge Gary seized upon it when sentencing the martyrs to swing. Many years later, Terry Robbins, the Weather Underground's late bombmaker, discovered the recipe and blew Officer Birmingham's cap off, not once but twice.

"'In giving dynamite to the downtrodden millions on the face of the globe, science has done its best work. This dear stuff can be carried in the pocket without danger, while it is a formidable weapon against any force or militia, police or detectives, that may want to stifle the cry for justice that goes forth from the plundered slaves.' Young Parsons said a mouthful there!

"'Dynamite is something not very ornamental but exceedingly useful just the same. It can be used against persons and things but it is better to use it against the former than bricks and masonry.' In other words, One Man! One Bomb! Heeheehee."

This was incriminating stuff—even if it was the best stuff. The brick-and-masonry disclaimer didn't sound right, however. Dynamite has historically been utilized by American workers for the purpose of structural rearrangement. Readily available in the construction trades and down deep in the mines where the sun never shines, dynamite was a prime ingredient in the destruction of company property, not the Capitalist class in person. Isn't that what guns were invented for?

In the Andes of Peru, the Maoist murder cult Sendero Luminoso, bereft of firearms but with access to dynamite thanks to their brothers in the mines, tried to obliterate the class enemy by slingshoting bundles of the stuff down upon them from the mountain heights—but in the gunhappy U.S. of A., revolvers and high-powered rifles with fine-tuned sniper scopes have always been the preferred tool of assassins.

With a gun, a would-be assassin can select his or her target with more precision. With a bomb, even in the best of scenarios, you are going to get collateral damage. Dynamite, TNT, C-2, Plastique and its reasonable facsimiles are as indiscriminate in their killing powers as George W. Bush's ill-named smart bombs.

Bombs are fundamentally dumb.

The first World Trade Center bombing was an ingenious "stunt," as the old labor bombers used to describe their work. It nearly knocked that tacky symbol of greed and globalization right off its foundation with minimal loss of life. Poetically, the blind Sheik's bomb was fashioned from fertilizer.

The second bombing was far more structurally traumatic—it literally melted the girders that kept the Twin Towers spiring into the heavens. The only hitch was that 3,000 souls evaporated under the rubble and most of them were not necessarily the class enemy.

"Kaboom!" Schnaubelt broke into my graveside revere with one further bomb from Parsons' repertoire.

"'Dynamite is a genuine boon for the disinherited, while it brings terror and fear to the robber class. A pound of this good stuff beats a bushel of bullets all to hell—and don't you forget it! Our lawmakers might just as well try to sit down on the crater of a volcano as to ever stop the manufacture and use of dynamite. It takes more justice and right than is contained in laws to quiet the spirit of unrest in this country.'

"That's all still true, bub. Dynamite is the Peoples' Tool."

Sounds like you agree with my amigo Alejandro back in Mexico City that 9/11 was a maximum moment in the class war.

"You're darn tootin' it was. 'Scientific violence' as envisioned by Comrade Johan Most in his superb doctoral thesis *Revolutionary Warfare—A Manual of Instruction In The Use and Preparation of Nitroglycerin, Dynamite, Gun Cotton, Fulminating Mercury, Bombs, Fuses, Poisons Etc.* can change the world.

"'It is only dynamite or some other blessed agent of God, wielded with heroic purpose, that earns redress of grievances.' 'Another mouthful! Deeds not Words!' I heard that from Most. I heard it from Lingg. More than anyone else, I heard it from my lovely Lucy.

"'Learn the use of explosives,' Lucy Parsons would preach to me. She exhorted the homeless to strap on a bomb and take out a Capitalist rather than throw themselves into the Chicago River in despair. 'Every dirty, lousy tramp must encamp on the steps of the palaces and shoot, stab, or bomb the splendiferous elites who lounged therein.' That's verbatim from Lucy's *To Tramps!*

"For Mrs. Lucy Parsons, our bombs were the Great Equalizer. The working class could never break its chains without the judicious use of dynamite. Whole nations would throw off Imperialism's yoke with this good stuff. 'One bomb in Westminster Abbey,' she lectured me, 'would be heard round the world.'"

But Eddie, Lucy, and Albert wrote these words for *The Alarm,* an erratically published pamphlet with minimal circulation, and they were used against them at the Haymarket trial. Unlike what your pal Most instructed, they were only words and not yet deeds—although that distinction did not much matter when it came time to hang the Martyrs.

Besides, you know yourself there is no evidence whatsoever that either Parsons ever threw a bomb in their lives.

"'What is dynamite?' Lucy once asked me. 'Why, just the latest discovery of modern science wherein power is placed in the hands of the weak and the downtrodden. 'Avail yourself of the methods of warfare that science has placed in the hands of the poor.' Lucy lobbied us to create a School of Chemistry in which these infernal arts could be passed on from one generation of anarcho-syndicalist youth to the next. 'The proletariat must be armed with the most recent scientific knowledge so that it will be able to assemble its own bombs,' she insisted.

"Let me explain, son. In those days, we still worshiped science. Before Albert Nobel invented dynamite, the class war had to be fought at close quarters, with clubs and knives. Dynamite gave us a scientific advantage. It allowed the workers to stay out of range of the bosses' muskets and bayonets. Dynamite could save the lives of many workers. Dear Lucy saw this clearly and she encouraged our work."

You know Eddie, I saw Albert Nobel invent dynamite in my fifth-grade Audio-Visual Aid class at Hunter College Elementary School, the Genius School. He was starring in a frayed black and white "educational" movie and the test tube slips out of Nobel's hand and kaboom! I remember that the scientist wore a white lab apron that never got dirty, even after he dropped the test tube. Nobel sported a kindly mustache and didn't seem like such an evil sort to me.

"Albert Nobel was a humanitarian. Before he dropped the test tube, he was just a poor scientist looking to cure the class war. He patented dynamite in 1868 but it never much caught on with old-world bombers. Dynamite really came into its own in the wide open spaces of America where there was a lot of topography to blast sky-high.

"Each year, Nobel improved his product—blasting caps were a qualitative leap—and took out new patents. Although he became a stupendously wealthy man and underwrote a million-dollar prize awarded annually for the advancement of Capitalism, Albert Nobel

was well-loved among the working classes for having fathered this elixir of liberation."

The four men gathered around the rickety table in the shed they kept down by the river. All four wore dark beards of various dimensions but you could not distinguish their features in the industrial dusk. Even if I did know their names, I would not tell them to you.

The men were drinking from large brown bottles of beer chased by shotglasses of rotgut whiskey. Every once in a while they would whoop and raise a toast in German. The occasion was Albert Nobel's 79th birthday—the old gent was still quite alive at the time. "To Science!" the men roared and downed their shots of rye whiskey.

The bombs were laid out on the workbench. There must have been two dozen of them in all, mostly pipe bombs and round black concussion grenades. Among those present was a machinist who had lathed most of the components.

The conversation turned hushed and serious. Which bomb should be used? The length of the fuse? These were crucial questions now that it had come to this.

The men drank some more and fell into silence, contemplating, perhaps, the destruction that each of the artifacts could cause. The fetid river, swollen by spring tides, slapped at the pilings. At last, the machinist put his hand on one of the round black bombs. He seemed to be reading it with his long fingers as if it were tea leaves or the Tarot.

"This will do," he said flatly, "This will do very well. This is the one. The father of all the pineapples. Our Adam."

In the beginning was the bomb, a loaded fist flying out of the mouth of the alley as if it had been spit up from the infernal darkness, the jumbo jets plowing into the sky-scrapers over and over again on the television screens.

"Even up in the towers built strong and high, we will find you," reads the crawl at the bottom of the screen.

Good Bombs, Bad Bombs

The four of us huddled in the half light of the glow-in-the-dark radio dial, staring at the little green numbers as we always did in the days before television stole our gaze. The dark awning of dusk had unrolled itself over the scorching August sky but it was still too hot to turn on the lights of the bungalow on Bayberry Lane. Ocean Beach was a sort of showbiz summer colony across the Great South Bay from Babylon on the sandy spit of Fire Island.

My grandmother Mamie wept softly on the sofa as grandmothers are obliged to do when history is being made on the radio. My little sister kept whomping me with a rubber baby doll. I don't know where my father was—we never did. Mom bit her lip and shushed us into silence.

"Sixteen hours ago, an American airplane dropped one atom bomb on Hiroshima," President Truman droned presidentially. "That one bomb had more power than 20,000 tons of TNT. It had two thousand times the blast power of the largest bomb ever used in the history of warfare. With this bomb, we have acquired a new and revolutionary increase in our powers of destruction. . . ."

"What's a bomb?" Susan wanted to know. "Johnny, what's a bomb?"

"It is an atom bomb. It is a harnessing of the basic forces of the universe," Uncle Harry explained to her. "The force from which the sun draws its power has been unleashed upon the earth."

"The sun?" Susan babbled, "The moom?," whacking me with her rubber dolly. "The sun and the moom, the moom and the sun," she sang gaily. "Do you want to go to bed?" Mom warned her.

"Having found the Atom Bomb, we have used it. It is an awful responsibility that has come to us and not to our enemy and we pray that He will guide us to use it in His way and for His purposes." My grandma's lips were moving as if she was saying Kaddish.

Who was this "His" guy anyway?

As usual, my mom knew all about the bomb. Mom knew everything about everything. "It is a very large and destructive bomb," she told us. "We dropped it on the Japanese because the Japanese dropped some bombs on us. When our bomb falls it kills a lot of people right away. Then it releases a poison called radiation and the Japanese who aren't dead already will get sick and die."

Mom had been reading up on the Atomic Bomb. She showed us a large black-and-white photograph on the front page of the *New York Times*. It was supposed to be the Atomic Bomb but it was really the great mushroom cloud the Bomb churned up when it exploded. I thought it looked soft and fleecy, the kind of cloud that angels float around on with their harps in the funny papers.

The photo did not show you what it looked like on the ground beneath the cloud. Mom told us that tens of thousands had been burned to death down there. No one yet knew how many. Truman believed that killing all those people was going to end the war with the Japanese and save lives. That was the hardest part to understand. How could you save lives by killing the people? Mom smiled. "Truman doesn't want to save the lives of the Japanese people," she explained.

Seventy-one thousand three-hundred seventy-nine were incinerated by the Atomic Bomb on August 5th, 1945 at Hiroshima "to save lives"; 49,305 at Nagasaki three days later "to save lives"; 83,783 on my seventh birthday, March 11th, when the U.S. bombed Tokyo with 16,000 tons of Napalm, yup, "to save lives." The year before, the allies saturation-bombed Dresden, taking another 135,000 lives "to save lives." The four bombings together total up to around 340,000 deaths, 99.99% of them civilians who just got in the way. Given the 3,000 vaporized up in the Twin Towers, there is an important karmic deficit outstanding. If I were you, I'd stay out of downtown skyscrapers for a good, long while.

"I've never been in a skyscraper" Schnaubelt reassured me, "and I don't intend to go now."

My parents knew some of the scientists who invented the Atomic Bomb. The physicist Robert Serber was the brother-in-law of the woman my father would eventually marry—his wife had gone to summer camp with my mom and Kathy Boudin's mother. They were all old commie-front friends.

During the war, we would write to Charlotte and Bob at a dummy P.O. box in Nevada. They never wrote back. We were not supposed to know where they really were because of something called National Security but the grown-ups told us that they worked in a super-secret place called Los Alamos, New Mexico, inventing a bomb that would kill Hitler. I imagined the scientists sitting around the table in sparkling white lab coats like Nobel had worn, smoking cigarettes and assembling pieces of this Kill Hitler bomb with screwdrivers. It seemed like a good bomb.

Like Serber, many of the physicists were Jews and left-leaning—a few may have even been members of the CP-USA at one time or another in the '30s and '40s. Their belief that they were building a bomb that would end Nazi tyranny was a terrible misreading of their bosses' race-based intentions. The all-white U.S. government would never drop an experimental bomb on Caucasians when the Japs had been placed upon God's green earth to guinea-pig it.

After Hiroshima, the Atomic Bomb didn't seem to be such a good idea after all.

Through Dr. Bob, who eventually became chair of the Physics Department at Berkeley, I met others who had invented the Bomb. The

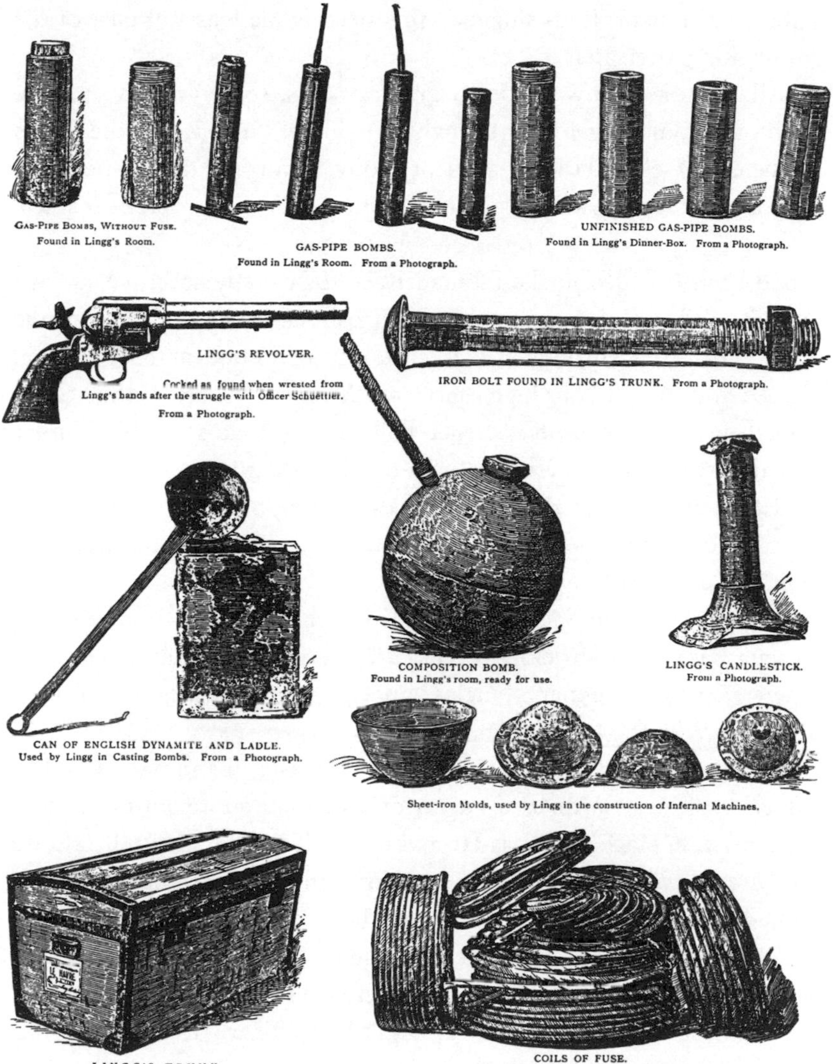

Gas-Pipe Bombs, Without Fuse. Found in Lingg's Room.

GAS-PIPE BOMBS. Found in Lingg's Room. From a Photograph.

UNFINISHED GAS-PIPE BOMBS. Found in Lingg's Dinner-Box. From a Photograph.

LINGG'S REVOLVER. Cocked as found when wrested from Lingg's hands after the struggle with Officer Schuettler. From a Photograph.

IRON BOLT FOUND IN LINGG'S TRUNK. From a Photograph.

CAN OF ENGLISH DYNAMITE AND LADLE. Used by Lingg in Casting Bombs. From a Photograph.

COMPOSITION BOMB. Found in Lingg's room, ready for use.

LINGG'S CANDLESTICK. From a Photograph.

Sheet-iron Molds, used by Lingg in the construction of Infernal Machines.

LINGG'S TRUNK. From a Photograph.

COILS OF FUSE. Found in the secret bottom of Lingg's Trunk. From a Photograph.

Nobelist Dr. I. I. Rabi invited us into his home on Riverside Drive for canapès. At age 14, I foot-raced Enrico Fermi on the beach near Brookhaven National Laboratories. J. Robert Oppenheimer gifted us with a Siamese kitten whom I baptized Kluzy after Ted Kluzewski, the

Cincinnati (ahem) Reds slugger—this sleek feline was still part of the family long after I left it.

All of these men were kindly graying souls, sometimes in slippers, who one would never have thought capable of "unleashing the forces of the universe" and the consequent agony, terror, and devastation that Fat Boy and Little Man have visited upon the Earth's people ever since.

I had been enrolled in the Human Race for exactly seven years four months and twenty-five days when Hiroshima ushered in the Atomic Age, and I grew through adolescence into manhood under its curse. "Duck and Cover!" our high school teachers would bark as the firebell trilled through the Bronx Science hallways and we scrambled under our desks, knees to chest, and held our breath, all of us budding scientists acutely aware that if the Russians dropped an Atomic Bomb right through the roof of the annex building, our desktops were not going to detain it.

My first years at Science were filled with such civil defense drills, evacuation routes, shrieking sirens. Who were they kidding? The kids knew we were all goners. Nuclear apocalypse was on the menu three times a day in the lunchroom.

You could hardly escape the mass psychosis at the movies. *On The Beach,* with Ava Gardner cast away on a desolate shore, intimated that the only safe place now was far-away New Zealand. Harry Belafonte in *Three Against Tomorrow* crept warily through the ruins of abandoned cities with two gorgeous white chicks at his side. The giant ants in *Them* had mutated after nuclear mishap. Doom was always on the eyeline and the mushroom cloud hovered directly overhead as if we were all Joe Btfsplks. "Oh Lord, Don't Drop That Atomic Bomb On Me!" Charlie Mingus yowled.

"You brought me into a world that is about to blow itself up," I accused Mom and Dad. "I didn't ask to be born." The impending truncation of my life made for precocious existentialism. Some social scientists reason that this is why so many of my generation went beat.

• • •

Later, in my twenties, as my revolutionary hormones began to percolate, I came to draw distinctions between bad bombs and good ones. Bad bombs fell from the sky, dropped by evil imperialists upon the proletarian masses in order to dominate the globe for maximum profit. Good bombs were thrown on the ground by working-class heroes to defend themselves and their class from enslavement. Howard Fast introduced me to the Haymarket bomb at an early age and that "original pineapple" dogged me as I journeyed through the Movement. But, like Lucy and Albert, although I talked a good bomb game, the only ones I ever threw were packed with words.

The bad bombs thundered down from B-52s, tearing apart the water buffaloes and the rice paddies, the house dogs and the hootches, whole villages disappearing into ugly craters smoldering deep in the Vietnamese jungle. Then the dusters came in to defoliate and distribute the cancers. Forget about the real estate. The daily body count was all that mattered.

The pilots never saw what it was that they bombed, the roofs falling in, the earth splitting open, the sudden, helpless terror in the disarranged darkness, the whimper of a broken baby on her dead mother's tit. The pilots flew very high above the clouds and their bombs were guided by technologies for which they had no responsibility. They were just doing a job. Making the World Safe For Democracy. "Saving Lives."

Napalm bombs, phosphorous bombs, carpet bombs, cluster bombs, fragmentation bombs, seismic bombs, dirty bombs, clean bombs, dumb bombs, smart bombs, germ bombs, depleted-uranium bombs, bombs that suck up all the air, bombs that paralyze all the computers, the Hydrogen Bomb, the Neutron Bomb, which kills all the people but leaves private property intact, the Mother of All Bombs, the MOAB, like God Herself, all of them as patriotic as the cherry bombs that blow up the sky each Fourth of July.

I have grown old under the bombs that one U.S. president after another has caused to fall on defenseless civilians, almost always of color. Iran goes blam, Lebanon goes boom, Sudan, Salvador, Libya, Laos, Nicaragua, Korea, Cambodia, Kosovo, the Congo, Grenada, Guernica, Panama (35,000 victims in the barrios of Chorillo and San Miguel), Somalia, Afghanistan where the wedding-party guests were whirling under the starry heavens when the Yanquis dropped the Big One.

"It was like a bomb," the farmer Gholan told reporters, describing how a crate of untoasted Pop Tarts dropped by an American plane had crashed through his roof and killed his poor wife.

The first Bush's bombs burned down the house at the Almariya Shelter, Baghdad, Valentine's Day, 1991. Four-hundred seven souls fused into one great ball of blackened ectoplasm. More than a decade later, you could still see their shadows burned into the shelter walls. It was 9/11 before 9/11, an act of pure terrorism to persuade the Iraqi people that their government could no longer protect them. "George Bush, we know you—your daddy was a killer too!"

The U.S. media reported the first Gulf War as if it were good clean family fun, an exciting, educational video game for all ages. The murdered and the maimed never showed up on TV dead or alive. Even if they are the enemy, blasted cadavers don't sell much commercial time.

Weeks after Saddam had been driven back to Iraq, I flew into Kuwait City with a battery of lawyers at the behest of the Palestine Aid Society to investigate abuses against the beleaguered Palestinian community. During our stay, I was taken to visit the infamous Highway to Hell where on the evening of February 27th–28th 1991, wave after wave of U.S. warplanes screamed in off the Gulf, massacring 22,000 (U.N. estimates) souls fleeing north in the night through the desert. Some were Iraqi soldiers who had thrown down their guns and others civilians who feared retaliation by the Al Sabah family mafia. All of them were protected by the Geneva Conventions. Each death was a war crime. "It was like killing fish in a barrel," one flyboy bragged to CNN.

In the days after this terrible killing, the Marines were sent in to haul the charred and riddled corpse from the decimated vehicles and bury them in mass graves out in the desert with what was left of their heads pointed towards Mecca. Then the Yanqui troops went to work, spray-painting the torched cars and trucks with sports slogans ("Go Redwings!") and the ever-popular "Saddam Sucks!" To the Marines, it was all a fucking game.

We walked the shoulder of the road, hunting souvenirs. I saw a baby's car seat, a woman's high heel shoe, a torn book whose fly leaf was splotched with encrusted sand that made it look like the map of a country I had never visited. There were cluster bombs everywhere. They had floated down on parachutes as if they were Christmas toys and when the kids picked them up, the shrapnel flew into their faces. Other bombs had burrowed into the sand, converting the desert into a death trip for all who walked there.

Some of these bombs were designed to blow off your feet, others your legs, still others your testicles and torso. The bombmakers sit in their cubicles in those same impeccably white lab coats, sipping coffee and designing these insidious instruments of death like so many secret Shivas.

"Let us rely upon the unquenchable spirit of destruction and annihilation which is the perpetual spring of new life . . . the joy of destruction is a creative one!" You know who said that, Eddie? Your old teacher, Johan Most.

The only good bomb is a bad bomb.

Bombing Baghdad

The second Bush war against Iraq would present me with a unique opportunity to experience the bombs for myself, to know what it is to live under their malignant aura, and to share in person the fatwa the White House has issued for so many of the world's peoples.

Being bombed in Baghdad also seemed to me an appropriate way to end this book.

Bombing was the leitmotif of the Iraqi invasion from the first pitch. As the aggression took shape in late 2002 and early 2003, Baby Bush, Cheney and Rumsfeld, Wolfowitz, Powell, Ashcroft, and the rest of the Yanqui ratpack bomb-talked Saddam with high-volume petulance. Three thousand cruise missiles would rain down on Baghdad within the first 48 hours of war "to save lives." To underscore their threats, the MOAB-9 was detonated above the Florida swamps and White House flacks began boosting Bush's "shock and awe" extravaganza. If Saddam did not forthwith fork over his make-believe arsenal of WMDs, George Bush, a born-again Christian with a fondness for Apocalypse, would unloose the wrath of his God upon theirs.

Early in January, I began to receive e-mails about the "Human Shield Action," a project initiated by a guilt-ridden Desert Storm Marine, Ken Nichols O'Keefe, who claimed to have been contaminated by depleted-uranium shells while in a support group on the Highway to Hell. Intrigued by his curriculum vitae, I surfed onto Ken's

Gandhi-studded web-page at a hustle called "The United Kinship Society." Transcripts of Nichols' interviews with not-so-major media and the Human Shields itinerary were posted. The plan, as much as there was one, was to drive a pair of bright-red London double-decker buses down to Baghdad and somehow place our bodies between Bush's bombs and the Iraqi people.

I signed on right away. The lure of the buses with their Keseyesque Pranksters flash from the past excited my ancient Beatnik pheromones.

"Well, it seemed like a good idea at the time," a disgruntled fellow passenger would later rue.

So I began to put my life in order. I had no illusions that Bush and his crew of cold-blooded killers would desist from dropping their death bombs just because a handful of international peaceniks had taken up strategic residence on the ground in Baghdad. I walked around Mexico City with my eye pasted on the sky. I became obsessed with the concept that George W. Bush had me targeted. This meditation slid me into an Iraqi headspace early on.

I packed my *kuffia* and flew to San Francisco to say good-byes. I even scrawled my last will and testament and read it out loud to my friends in a black mood, instructing my executors to dribble my ashes—if any ever should be located—upon your gravesite here so that we might be together until the end, whenever the hell that gets here.

"I was wondering about that myself. . . ."

I also distributed a statement of purpose that made it clear that I was heading out to Iraq not to stand "with the corrupt and undemocratic regime of Saddam Hussein" but with the "Iraqi people," a position I suppose that ultimately queered my mission.

I flew into Istanbul during the first week in February to hook up with the buses. It was snowing and I was clothed for tropical Chiapas. The buses would be arriving a little late, the Turkish comrade Tolga cautioned. The Mad Marine with the paper-doll slash marks tattooed around his neck inscribed "cut here," had unilaterally hijacked the caravan to Rome in a flawed bid to win the Pope's blessing. One bus had broken down during this difficult passage and the Human Shields were right now bunkered down in a squat outside Rome at an abandoned racetrack.

They were bickering to beat the band: Ken vs. his bus crew and the passengers vs. Ken The madcap cast included a claque of London clubbers, among them a manic Palestinian hairdresser who was daffy for O'Keefe; a pair of marble-mouthed Welsh anarcho anti-vivisectionists whom Ken had been unsuccessful in tossing off the bus because they wouldn't circle up and hold hands; a jaunty country squire fond of spouting Tennyson and a trim, former British diplomat with a penchant for horseflesh, both of them suffering bad cases of white man's and woman's burden; various altruistic backpackers on their first political pilgrimage; do-gooders, peacemakers, problem-makers, and probably MI6 agents.

There were also four separate crews of videographers aboard, filming every nuance of this goofy odyssey for posterity and commercial profit. No interchange between the entirely-too-human shields, no matter how petty, was insignificant enough to escape their probing lens, and their presence transformed the journey into a sort of reality show that could have been marketed as *Big Brother Goes to Baghdad*—indeed one shield, Gordon, a tall, spikey-haired heartthrob, had been a star of the Australian spin-off of that show.

What had I gotten myself into now?

The route through Turkey and Syria down to Baghdad took us through spectacular terrain, spinetingling climbs into snow-capped mountains, and perilous descents into the endless sweep of the desert. Much like the caravans of the Zapatistas that I have accompanied to Mexico City from the jungles of Chiapas, the roadsides were often lined with cheering throngs of supporters. Every ten miles or so, antiwar demonstrators would pop out of the highway like so many toadstools and we stepped off the buses into wild fandangos of dancing men and militant speeches at the end of which we all yelled *Savasa Hiyer!* No to the War!

Savasa Hiyer! Yanqui Go Home!" the few American shields chanted within shouting distance of Inchilik air force base in southern Turkey, from where U.S. planes would soon be sailing off to bomb our asses in Baghdad.

We were heroes rolling off to Iraq to somehow stay Bush and his bombs with our lumpy bodies. At every stop, we took on copious bouquets of flowers, and our hosts would feed us mountains of kabobs, lakes of hummus, and oceans of sweet tea. It was a hopeful moment in an otherwise hopeless time. Millions were on the march and it seemed like we might really be able to derail the Bush bombs. Indeed, we reached Baghdad on the maximum day of world condemnation for his mad aggression, February 15th, when 12 million souls are calculated to have pounded big-city sidewalks and back country highways in the most stentorian No to War! ever heard on this planet.

As the war approached, the Human Shield Action took off like a peace missile. By my calculation, we had arrived in Baghdad with 37 disheveled shields aboard the buses and now suddenly hundreds more were streaming into Baghdad or lined up in Amman and Damascus awaiting visas to join us.

At the apex of the Human Shield pandemonium, we counted well over 200 volunteers, citizens of 34 countries from Iceland to South Africa and Japan to Argentina, packed into three threadbare hotels in downtown Saddam City. Our tumultuous three- and four-hour evening meetings were simultaneous translated from English into Arabic, Turkish, Spanish, French, Italian, German, and sometimes Russian. We told ourselves that there had not been such a set of international volunteers gathered in one country to defend a besieged people since the International Brigades arrived in Madrid in 1936.

"We love you," The schoolkids blew kisses outside the Almariya shelter, site of Daddy Bush's Valentine's Day massacre. "We love you," the waiters told us, the street vendors, the moneychangers. "We love you," the minders told us too, "but you are very difficult to control."

Our spontaneous demonstrations of solidarity with the local citizenry startled our minders. We died-in on the boulevards of Baghdad and dead-marched handcuffed to the United Nations demanding to be prosecuted for "war crimes" as Donald Rumsfeld suggested was the fate of any shield who survived his rain of death.

"No more lies!" we woofed at the corporate media, conga-dancing from cubicle to cubicle at the International Press Center. We swirled through Martyrs Square with the Turkish comrades, circle-dancing and pounding on drums and tambourines—*Savasa Hayir!* And when the young Iraqis who lounge around that public plaza joined in, you could feel the anger in their blood boiling.

All this improvised marching did not look right to the Peace and Friendship Organization, the NGO that had invited the Shields to Baghdad, or to the government for which it stood. Spontaneity is equivalent to subversion to entrenched regimes—I have lived for years under the Mexican PRI, whose style of rule was not much distinct from the Baath Party's.

Looking back now, I suppose the minders feared civil society might take a cue from our exuberance—which indeed it did in the days after Saddam fell nose-first from his pedestal in Paradise Square.

As the Saddamites grew dour and bossy, suggesting that those who did not fully cooperate with their designs for the Human Shield Action were free to leave, it struck me that being bombed in Baghdad might not be as easy as I had once contemplated.

The big beef was about where we were going to be bombed. The Peace and Friendship Organization was insistent that we take up positions at key state infrastructure sites that had been blasted by the first Bush. But the Shields were reluctant. Many volunteers feared manipulation and even hostage-taking. We were worth more dead than alive to Saddam, embedded reporters suggested—the corporate press was already baiting us as his willing fools.

Instead, the Shields proposed to plant themselves in front of more human-directed installations like hospitals (separate Turkish and Catalan groups had come to set up tents in the parking lot of the Saddam Children's' Hospital, where the government kept its dying babies on permanent display), schools and orphanages, and the precious archeological sites of civilization's cradle, the Iraqi National

Museum, and treasures like Ur, the birthplace of Abraham, which had been badly damaged during Gulf War I. The poet in me cried out to be buried under the collapsing walls of Babylon.

Subsequent events proved our instincts to be correct but our minders would not hear our supplications. No one visited these ruins anymore. We would only be in the way at the hospitals. Schools are not in session during wartime. So we agreed to do our hosts' bidding and cover the state-infrastructure sites in the unfounded hope that if we did a good job, we might later be allowed to go to the sites that had been denied us.

During the final week of February, more than a hundred Human Shields were dispatched to two Baghdad water-treatment plants, a pair of power plants, a grain-storage site, and the Daura oil refinery, all of them civilian facilities so designated by the United Nations Development Program, to await Bush's bombs.

Once out on the sites, we marked them in 16-foot-letters that Bush's bombers, could clearly decipher: "This Site Protected By Human Shields." We faxed the White House to inform Bushwa that there were now dozens of Human Shields, some his own countrymen and women at the Daura Refinery, the 17th of April water-treatment plant, the Taji food-storage warehouse, and the Aldura and Baghdad South power plants. We passed along the geographical coordinates of each site to the American president and reminded him that he would be in violation of the Geneva Conventions by attacking such U.N.-designated civilian facilities.

Then we asked our friends and families to bomb the White House with e-mails and phone calls, imploring Baby Bush not to pull the trigger. "We can't protect those who call themselves human shields," Rumsfeld sneered, threatening to have us shot down like dogs or dragged off to Guantanamo as enemy combatants if we miraculously emerged from the rubble of Iraq.

Curiously, whether due to the poor aim of the U.S. air campaign or to our presence, none of the sites where the Shields positioned themselves were bombed.

• • •

We took up residence under the roar and whistle of the stacks out at the Daura refinery in the west of the city, which old man Bush had battered so badly back in 1991 that it burned for 42 days and nights. A score of us packed into an oil workers' guesthouse with only one toilet on a quiet street populated by refinery engineers. Muslim and Christian families resided on either side and invited us to sweet tea. Soccer balls and scampering kids bounced in and out of the courtyard. Each morning, I walked with the children to the grade school, teasing them in English. "We love you" they would call from the schoolhouse gate and I swore that if the American bombs harmed a hair on their heads, I would take George W. Bush's scalp in revenge.

Despite the sulfur-yellow pall that seared one's lungs and the frightening fireballs of toxic waste vomiting from the stacks at unscheduled moments, the Daura refinery seemed an honorable place to die. I would make my stand here with the valiant Human Shields, our corporeal remains toasted like oozing marshmallows under Bush's promised blizzard of bombs.

I was up on the roof of the refinery engine house painting in HUMAN SHIELDS in industrial black paint with Tolga Termuge, the Turkish Greenpeace activist who had become a sort of surrogate son during our travels. We had just completed the H-U and half an M when our minders summoned us down from the roof to read us the riot act. The Human Shields were accused of "usurping the function of an NGO," i.e. the Peace & Friendship Organization, and our presence was no longer demanded in Iraq. Five of us Tolga, Eva, the Slovenian woman who had sparked the spontaneous demos, Gordon, the spikey-haired *Big Brother* star, and Ken, the crazed leatherneck who had provoked the fury of Saddam's heavies by suggesting that we were being held hostage, were asked to leave the country before the day was out.

"But you can't do this to me!" I blubbered. "I came here just to be bombed. Bush already has a bomb with my name written on it.

You cannot deny me this honorable death! It's the final chapter of my book!"

The minders, who scant days later would themselves be driven into hiding by the U.S. bomb show, were unsympathetic. We were told to assemble at the Palestine Hotel in downtown Baghdad later that afternoon for "voluntary departure" to Jordan. This decapitation of what in effect had been the logistical leadership sent an ominous signal to the remaining Shields in Baghdad. Uncle Saddam was in control now. You had better mind what the minders tell you.

But in the big picture, Saddam Hussein was not the primary threat to public peace on the planet earth. That foul distinction belonged to George W. and his bellicose-Board of Directors. Tolga and I and Gordon quickly consented: The gig was over and to resist the deportation order and be hauled off to some desert dungeon would just hand Bushwa fresh ammo to attack Iraq. In the very worst-case scenario, the one cyanide pills are reserved for, the Marines would be dropped in to rescue us.

Meanwhile, Ken and the hot-blooded Eva, protesting that the Iraqis had "rubbished our movement," ran off into the Baghdad night and security forces were dispatched to round them up.

Hours later, cruising through the darkened desert that the "Coalition" would soon scar with its stupid smart bombs, I was still stewing in my own juices. Each kilometer was taking me further from my destiny. Oh, the shame of it all! Weeks ahead on the streets of Mexico City or San Francisco, friends would hail me as if they had bumped into a ghost. "But we thought you were being bombed in Baghdad. . . ."

"It's a long story," I would lamely explain.

"It certainly is," yawned Schnaubie. "See that it ends soon . . ."

Fortuitously, our leave-taking did not alter the Human Shields presence in Baghdad, and other brave souls stepped forward to carry the load. On the night of our unceremonial exodus, even as we were being ferried to the border, we crossed paths out on the desert highway with a band of Mexican *Escudos Humanos* heading up to Ali Baba City to fill our shoes.

And in the end, the Saddams, just as they did not deploy their imaginary WMDs or set fire to their oil wells, did not bother to chain the Shields to their sites and take them hostage as Ken and the whores of the press had predicted.

I went back to San Francisco to try and stop the bombing but the house was stacked against us and it was a fucking remake of *High Noon* with Bush dealing five-card stud in the town saloon and advising Saddam and his sons to be out of Dodge before sundown. The Sheriff twirled his pearl-handed six-shooter and the Security Council ducked under the table. Sundown came. The bombing began.

The morning after, thousands of us threw ourselves into the intersections of downtown San Francisco, blocked the freeway off-ramps, locked ourselves in at the doors of the bloodiest war profiteers. Two hundred of us shut down the Bechtel Corporation, a million-buck-a-minute conglomerate with contracts to "reconstruct" Iraq once Bush's bombs had deconstructed it. I hooked arms with Father Looie and Sister Bernie and the goons in blue led us off to the pens down on the docks where thousands of us were booked and eventually released to do it all over again. I was still furious that Bush had started to bomb Baghdad without me.

The Baghdad blitz stirred up the same patriotic loony tunes it always does in the Land of the Tree and the Home of the Grave. The Stars and Bars undulated just as viciously as they ever had after Haymarket or when McKinley got plugged or when the Yanqui Doodle Dandies went off to fight America's foul Imperialist wars or when they executed the Rosenbergs or when they napalmed the Vietnamese children or when the jumbo jets plowed into the skyscrapers over and over again on the television screens. Iraq was Bushwa's delusional payback for the psychic wound 9/11 had inflicted on the notion of U.S. invincibility. Even if no reasonable evidence would ever be unearthed of Saddam's Weapons of Mass Destruction or a hookup with Osama bin Laden, his guilt was a foregone conclusion. It wasn't all that different from the public hangings of the Haymarket martyrs.

So they bombed Baghdad and I was not invited to the party. The missiles whistled in, the bunker-busters dropped from the bellies of the B-52s like megaton turds of death, the rockets glared red and the bombs bursted in the air. The sky over Baghdad blazed like a Christmas tree on the Fourth of July and back in Mexico City, I could not sleep as the MOABS detonated dully inside my pillow.

Unlike Gringolandia, where the Grand Guignol images of the evisceration of Iraq were whited out, the slaughter was delivered in living crimson in Mexico. Al-Jazeera beamed in images of Yanqui butchery, the charred marketplaces, the wailing mothers digging at the rubble with bloody stumps of fingers.

The hospitals swelled with children punctured in a thousand gaping, festering places by the fragments of Yanqui cluster bombs, and Faith Fippinger, with whom we had lived at the refinery, picked up the amputated little arms and legs and threw them at the snarling dogs on the patio. When she returned home to Florida, Fippinger, a 62-year-old teacher of the blind, was threatened by the Bushites with 12 years in prison and a million-dollar fine for "trading with the enemy."

How many died in the American bombing of Iraq? 10,000? Ten times 10,000? The Pentagon took no body count and miniaturized the killing, insisting the butchery had been the most precise in the history of warfare. I wore my red kuffia in mourning every day for months in the streets of Mexico City, and the neighbors would sadly nod and pat me on the back in passing.

Saddam himself crumpled like a paper bag. That's the way it always is with U.S.-installed tinpot tyrants who long ago wore out their welcome with their own people. Billions would eventually watch a bleary-eyed Saddam having his teeth checked by a yanqui dentist on TV—but the resistance has endured. No occupying army has defeated aroused nationalists in any modern war.

One morning, the American tanks entered Baghdad to take down the monumental Saddam statue in Paradise Square, the defining photo op of this ill-named "war." As they advanced across the Tigris, the

Marines opened up on the Palestine Hotel, which during Bush's bombing had become the last refuge for the intrepid journalists who had remained to record the atrocities. Three reporters were murdered outright and the Al-Jazeera offices bombed as the invaders tried to muzzle the messengers.

Then the U.S. troops burst into the square, herding their Kurdish extras to cheer them on as they took down the statue of Saddam, and suddenly a handful of Human Shields marched out of the hotel lobby waving a bedsheet that read "Killers of Iraqi Babies! Yanqui Go Home!" The Shields stood on the narrow sidewalk chiding the Marines. "Shame! Shame!"

I saw this all on Mexican television, at the bottom of the screen, and a bomb of tears burst so profusely from my damaged eyeballs that it took two of my American flag snotrags to mop it up. How proud I was to be back in Baghdad with the Human Shields digging out from under Bush's bombs!

Bombing Paradise

"The very best time to bomb is during the holiday season. Yom Kippur and Ramadan are excellent opportunities," E. B. Schnaubelt counseled.

There's never a good time to bomb, Ed. Kissinger and Nixon dropped more bombs over Vietnam, Christmas '72, than ever had fallen before in the history of aerial bombing—and the Vietnamese don't even celebrate Christmas.

"I was thinking more along the lines of the coming Christmas bombing of George W. Bush's sprawling dude ranch near Crawford, Texas, just a stone's throw away from Waco, where Reno's F.B.I. firebombed the Koresh crazies.

"You know, the Bush family gets together at Christmas time—they'll all be there, I bet. Dubya, the Old Man, Mama Barbara, Laura, the two drunk daughters, maybe even Jeb and Columba. Noelle too if she can get a holiday furlough from the detox center. And if we get lucky, maybe even the nephew, George III who's on deck for 2016 after Jeb finishes his second term. It would be like a preventive strike! Kaboom! Ten Bushes in one bunch! Their expensive body parts scattered all over the range! *Inchilah!* "

"Pipe down!" I barked at the crazy old anarchist. "Pipe Bomb!" he piped back. This kind of repartee was definitely not appropriate in post-9/11 America. Old Glory furled over the Trinidad cemetery to remind us that we were being watched. "Glen Saunders" filmed through a knot hole in his fence. Special Forces would soon be cordoning off the town, the black helicopters closing in to thwart yet another terrorist plot to wreck America!

How would you do it? I whispered to the already assassinated would-be assassin. I was curious.

"How would I do what?"

Why, whack Bush, of course.

"A bomb! What else? Bush bombs us, we bomb Bush. Allah Akbar! God Is Great! Bomb Is Great Too. Any other dumb questions, son?"

Yah, what would you put in your bomb?

"Dy-na-mite! That's the best stuff. Oh, I might add a few vitamin supplements. Lathe up a few pounds of shrapnel so that the Bushes can together experience the excruciating torment their cluster bombs visited upon small Iraqi children in the name of liberation and petroleum. Toss in some screws and nails, the blasting cap, and run a short fuse to my Mickey Mouse watch. I suppose I could throw in a splash of Bubonic Plague, a dash of Ricen too—that should really clean them out! Spread radiation all over it, make it a real dirty bomb."

You really have all this stuff? I asked amazed.

"Sure. Where do you think all the anthrax in the mail was coming from? I posted the envelopes from the dead-letter office down here."

Holy shit, Eddie, you have the WMDs? How did you get your hands on them?

"Why your old buddy Saddam, of course! Where did you think he was hiding them? Hans Blix would never have trekked out here to frisk my bier. When it came to underground excavations, Saddam was a genius with a backhoe!"

Schnaubelt's preposterous plot whetted my fevered imagination. I have not been above entertaining such vicious fantasies.

So where would you plant this bomb? Have you cased the Bush ranch lay-out yet?

"I'm thinking the Christmas tree, the TV set, or the barbecue pit. Maybe I could just strap it to my body and crash the party."

Eddie, you don't have a body. . . .

"A car bomb then! Kaboom!"

You don't drive, either.

"Maybe I could fly in like Mohammad Atta and the boys?"

I don't have anymore frequent flyer miles.

"God Is Great! He will point the way! Perhaps He will guide us to hijack a cropduster and dose the sky with Sarin gas."

Do you have any useful advice for young bombers?

Be sure that you wear tight socks that will hold on to your shoes and not let them slip off. All this can be learned by studying the Holy Koran."

Jesus, Eddie, have you switched to Islam or something?

Waffa etched her mouth carefully with the lipstick. Not too much. She had to look virtuous this morning. I look more like a vampire, she laughed to herself in the mirror.

Waffa slipped the burkah over her slim, pregnant body. In her womb, the coils clasped the blasting cap with the tiny hands of her unborn baby. Her time was nearing.

At the checkpoint, the young soldier only glanced at her ID, then shyly looked her in the eye and flirted. The soldiers had only been there a short while and did not understand yet the danger they were in. How much we hated them.

The boy handed the card back to her at last and she smiled demurely, not showing her white teeth. How much she wanted to lunge at this ugly blond child and tear open his throat.

After they murdered Nabil, she had gone to the comrades and asked for this work. It was to complete his mission. They had never sent a woman before and they had to consult with the Imans. In the end, they said yes. She and Nabil had lived openly together and now no man would take her. It is better that she be sent. It will show the world we do not keep our women locked up in the kitchen. She knew it had been a political decision.

Waffa remembered the street to go to, the one with all the pizza places. She had been there several times. The comrades had accompanied her to show her exactly where to stand. But for some reason, today she could not find it. Every bus seemed to take her in another direction.

Then the soldiers came aboard and began to put their hands on the women and the baby in her belly kicked hard. Now she felt it coming and began to moan and shake. The soldier touched her on the shoulder and asked if she was ill. Don't touch me, you devil she screamed, pushing down hard on the detonator inside her panties and then, in one great gush of blood and shit, she gave birth and her son tore the bus apart, propelling deadly fragments of metal into the crowded street where dozens would be mutilated beyond recognition.

> *The blood nourishes the struggle. Every drop of blood of the martyrs will multiply a thousand fold and transfuse the body of our revolution.*

Bombing America

9/11 had happened before, human plasma splashed all over Wall Street, secretaries somersaulting onto the sidewalk like rag dolls, shrapnel flying around like buzzsaws, shards of glass sharp as daggers raining down from the surrounding skyscrapers, the blood slithering down the steps of the New York Stock Exchange.

Like 9/11, the blast stopped all trading on the Big Board, a direct hit on the heart of American Capitalism. When the pall cleared and the victims hauled off, the body count was fixed at 40 dead and 300 injured but no one could ever say for sure. Millions were lost when trading was halted on the killing floor.

Whodunnit? What happened on September 16th, 1920 just three blocks from where the fall of the World Trade Towers would entomb thousands eight decades later? Hullo?

This much is publicly known. A little before noon, a horsedrawn wagon hauling dynamite and sash weights pulled up in front of J.P. Morgan & Co. at the corner of Wall and Broad. The driver, claiming that he was looking for a construction site and must have written down the wrong address, disappeared to make a telephone call and was never found again. Two roasted horse hooves were later located in front of Trinity Church one block west.

Attorney General Mitchell Palmer, whose own Washington D.C. front porch had just been blown off in apparent retaliation for the brutal roundup of the American Left to which he lent his name, did not hesitate to jump to conclusions and fingered the Reds. The blast was "a plot to wreck Capitalism," affirmed chief investigator William Flynn of the Secret Service.

"Free the American prisoners or it will be sure death for you—we won't tolerate it any longer!" read a scrawled note purportedly found on the street five blocks north and signed off by the pseudonymous "American Anarchist Fighters." Eighty bombs each bearing similar messages, wrapped in Gimbel's Department Store boxes, had recently been mailed to prominent American capitalists. Palmer and Flynn both linked the Wall Street bombing to the arrest weeks earlier of Sacco and Vanzetti in Boston.

Was the notorious 1920 bombing of Wall Street really a bombing at all? Subsequent evidence amassed by the New York Police Department suggests that the most lethal bomb to smite the heart of American Capitalism prior to 9/11 may well have been a stupid accident. Construction sites in the neighborhood routinely ordered wagonloads of dynamite. Although the anarchist leads were ardently pursued, no arrests were ever made, a rare exception in an era replete with frame-ups and false accusations.

By nature, bombers are sneaky and hard to figure. No one will take credit for a political bombing or three groups at once claim to be the sole perpetrator, each with separate manifestos of responsibility. There are many more threats than there are bombs and probably many more duds than bombs that actually go off. Over time, more bombs have probably been set by police agents than by bona fide revolutionaries. How many innocent "bombers" have been framed by the government and hung by the neck or other extremities until they were dead for setting bombs they had never actually set?

Contrary to Schnaubelt's newly embraced Muslim credo, bombing is as American as rhubarb and the electric chair. Indeed, Americans were bombing each other before they were even Americans—or at least had the papers to prove they were. The Molly McGuires out in the coal fields of Pennsylvania bombed bosses, stoolies, and Pinkertons with great glee in the 1860s and '70s. Rough workers bombed the Pittsburgh railyards during the great strike of '77, demolishing $5 million worth of the railroad tycoons' precious equipment. A decade later, in 1886, the Adam of all the Pineapples, its rouged tail incandescent in the black night, flew from Crane's Alley, Chicago and irrevocably altered labor history.

Big Bill and the Western Miners ate dynamite for breakfast and bombed the bosses eye for eye. Hayward was found not guilty of blowing the governor of Idaho into the next world but never went to trial for the Bunker Hill lead mine job six years earlier.

The McNamara brothers took out *The Los Angeles Times* on October 1st, 1910–23 succumbed back in Ink Alley just as they were putting the paper to bed and Colonel Otis, the biliously anti-union owner of the *Times,* decreed eternal vengeance on American labor. Tom Mooney, already tried and acquitted three times for bombing Pacific Gas & Electric power stations, was fingered for setting a satchel bomb against a saloon wall on Stuart and Market streets in San Francisco that killed ten on Preparedness Day, July 16th, 1916.

You can be sure that if Mooney didn't do it, some other American did. It's in the blood. Americans are convinced that they have a constitutional right to bear bombs.

The sirens scraped against the downtown Manhattan night like chalk on a blackboard as the ambulance driver tried to dodge through the clotted crosstown traffic. He need not have hurried. The three young victims were killed instantly in the explosion, a blinding sheet of light and then a monstrous thud. The neighbors gasped as they stumbled from the destroyed tenement on 13th Street and Lexington Avenue, a block from Union Square, and less than a quarter mile from 15 West 11th Street where 58 years later the Weather Underground would blow itself into the revolutionary bombers Hall of Fame.

There are extraordinary coincidences between the two events. In both cases, three young white radicals apparently fumbled bombs destined for the consumption of the capitalist class. In the July 14th, 1914 blast, Arthur Caran, Charles Berg, and Karl Hanson, all disciples of Berkman, were said to be preparing a gift package for John D. Rockefeller to thank him for the massacre of women and children in the Ludlow, Colorado miner's strike.

"I was against it from the beginning. I told Sasha I would have nothing to do with it," Emma Goldman alibied. "I do not believe that the means justify the ends."

Despite Emma's objections and Berkman's contrition, the three would-be bombers were hailed as heroes at a Union Square rally and what remained of their anatomies were driven up to Yonkers to be buried under a big stone fist.

"What labor needs is dynamite, the only means to make the plutocrats and the white-collar mob know they are hated." The McNamara boys, who ran the Ironworkers operation out of Indianapolis made dynamite into a religion. During their rule, the Ironworkers Union is thought to have ordered the bombing of 150 building sites and bridges in their decade-long vendetta against the National Erectors Association, snuffing an occasional night watchman with their stunts. In their spare time, the boys delighted in tossing scabs from the upper stories of tall buildings under construction in and around Chicago.

"My men starved before dynamite," J. J. McNamara told the presshounds one last time before he was shipped off to San Quentin—in fact, the bombs had doubled structural ironworkers' wages by 1910 to $4.50 a day.

Between 1910 and 1930, the American Federation of Labor, an association of right-wing craft unions, planted, threw, or otherwise caused to explode more bombs than the U.S. Revolutionary Left will ever dream of detonating. So many bombs went off in Chicago between 1920 and 1924 (220), it's a miracle anyone ever got any sleep. American labor bombers coined the phrase "racketeers" (because they made such a racket). They were experts at "dropping the big cough" so efficiently that they could strip the storefront off a building without disturbing the customers shopping inside.

Labor bombers took out clothing stores, sweatshops, printing establishments, paint factories, smoked-salmon dealers, movie theaters (the musicians union so moved in the Midwest after talkies displaced their members). Coal and gas companies were favorite targets, mostly to run off the scabs that had been hired to break the United Mineworkers Union. On February 13th, 1930, striking miners actually dropped nine bombs upon a mob of scabs from a rented airplane in Harper County, Kentucky, the first known aerial bombardment in a labor dispute.

As noted, not a few of these bombings were designed to discourage the contracting of non-union laborers, many of whom were too often Afro-Americans. "I can hire one half of the working class to kill the other," Jay Gould was fond of boasting.

During World War II, Americans were too busy bombing the Japs and the Nazis to bomb each other. But the boys came back home after a while and soon the KKK picked up the dynamite. Black churches in the segregated south were fair game for the Ku Kluxers in their virile defense of Aryan Womanhood. Four black girls were blown to kingdom come after bible class at the 16th Street Baptist Church, in Birmingham, Alabama in September of 1963, and God didn't bat an eye.

In America, the bombs come in all flavors—racist bombs, fascist bombs, Jesus bombs, anarchist bombs, anti-abortion bombs, revolutionary communism bombs, union bombs, Capitalist bombs, criminal bombs, and just plain old grudge bombs.

Bombs are advertised as being excellent for settling grudges. My favorite all-time U.S. bomber, George "the Mad Bomber" Metesky, blazed a small trail of destruction in the late 1940s, blowing up the back rows of Times Square moviehouses in the dark and occasionally herniating a slumbering transient. He was out to settle a grudge. He had wild hair and crazy pop eyes in the *Daily News* photos when he was snagged. His beef? Something to do with being fired unjustly from the gasworks.

They had kept the telephone arrangement for years. When he was out on the road, Pablo would be sure to call exactly at 10 PM. It was her job to be there. If he did not call, she would wait two hours, go to the nearest pay phone and dial the drop number. If no one answered, she was to pack up the kids and put the burn bag in the incinerator. Then she and the kids would take the car and drive as far west as they could. Once on the coast, she would head up U.S. 101 for the Oregon border and lay low in the cabin atop Spy Rock Road until further notice.

She was always ready for this eventuality. She always had the kids' stuff packed and the old station wagon gassed up. Twice before he had failed to call and the drop number was left uncovered. Both times were false alarms, but it had taken her months to make contact with Pablo again.

She woke the kids as gently as she could. They knew the drill by now. Still, they were cranky and fussed with their clothes. She fed them the last of the Fruit Loops and the dregs in the orange-juice container. Nothing else in the fridge. She promised them breakfast burritos down the road. Pablo was right. She was a lousy mom.

She handed Haymarket her Myrtle the Turtle and the little girl burst into tears and threw herself down on the floor. She scooped up the sobbing child and tried to tell her how nice it would be back in the country. You like the country, remember?

History was already out in the car. Like his father, he was always ready to go.

She packed the papers in the incinerator and watched them curl into ash, cursing the cadre and their dumb symbolic jobs under her breath. They never did any real damage anymore—a bomb in a toilet or a broom closet at a Fortune 500 corporation. Ha! That will really bring down the system. Since she hooked up with Pablo after Chicago, her life had been all "do the job, pack up and go," the Big Getaway. Was he ever around to take responsibility when it was time to leave?

Now she would be a wilderness mom again, up there on the hillside with the dope growers and their ripoff paranoia, trying to home-school Haymarket and History—if that was going to be their names this time. That's where she was the day the comrades hit the Big Top. Out on the hillside weaving fucking wildflower crowns with the kids.

She had always loved doing the bombings herself. She said it was like mailing an armed love letter to God. But after History was born, Pablo had gotten protective and made her stay home.

She had first begun to do the bombs because she was just so sick of meetings. She couldn't go to one more. People always spoke to hear themselves talk—it was all ego and power-tripping. Then she went to see The Battle of Algiers *and Ali-le-Point pointed out the way. Enough talk. We have to bomb so the people will not think the resistance is dead. We must show them that we are still here. Only Ali Le Point was pure.*

The cadre had been patient with her and she had proven a nimble bombmaker in her time, able to whip together a lethal device with a pair of snips, a nine-volt battery, her trusty Westclock, and a few sticks of the good stuff. In the old days when she was still a punked-out bike messenger, she would hop on her trusty Schwinn and drop the packages off at corporate offices in downtown San Francisco and read all about it in the Chronicle *the next morning. She had gotten so good that her mug now stared back at her from the post office wall.*

She knew she was still good, better than the others who sometimes lost their nerve. Even Pablo. And here she was playing big mama, herding the kids into the car for the big getaway all over again. She hit the ignition and the engine sputtered and ultimately caught. It just wasn't fair having to always leave like this, she muttered to no one at all as she pushed off into the bottomless American night. Not fair at all. . . .

The need for immediate gratification is in the back pocket of every pair of American genes and bombs really fill the bill. The Weather Underground hardly invented American bombing but they curled cozily into its grand tradition. The Weathers were indeed as American as Donald Duck, whose voice was performed by beach-boy bombmeister Jeff Jones's pop.

With their uncanny ability to melt back into whitebread America, the Weather Underground utilized skin privilege as a weapon of war. Where on earth was Bernadine Dohrn, the most dangerous woman in America? You'd see her down at the Mission P.O. in her tight leather pants (I once jerked off to her wanted poster.) But even if she was living just down the block—which it turns out she sometimes was—you were never going to spot her out on the street.

Armed with their E. P. DuPont *Blasters' Handbook* and 125 pounds of dynamite lifted from a Maine quarry, they raised the stakes and were the only perps to blow the Pentagon until Mohammad Atta and his Hashashin dropped in.

The Weathers promised "responsible terrorism" and "principled violence" and always made a warning call once the pickles were on the premises. They injured few and killed no one other than themselves. Diana Oughtan, Teddy Gold, and Terry Robbins—Presente!

The Weather Underground was not alone in this armed subversion. Other shadowy cadres were creeping through the night—a collective out of Portland, Maine led by Ray Luc Levoisier bombed corporate headquarters and military bases well into the 1980s. Autonomous collectives like the Red Hawk Tribe out of Denver prowled the interior of the country. Carleton Armstong (now the proprietor of Che's Lounge, a hip Madison venue) and two co-conspirators levitated the math building at the University of Wisconsin in June, 1970. The New World Liberation Front took out more PG&E substations south of San Francisco than even poor Tom Mooney.

Although when it came to bombing, the two-tone Symbionese Liberation Army were master bunglers, the Puerto Rican Frente Armada de Liberacion Nacional (FALN) and the Black Liberation Army (BLA) proved that setting bombs was not just a white guy's sport, like bowling.

The Arab influence in American bombing surfaced with the Blind Sheik's fertilizer business at the World Trade Center in 1993 and the

Oklahoma Federal Building bombing, that same year. Timothy McVeigh, a Desert Storm vet who must have picked up some tricks out in the Gulf, snuffed 168 civilian lives, a lot of them kids, at the time the highest number of Americans ever slaughtered in a domestic bombing. McVeigh also exploded a fertilizer bomb—payback to Janet Reno and the F.B.I. for having torched 41 members of the deranged Koresh clan. Who won?

Since then, the Jihad squad seems to have bought the franchise.

Has American bombing gone downhill in recent seasons? Take the Columbine kids, Dylan and Eric. They carried bombs and even fantasized about crashing a jumbo jet into the Twin Towers long before Osama and his boys pulled it off. What were they so pissed off about? Their schoolmates didn't like the way they dressed.

Or take 19-year-old Lucas Holder who in 2001 drove a carful of pipe bombs on a Charles Starkweather-like death trip through the breadbasket of America, blowing up mailboxes and an odd carrier as he traveled west. When captured. he told the Highway Patrol he had been mailing letters to Kurt Cobain.

Bomb in the Earth

The four men had been hunched over the unsteady wooden table for hours, sipping rotgut whiskey (the beer was long gone) and smoking cheap cigars. Their bearded features were veiled by the half-light of the kerosene lamp. The men did not talk much, studied instead the intricate smoke plumes of their glowing cigars. The fetid river lapped forever at the busted spilings.

Then, the youngest of the group, a fierce manchild with coals for eyes, hissed in German—"See, this is the bomb we have chosen. I am the one who made this bomb. Now who will be the one to throw it?"

"Ya, I will, of course" the tall man with the ginger-colored beard answered impatiently. "Ya, me too," echoed his brother. The fourth conspirator, a sort of silent partner, simply raised his hand to volunteer.

How shall we decide, the bombmaker wanted to know. "We must draw straws," the tall man said. "Ya, draw straws," his brother seconded, and went to fetch the broom.

He stood in the shadows at the mouth of Crane's Alley, sweating profusely. He felt like he was on fire inside. He had on his winter overcoat and it was the middle of spring. Besides, he'd heard enough of the speakers on the platform. They made him sick with their endless ranting. It was time to act, not to spout more words. Not after what happened yesterday at McCormick's. He caressed the cool black billiard ball of a bomb inside his overcoat pocket. "Soon my darling, soon," he murmured as if she were the whore mama of all destruction. He was surprised to discover that his penis was swelling.

Then Bonfeld and his goons burst out of the precinct up Desplaines, firing their revolvers into the crowd and clubbing the workers around the speakers' wagon, and he knew this was the moment he had always been waiting for, the rhyme and reason of why he had been placed here by the hand of God, his dream and his destiny. His heart soared!

The Adam of all Pineapples sailed out of the mouth of the darkness, its rouged tail illuminating the trajectory into the moment that would change the history of the American working class forever.

Who? Who was it? Who threw the bomb, Eddie? You must know. There were only four men in Lingg's cabin that night. Lingg said he would not do it, that one of you had to throw it. Who drew the short straw, Ed?

You told me yourself Rudolph did not throw it. You said the same of Meng, who certainly was the fourth man in the room. That leaves only you, my old friend. You were the one who selected the bomb to be used. Did you throw it too? Did you throw the bomb at Haymarket, E. B. Schnaubelt?

"E. B. Schnaubelt did not throw the bomb at Haymarket," the voice from the grave pronounced gravely. "I swear it on my brother's grave. I can testify to this because I am his brother and his best friend and alibi. "

Wait! I shook the Murdered By Capitalism cenotaph perhaps a little too rudely. Can you run this by me again, buddy? You say E. B. Schnaubelt is your brother? You're not Eddie Schnaubelt down there?

"Heeheehee," the voice from the grave giggled. "That's right, kid. Rudolph Schnaubelt, bomb man to the stars, at your service and raring to go. Got a job you want done?"

But-but-but I sputtered, still clutching his marker.

"We switched identities at the train station, remember? I became Eddie and Eddie became me and caught a train to Canada. Eventually, he made his way to Buenos Aires and opened a metal shop in the port and fashioned a bomb or two for the dockworkers' union whenever they needed a boost.

"I came out here with that fink Henry, got Murdered by Capitalism, and became a bomb in the earth. John Law could never find me down here although "Glen Saunders" got close. Heeheehee. Talk about going underground! Hey, you better stop shaking my stone, boy. The sticks are all wired up to the blasting caps. You don't want to do that. You don't want to—

"Oh, fuck. . . ."

KABOOM!!!

Epilogue: The Days of the Dead of the American Left

'Twas the Days of the Dead
of the American Left
and the masses were decked
in their best Sunday bones,
the Schnaubelt boys cloned
to my unfleshed elbows
as our working-class heroes
stomped through the tombstones.
At the head of the line,
fellow worker Joe Hill rhymed
criminal couplets into the ear
of a comrade who looked mighty familiar,
lanky and long-haired, a carpenter for hire,
whom the finks and the stoolies had conspired
to sell out to the Big Boss of the Romans
for thirty lousy simolians.
Jesus Christ raised his fist
like a good working stiff

while the Carpenters' Union band
with Louis Lingg on Baby Grand
tootled "Solidarity Forever."

They came like a torrent,
the bones of the Left,
the Haymarket Martyrs
with ropes round their necks
dancing the cursed hangman's jig.
Next came Huey and Eldridge offing the pig
and in the Panthers' riotous ranks
still stinking of arson
strode a smiling skeletal Lucy Parsons.
Albert Jr. in tow, apparently pardoned—
for death had not his mother's heart hardened,
then with a wink to both Schnaubie boys,
she vanished into the swelling noise
as mountains of martyrs hove into view,
Mooney and Billings, Julius and Ethel,
their shaved heads shining like precious metal.
Sacco and Vanzetti, Tresca and Gurley Flynn,
Frank Little, Judi Bari, and Ralph Chaplin,
Gene Debs bony as any Mexican *calaca,*
Gil-Scott Heron rapping with La Flaca,
Commies and anarchos kissed and made up,
the years had flown, it was time enough,
William Z. Foster waltzed with Red Emma,
Voltairine took Gus Hall out to dinner,
Irving Abrams and Mao Zedong
played Chinese Checkers,
Dr. Ben Reitman passed out prophylactics
to comrades who felt a little too hectic,
Nina Van Zandt danced with a horse,
Fidel Castro and Tina Modotti had intercourse,

Leon Czolgocz masturbated into a barrel,
Federico Esmith diddled Colin Nancarrow,
Phil Mehlman got hitched
to Fanny Moony Sellens.
Along came the San Quentin 6
and the rest of the felons,
Cannonites and Schackmanites
mixed it up with Saddamites and Sodomites
It was one great confusion I tell you,
just a big mix-up.

Sojourner Truth and Harriet Tubman
joined Lenny Bruce and Peter Kropotkin
for a live-wire Dia de Los Muertos love-in,
Big Bill Hayward rode little Miss Mary Marcy
around the boneyard like they were playing horsy,
Sweet Honey In the Rock struck up a song,
Ol' John Brown and Vince Hallinan sang along,
then Mother Jones and Mother Bloor chimed in,
Abbie Hoffman, Jerry Rubin, and Abraham Lincoln,
Maria and the rest of the Schnaubelt tribe.

Their rebellious clan kept the fire alive,
Pete Seeger, Izzy Stone, and Malvina Reynolds,
Johan Most made the cemetery tremble
as his bombs burst at maximum level,
but the comrades only stepped up the revel,
the tequila arrived with the Flores Magones,
Jack Reed and Villa were *meros chingones,*
Warren Beatty schtuped Louise Bryant
while Clarence Darrow signed up clients,
Jack London and J. Robert Oppenheimer
competed at Scrabble without a timer,
Karl Marx hugged Groucho, Gummo, and Zeppo
(Harpo and Chico got left at the depot),
and Vladimir Ilyitch confessed to John Lennon
that "Give Peace A Chance" was as good as a cannon,
Howard Fast and Tom Paine wrote a new screenplay
Muhammad Ali declaimed to Denmark Vesey,
not about to be outdone by all the fun,
the beats came with their big guns,

Kerouac, Kaufman, and Gins-bomb,
to slam with Burroughs, Bukowski,
DiPrima, Micheline, and Belchowsky,
it was better than chopped liver
or having your eye put out very gently.

Sasha Berkman and Timothy Leary
smoked a joint and got terribly cheery,
Zippy the Pinhead and the Molly McGuires
roasted Pigasis over the bonfire,
"No pork!" Bob Dylan and Ralph Nader protested,
"Como no!" Sub Marcos and the SLA contested.
Dorothy Day lay with the Weather Underground.
Patty Hearst and Bishop Romero even got down,
Wilhelm Reich invited Hegel to his orgone box,
rocked the old philosopher down to his socks,
Houdini taught George and Jonathan to disappear,
Thomas Pynchon polished the last keg of beer,
but just as the party was getting a bit old,
our numbers were increased one-hundred fold:
Marcus, Malcolm, Martin, Meredith, and Medgar
marched with their bones tethered together,
Peltier and Crazy Horse came to take back the land
from the redwood forest to the New York Island,
its all yours, sang Cisco and ol' Woody Guthrie,
Mario Savio was one of the first to agree,
Me too! yodeled Che G. high up a redwood tree.

So it came and it never ended, a river of souls
of those who never surrendered,
William Patterson, Bobby Hutton, Conrad Lynn
Bill Epton, Claude Lightfoot, Henry Winston,
young Schwerner, Cheney, and Goodman,
Stokley Carmichael and Dr. Spock all in line,

the Hollywood 10, the Chicago 8,
and the Catonsville 9, right behind,
Decca Mitford and Rutilio Grande,
Oscar Collazo with his machine gun handy,
the Borinquines came with national force,
Lolita Lebrun, Young Lords, Don Pedro of course,
the Salsa sizzled and the Chelas flowed,
the Calaveras boogied like the dead of old,
I even spied a pair of legs dancing alone,
must have belonged to Brian Willson.
And trucking about were a thousand footnotes,
Red Jake, Haywire Sven, ol' Jonesy Jones,
Harry Hayward, Harry Bridges, and Nick Boudois,
Fred Hampton, the Berrigan boys, and Dr. Dubois,
Luc Levasseur, Sam Melville, and Ruchel Magee,
Mike Gold, Malatesta, and Eugene McCarthy,
George Rathbone, Charles Meyer, and Studs Terkel,
Mort Shafner, Earl Browder, and Robert Reitzel,
Diana, Teddy, Terry, and Zero Mostel.

The feets to the notes of this apocalyptic tome
written by Schnaubelt and Ross and their bones
wiggled and woogled up such a lather
that "Glen Saunders" himself jumped into the blather,
and the dead who were not done began to hum,
Rob Williams, E. Gruening, the Scottsboro guys
Emmit Till and Rex Ingram at the Big Fish Fry,
streetcorner a capela they hummed and they hummed
Upton Sinclair, Wesley Everett, ol' Charlie Tom,
the Ludlow dead, they hummed like a bomb,
a magnificent hum, like B-52s
or maybe a Psalm
and then the clouds parted
and there was my Mom!
She was lost in a swarm
of Spanish war vets with no teeth
all of whom had become strong olive trees,
Paul Robeson on her right, rumbling Kaddish,
Billie Holiday on her left cooing "God Bless
The Child Whose Got His Own,"
whose got his own . . .
Johnny! Mom waved, she didn't have a face,
what the hell are you doing up in this place?
I'm dead, mother dear, I lived many a year
and what I learned in that skein
is that life's full of struggle and pain
and the revolution won't last
if it's not a good blast,
full of stories and laughing and lovers.
Well, come with us then,
my fine rebel of a son,
bring the Schnaubie boys with you,
we're heading downtown
to picket a bum

who won't give the workers their due.
And so bone to bone,
we linked up our arms,
me and my Mom's,
and we marched on and on.
An endless procession
right into the sun
where the revolution
never stops rising.

Index

F

G

H

John Ross is a long-time Mexico hand for *Noticias Aliadas* (Lima), *Texas Observer, San Francisco Bay Guardian*, and the *Anderson Valley Advertiser*, amongst other screwball publications. He is the author of five volumes of non-fiction (*Rebellion from the Roots* won an American Book Award) and *Tonatiuh's People*, a novel of the Mexican cataclysm. Ross also publishes a weekly on-line screed, "Mexico Barbaro" (now "Blindman's Buff"), a mordant view of political outrages south (and east, west, and north) of the border reported from the grass roots. John Ross is the author of nine chapbooks of poetry, both in and out of print, the most recent of which is *Against Amnesia*.